Mutual Images

Essays in American-Japanese Relations

Edited by Akira Iriye

Harvard University Press
Cambridge, Massachusetts
and London, England
1975

Library of Congress Cataloging in Publication Data
Main entry under title:
Mutual images.

  (Harvard studies in American-East Asian relations ; 7)
  Papers presented at a binational conference held on Kauai, Hawaii, in
June 1972.
  Includes bibliographical references and index.
  1. United States—Relations (general) with Japan—Congresses. 2. Japan
—Relations (general) with the United States—Congresses. 3. United States
—Foreign opinion, Japanese—Congresses. 4. Japan—Foreign opinion,
American—Congresses. I. Clapp, Priscilla. II. Iriye, Akira, ed. III. Series.
E183.8.J3M85   301.29'73'052   75-4625
ISBN 0-674-59550-5

Mutual Images: Essays in American-Japanese Relations

Harvard Studies in American-East Asian Relations 7

The Harvard Studies in American-East Asian Relations are sponsored by the Committee on American-Far Eastern Policy Studies of the Department of History at Harvard University.

*This book was sponsored by the
Joint Committee on Japanese Studies of the
Social Science Research Council and the
American Council of Learned Societies*

Contributions by

Priscilla A. Clapp
Nathan Glazer
Morton H. Halperin
Neil Harris
Akira Iriye
Harold R. Isaacs
Shunsuke Kamei
Hidetoshi Katō
Kimitada Miwa
Michio Nagai
Don Toshiaki Nakanishi
Takeo Nishijima
Shōichi Saeki

Acknowledgments

This volume is the product of an experiment in trans-Pacific scholarly exchange. The authors of the essays were participants at a binational conference held on Kauai, Hawaii, in June 1972 to discuss various aspects of Japanese-American perceptions of one another. The conference had been suggested by Professor Kuwabara Takeo of Kyoto University, and the meeting was supported enthusiastically by the members of the Japanese-American Committee on Cultural and Educational Interchange, and by Professor Ernest R. May of Harvard University, who attended a planning session a year before the conference.

The research that led to the essays, the conference itself, and the editing of the volume have all been possible because of international collaboration. The participation of the Japanese scholars was supported by the Japan Society for the Promotion of Science; the participation of the Americans, as well as the holding of the conference itself, was made possible by funds granted to the Social Science Research Council by the Bureau of Educational and Cultural Affairs, Office of East Asian and Pacific Programs, U.S. Department of State. The Joint Committee on Japanese Studies of the American Council of Learned Societies and the Social Science Research Council sponsored the project and provided the necessary staff support. To these organizations and individuals the conferees are indebted for providing a unique opportunity to engage in truly binational scholarly interchanges.

Acknowledgments

The study of Japanese-American relations is still at a primitive stage of development because so much that scholars publish in one country remains unknown to those in the other. A symposium volume like this, it is hoped, will demonstrate the possibility of raising the level of scholarship in both countries through direct interactions and mutual influences. But the editing of papers given at an international conference is often more difficult than writing them. I am grateful to all the authors for their cooperation and patience throughout this process, and to Dale Finlayson for going over the entire manuscript with the care and insight that have earned her the admiration of those who have benefited from her assistance. At the proofing and indexing stages, I have been fortunate to have the help of two graduate assistants: Anthony Cheung and Douglas Day.

Akira Iriye

Note on Japanese names. Throughout this book Japanese proper names are given in the traditional manner, that is, the family name first and the given name last. However, the names of the Japanese authors of these essays as they appear in the table of contents and at the beginning of each essay are given in the Western fashion.

Contents

Contents

Foreword

The origins of this book go back to 1961, when President John F. Kennedy and Prime Minister Ikeda Hayato met and decided to establish a U.S.–Japan Conference on Cultural and Educational Interchange. The Conference has been convened periodically in Japan and the United States, and at its third meeting (1966) the conferees recommended that joint research projects be developed by Japanese and American scholars. To implement the recommendation, the Japan Society for the Promotion of Science created, in 1968, an "advisory committee on the U.S.–Japan cooperation program in the humanities and social sciences."

As a member of this committee, I proposed that a research conference be organized to study mutual images between Japanese and Americans. I had been interested in the question of images ever since Professor Katō Hidetoshi of Kyoto University interviewed some young Japanese farmers who had been sent to the United States soon after the war to study agricultural technology. I had felt that these men were far more representative of Japan than urban intellectuals whose views of America were well known. It was rather these ordinary Japanese, growing up in the country and without much bookish knowledge, whose contacts with the United States would provide a solid foundation for friendship between the two countries. My idea, therefore, was to have first-rate scholars undertake studies of images held by diverse groups of Japanese and Americans.

I am very happy to say that my suggestion resulted in a conference at Kauai, Hawaii, in June 1972, in which Japanese and American scholars participated after they had spent the preceding two years working on their individual studies of mutual images. In addition to those who wrote papers, Professor Harold Isaacs and I attended the conference as discussants. I am grateful to the participants and to the Harvard University Press for preparing this volume so soon after the conference. (A Japanese-language edition is to be published through the auspices of the Japan Society for the Promotion of Science.)

I believe the book contributes significantly not only to scholarship but also to understanding and friendship between the two peoples.

Kyoto   Takeo Kuwabara

Mutual Images

1   AKIRA IRIYE

Introduction

The study of images in international relations has made vast strides in the last several decades. It is a rare year when international symposia of one kind or another are not published, dealing with the subject of how nations view one another. In 1972, for instance, one issue of *Daedalus* was entitled *How Others See the United States* and contained articles by foreign observers discussing various facets of contemporary American life. Two non-American historians of the United States, Saitō Makoto of Japan and Sigmund Skard of Norway, coedited a book examining the images of America in Japan, India, Western Europe, the Soviet Union, and Australia.[1] These symposia revealed the recognition by scholars of many countries of the fundamental importance of images in relations among peoples.

American and Japanese scholars have been among the foremost students of mutual images. Reasons for this vary, but in both the United States and Japan there has been an extraordinary concern with the uniqueness of national character and experience. Such a concern has led historians and social scientists to ask two related questions: is there a characteristically American (Japanese) way of looking at the world? And, how is national uniqueness viewed by outsiders?

The study of U.S. diplomatic history as a discipline blossomed in the 1930s, and it is interesting that some of its most illuminating works were analyses of images. Charles A. Beard's *The Idea of National*

Interest (1934) blazed the trail by developing a new method for studying America's foreign relations. His concern with the question of how different segments of the population had defined the national interest was essentially a concern with studying ideas and assumptions men and groups had about their country's place in the world. Albert K. Weinberg's *Manifest Destiny* (1935) and Harley Notter's *Origins of the Foreign Policy of Woodrow Wilson* (1937) reflected the same thematic interest, Weinberg describing how Americans developed ideas of and justifications for territorial expansion, and Notter trying to examine in great detail the fundamental assumptions underlying Wilsonian foreign policy. All these books revealed the authors' interest in finding out in what characteristic ways the American people had responded to world problems. From the vantage point of the 1930s, such an interest was a reflection of the intense national questioning about the wisdom of the past course of American foreign policy. In trying to understand how the nation had got where it was, these writers turned to the study of ideas, to examine what assumptions and attitudes had characterized the people as they related themselves to the outside world.

The search for characteristically American ways of perceiving international relations was continued after World War II, this time reinforced by a certain consensus about the failure of interwar U.S. diplomacy but also reflecting a confusion about the role of the country in the postwar world. The years immediately after 1945 were the most fruitful period in this regard, producing historiographical landmarks such as Hans Morgenthau, *Scientific Man vs. Power Politics* (1946), his *In Defense of the National Interest* (1951); Dexter Perkins, *The American Approach to Foreign Policy* (1951); George Kennan, *American Diplomacy, 1900–1950* (1951); and Robert E. Osgood, *Ideals and Self-interest in American Foreign Relations* (1953). These writings embodied a national-interest approach, and the authors were essentially apologists for the *raison d'état*. But they were also interested in the way the national interest was defined, articulated (Perkins), or subverted (Morgenthau, Kennan, Osgood) by the American people. The last three were instrumental in popularizing the notion that there had been a strain of idealism in American foreign relations which had often beclouded a rational perception of the national interest. In their view the American people and their leaders, especially in the twentieth century, had been too ignorant, impatient, or sentimental in appraising factors at play in world politics to evolve a realistic foreign policy. They had tended to superimpose their image of how individuals did or should behave—derived from Judeo-Christian and Enlightenment concepts—upon relations among nations. They had been prone to assume that other peoples were motivated by the same considerations and acted in the same manner as Americans. Perkins, on the other hand, found in such a trait an essence of American humanitarianism, which, combined with more pragmatic concerns, had produced a basically successful record of the country's foreign policy.

The 1950s also saw the publication of a number of first-rate monographs which analyzed specifically how Americans and other peoples had viewed one another. Frederick Barghoorn's *The Soviet Image of the United States* (1950) tried to describe the way a government manipulated public opinion by controlling images the people had of another country. By stressing the role of propaganda and the government-controlled press, the author implied that Soviet images of the United States had not been uninhibited expressions of popular sentiment but had fluctuated according to the needs of the state. Another book published in the same year, Henry Nash Smith's *Virgin Land* (1950), however, was a study of spontaneous popular notions. It analyzed images of the American West that Americans held in the first half of the nineteenth century. According to the author, part of the national imaginings about the West was bound up with expectations about the Orient beyond the wilderness. To think about the American West, then, was to have a vision of the East. This close connection between one's image of one's country and of a distant land was elaborated by John Higham's *Strangers in the Land* (1955), which studied the American people's responses to the coming of foreigners. A thesis of the book was that the Americans' attitude toward immigrants was as much a product of socioeconomic conditions in the country as a reflection of personal prejudices.

By far the most significant studies of images in the 1950s were Durand Echeverria, *Mirage in the West* (1957), and Harold Isaacs, *Scratches on Our Minds* (1958). The former traced, according to the subtitle, "the French image of American society to 1819." It was an excellent empirical study of how the *philosophes* developed their

"American dream" and how, in French minds, the American and the French revolutions became conceptually intertwined. But the author's conclusions were even more important in terms of their implications for the methodology of the study of images. He wrote, "[The French] always saw not what was there, but what, consciously or unconsciously, they were compelled to see. They discovered each time only a reflection of their own aspirations or of their own fears and prejudices." His study of the French-American perceptual interaction led the author to the view that "the picture others see of us [is] created not by what we are, or what we think we are, or what we wish to be, but instead by what we seem to mean in terms of the private hopes and fears of those we seek to impress." [2]

Isaacs came to more or less the same conclusions in his study of American images of China and India. He, too, stressed the fact that in viewing others one was viewing oneself. But Isaacs contributed a methodological innovation; he carried out intensive interviews with nearly two hundred people, representing different age and occupational groups, and sought to determine how one arrived at an image of China or India. In addition, the author gave a historical overview of changing American perceptions of these countries, a sort of collective national perception, some of which formed part of an individual's images. American images of China were a particularly fascinating subject, as they had undergone violent fluctuations as a function of the traditional love-hate relationship between the two peoples, but also as a manifestation of the fact that for most Americans China was merely a "scratch" on their minds. Thus they did not have to come to grips with the internal contradictions in these images.

These historiographical breakthroughs were followed by further monographic work. To name only a few outstanding examples from works that appeared in the 1960s, Christopher Lasch's *The American Liberals and the Russian Revolution* (1962) was an ambitious attempt to establish a connection between one's view of the Bolsheviks with one's attitude toward the war against Germany. The author's basic problem, "why liberals found it so difficult to understand the Russian revolution," led him to an analysis of the American liberals' self-image, one aspect of which was "the assumption that the ideological alignment of a nation dictated its foreign policy." Lasch also gave a provocative discussion of the concept of "efficiency" as Americans

applied it to Germany before and during the war.[3] In 1963 two books
—Tang Tsou's *America's Failure in China,* and Frederick Merk's
Manifest Destiny and Mission in American History—further elaborated on the theme of national images. Tsou's was a comprehensive
account of American perceptions of China during and immediately
after World War II. Under the influence of the "consensus" school
of American history, the author developed the thesis that the country's liberal tradition had made it difficult for Americans to understand a society devoid of such a past or a movement like Chinese
communism which thrived on dogmatic rigidity. Merk's book was a
study of American self-images. It showed how different perceptions
about the nature and composition of American society led men to
espouse opposite causes externally. Those who conceived of the nation
as a federally organized entity made up of distinctive states supported
a limitless expansion of the United States, whereas those who thought
of America in terms of certain principles were content to see their
country stand as an example to the rest of the world. Such an analysis
served to refine conceptual tools in the study of American foreign
relations.

Public opinion concerning foreign affairs was the focus of five excellent monographs in the mid-1960s: Alfred Hero, *The Southerner
and World Affairs* (1965); A. T. Steele, *The American People and
China* (1966); Manfred Jonas, *Isolationism in America* (1965); Robert Divine, *Second Chance* (1967); and Peter G. Filene, *Americans and
the Soviet Experiment* (1967). Each author in his own way was
trying to detect what determined the American people's responses to
foreign policy questions. Hero and Steele noted the widespread ignorance and indifference among segments of the population concerning external issues, while Filene related American images of the Soviet
Union during 1917–33 to intellectual, psychological, and economic
needs of the people to accommodate Russia into their world views.
Thus the *Nation* magazine asserted in March 1917 that the United
States, as the first large modern democracy, was "more qualified than
any other nation to understand the aspirations of the Russian people,"
while twelve years later its editor, Oswald G. Villard, wrote that the
Soviet Union might be the freest of all countries, since "it has been
spared the curse of Anglo-Saxon hypocrisy."[4] The reverse of this tendency to imagine a promised land abroad as the antithesis of domestic

ills was the isolationist thinking of the 1930s which, as Jonas noted in his book, was morally relativistic and refused to apply value judgments to world problems. Images of other countries were colored by a determination to maintain autonomy and unilateralism of American national behavior. Divine's study of the resurgence of internationalism during World War II traced the manner in which such an inward-looking attitude was transformed in a short span of time. Examining opinion polls as well as writings and speeches by policymakers and opinion leaders, the author showed that the new internationalism was a complex phenomenon consisting of various layers of attitudes concerning American relations with other countries, in particular the Soviet Union and Great Britain.

The vogue of revisionist history, which approached a crescendo in the late 1960s and the early 1970s, had important implications for the study of images. Writers such as William Appleman Williams, Lloyd C. Gardner, N. Gordon Levin, Gabriel Kolko, Carl P. Parrini, Richard Freeland, and Bruce Kuklick were as interested as earlier authors in seeking underlying themes in U.S. foreign relations. Most of the revisionist historians saw uniqueness in America's search for a world order in which multilateral economic relations would provide stability and promote peace. Such a world order reflected, according to this interpretation, not only America's affluence and economic superiority over other countries but also the national dogma of free-enterprise capitalism and liberal democracy which were to be exported overseas. These historians criticized the Morgenthau–Kennan–Osgood interpretation for its alleged failure to see consistency underneath the seeming oscillation of the American mind between realism and idealism. But they were equally concerned with the American images of the world. The tradition of economic expansionism and liberal exceptionalism, according to Williams, Kolko, and others, provided the intellectual milieu in which Americans looked at foreign lands. For example, the symbolism of the China market was a key aspect of the ideology of American expansion, as was the view of the European countries as an embodiment of the Old Diplomacy and of revolutionary Russia as a threat to the liberal capitalist order for which the United States stood. Moreover, Levin, Parrini, and others argued, there was a close identification between American self-images and perceptions of the international community. There was a synthetic view in which American interests and ideals were compatible, even identical, with those of the entire world. In Parrini's words, American leaders after World War I endeavored "to make American interest the world's interest. If they could do that, they could give potentially competing nations a stake in stabilizing and securing a system which was in the first instance beneficial to the United States." Herbert Hoover's opinion in 1920 that the expansion of American investments abroad was "the most beneficent operation that can be done to humanity" said as much about Hoover's image of the world as about his concern with the country's welfare.[5]

One subject that commanded the growing attention of historians, revisionist and otherwise, was the Spanish-American War and the subsequent insular imperialism. This was understandable in view of the intense concern with American expansionism and imperialism that had been abetted by the war in Vietnam. Here again some of the best studies dealt with images. Robert L. Beisner's *Twelve Against Empire* (1968) gave an excellent treatment of twelve prominent Americans' perceptions of the country's foreign relations. Ernest R. May's *American Imperialism* (1968) did the same for those who supported or acquiesced in imperialist expansion, as did David Healy's *U.S. Expansionism* (1970), while E. Berkeley Tompkins' *Anti-Imperialism in the United States* (1970) covered a wider time span than Beisner's book. The racial ingredient in the debate was singled out for treatment by George P. Marks, *The Black Press Views American Imperialism* (1971) and Rubin F. Weston, *Racism in U.S. Imperialism* (1972). Although their interpretations of turn-of-the-century imperialism varied, all these historians shared a concern with the sources and characteristics of American attitudes, assumptions, and images. In each instance, imperialism or anti-imperialism was seen as a highly subjective phenomenon, reflecting individual Americans' perceptions of where the country stood in the world arena and whether it should behave as a champion or enemy of the policy of power and empire.

Scholarly concern with American images has not abated. The combination of revisionist scholarship, skepticism concerning traditional assumptions about United States foreign policy as a consequence of the Asian war, and the sheer accumulation of monographs has been conducive to producing more and more detailed studies of the subject. For instance, Kenneth Shewmaker's *Americans and the Chinese*

Communists (1971) offered a well-documented account of every American who had contact with Chinese communists before 1945 and traced the way his image of the latter was developed; Thomas G. Paterson's *Cold War Critics* (1971) examined the attitudes and ideas of a few individuals who had serious doubts about the containment policy of the late 1940s; and John Lewis Gaddis' *The United States and the Origins of the Cold War* (1972) gave a careful analysis of Franklin D. Roosevelt's perception of world order during World War II. One of the best studies of interwar foreign affairs was John P. Diggins, *Mussolini and Fascism: The View from America* (1972), a thorough and systematic analysis of cultural, political, and psychological factors underlying American perceptions of Italy. From articles in scholarly journals, doctoral dissertations in various universities, and manuscripts submitted to presses for publication, it seems possible to say that the importance of studying images is now taken for granted as a starting point for any study of foreign relations, and that an impressive number of scholars in the United States are currently engaged in further exploring and refining the subject.

In Japan the study of images has been of much more recent origin. There is no precise Japanese word for "image" and the transliterated word, *imeiji,* is often used for the purpose. But this has not deterred Japanese scholars from developing their study of national images. Like their American counterparts, Japanese writers have been intensely interested in the problem of the cultural identity of the country. This is in part a reflection of the sense of uncertainty about Japan's place in the contemporary world. As Wagatsuma Hiroshi wrote in 1970, "Japan today is the only country in Asia that has fully developed a 'modern' society with the third largest industrial complex in the entire world. Arising from this industrial accomplishment, however, there is an important question the Japanese must answer. It is the question of the national purpose of the country, or the cultural identity of the nation." [6]

The search for identity, however, is not a new phenomenon. By the middle of the nineteenth century Japan's intellectual leaders were already grappling with the same question. The overall nature and specific manifestation of this quest have been explored by recent monographs. A good example is a collection of essays edited by Hashikawa Bunzō and Matsumoto Sannosuke and published in 1971 as

Kindai Nihon seiji shisō shi (History of political thought in modern Japan). One of the contributors, Uete Michiari, traces the dialectical relationship between Japanese images of China and of the West. His thesis is that the Confucian world order that had provided the intellectual foundation of Japanese thought had transformed itself in Japan before the coming of Westerners, so that instead of holding on to an ethnocentric world view as happened in China, the Japanese were able to differentiate between "China" in the abstract Confucian sense and the actual Ch'ing empire. As soon as they recognized the superior power of the West, they simply transferred "China" to the latter. However, there still persisted a hierarchical conception of the countries of the world. Instead of putting China at the apex, the Japanese came to perceive differences among nations in terms of their relative strengths and weaknesses, with the result that the West was accorded the highest status because of its power. Such an image of the international community, Uete argues, was a far cry from the universalistic concepts of international relations that had developed in western Europe since the seventeenth century.

Another contributor to the volume, Matsunaga Shōzō, describes the images of Western nations held by the *Jiyū minken* (liberty and the people's rights) group in the 1880s, while Motoyama Yukihiko traces the evolution of pan-Asianism, and Kano Masanao that of Japanese imperialist ideology. Other authors deal with Japanese intellectuals and politicians in the nineteenth and twentieth centuries who sought the essence of national life. They wanted their country to be unique and proceeded to look for factors in Japanese history and society that justified their faith.

There have also been excellent biographical studies. Satō Seizaburō's 1965 monograph on Kawaji Toshiakira, an official of the Tokugawa shogunate, considered the "frame of reference" of an Edo official and tried to understand him in terms of his intellectual framework. It was a study in late-Tokugawa world views and did much to illuminate how a highly intelligent official sought to reconcile his awareness of the superior power of the West with his feudal ethic of loyalty. Also in 1965, Mitani Taichirō published an important study of Hara Kei, in which Hara's foreign policy decisions during 1918–21 were related to changes in his perceptions of the world, in particular the United States. In another essay written in the same year for a volume edited by Kamishima Jirō and entitled *Kenryoku no shisō* (Ideologies of power), Mitani followed Hara's earlier intellectual development, focusing on his images of the outside world. Another article in this volume, Hagihara Nobutoshi's study of Mutsu Munemitsu, offered a fascinating account of the interaction between the Japanese diplomat's concept of power in international society and that in domestic politics. All these monographs were alike in showing the writers' concern with Japanese self-perceptions and world views as a key to modern Japan's westernization and imperialism.

Because the study of Japanese images requires an understanding of both Chinese classics and Western thought, inasmuch as these provided the vocabulary for Japanese to express their ideas and feelings, it is not surprising that some of the best works on the subject have been written by specialists in comparative literature. Shimada Kinji, sometimes regarded as the dean of comparative literature in Japan, has published intellectual portraits of two Meiji military figures, Hirose Takeo and Akiyama Saneyuki. They were professional naval officers, but they were also deeply immersed in classical and Western education. One had spent some time in Russia, the other in the United States. By examining their letters and other writings, Shimada tried to understand what it was like for young men of the late nineteenth century to be exposed to Western civilization. Fundamentally, these were studies in the formation of images, central to which would be such themes as ego-identity, nationalism, and the pursuit of more universalistic objectives like love and beauty.

Younger specialists in English, French, and German literature have made significant contributions to the study of Japan's search for identity. Haga Tōru's account of the late Tokugawa missions overseas, *Taikun no shisetsu* (The Taikun's embassies, 1968), is much more than a chronicle of these embassies. Haga is more interested in portraying the cultural shocks the Japanese samurai experienced when they went to Europe, as well as the way they sought to accommodate them to their world views. Kobori Keiichirō and Hirakawa Sukehiro, both students of German and comparative literature, have traced the career of Mori Ōgai, one of the outstanding literary-scientific figures of Meiji Japan, through his exposure to the turn-of-the-century West. Etō Jun, the literary critic, has done the same for Natsume Sōseki, whose encounter with Western civilization took place in England. The contrast between these two novelists was a product of their different personal and educational backgrounds and their experiences in Germany and England. To understand what went on in their minds one must be thoroughly familiar with German and English literature, music, and philosophy of the period. This is a formidable task for any student, but these monographs suggest that important beginnings have been made and that there is no shortcut to the study of intellectual and artistic interaction between peoples. They also show that the study of images at one level is a study in cultural epistemology. Not only the specific content of an image but the way it is formed and articulated in one culture and reconstructed in another must be examined.

Besides these achievements by pioneering scholars, American and Japanese writers have produced important monographs specifically dealing with mutual images between the two countries. In the United States numerous books and articles have traced American images of Japan since the nineteenth century. Among the more generalized works, William L. Neumann's *America Encounters Japan* (1963) stands out. The author makes use of novels, newspapers, and opinion polls as well as official documents to trace the changing perceptions of Japan held by generations of Americans. He particularly notes the role of special-interest groups such as labor unions, the navy, and missionaries who had much to do with spreading unfavorable views of the Japanese. This book is short on cultural relations, for which, however, there are two excellent studies, also published in 1963: Lawrence W. Chisolm, *Fenollosa: The Far East and American Culture,* and Clay Lancaster, *The Japanese Influence in American Architecture.* To date the only work on Japanese-American mutual images that utilizes Japanese sources has been Robert S. Schwantes, *Japanese and Americans* (1955), but the book covers much more than images and is better as an introduction to the subject than as a substantive monograph. My own attempt at studying images has resulted in two books: *Across the Pacific: An Inner History of American-East Asian Relations* (1967), and *Pacific Estrangement: Japanese and American Expansion, 1897–1911* (1972).

In Japan the publication in 1954 of the six-volume *Nichi-Bei bunka kōshō-shi* (Cultural relations between Japan and the United States) marked the beginning of a serious scholarly effort to study the subject. Despite its title, the series dealt more with formal (diplomatic, economic, military) than informal aspects of Japanese-American relations. One of the authors of the series, Kimura Ki, later expanded his study of the literary relationship between the two countries and published an encyclopedic volume, *Nichi-Bei bungaku kōryū-shi no kenkyū* (A history of Japanese-American literary relations, 1960). His approach was more episodic than analytical, however. By far the best scholarly works on the impact of American literature on Japan have been written by Kamei Shunsuke, whose essays on Noguchi Yonejirō (Yone Noguchi), Walt Whitman, and the "literature of nationalism" in Meiji Japan have contributed much toward illuminating specifically how American literary figures and products were viewed by Japanese intellectuals and in what ways they contributed to the formation of an image of the United States in Japan.[7] In another series, called *Kindai Nihon no meicho* (Famous books of modern Japan, 1966–   ), which reprints writings by Japanese and foreigners on Japan, American images of and influence on Japan have been skillfully traced. One of the volumes is edited by Nagai Michio and discusses America's role in modern Japanese education, and another, edited by Katō Hidetoshi, describes foreign views of Japanese culture, including those of Lafcadio Hearn and Geoffrey Gorer.

One of the first attempts at frontally dealing with the question of Japanese-American mutual images was a 1967 issue of *Kokusai seiji* (International politics), which was entitled *Nichi-Bei kankei no imeiji* (Images in Japanese-American relations). It contained several essays by historians and political scientists, studying the subject in different time periods. Among the more recent works notable for discussions of mutual images have been Saeki Shōichi's *Uchinaru Amerika sotonaru Amerika* (America from inside and outside, 1971), and Miwa Kimitada's *Matsuoka Yōsuke* (1971). The former, like the same author's *Bungakuteki Amerika* (Literary America, 1967), is a collection of essays, including a highly suggestive attempt at locating the origins of certain Japanese stereotypes about America. The latter is a biography of an American-educated Japanese diplomat who was an architect of the Axis alliance. It offers a fascinating account of how a man who spent nine years of his youth in the United States later turned against the country.[8]

Finally, the publication, in Japan and the United States, of *Nichi-Bei kankei-shi* (issued as *Pearl Harbor as History* in English, 1971–1972) has been a major event not only in the study of mutual images but in the history of scholarly collaboration between the two countries. The book was an outgrowth of a 1969 binational conference that took place near Lake Kawaguchi, outside of Tokyo. Japanese and American specialists participated and presented papers dealing with the two countries' relations during the 1930s. While all the papers by implication dealt with images, four in particular—those by Kakegawa Tomiko, Mitani Taichirō, Dorothy Borg, and Ernest R. May—discussed the images held by mass media and intellectuals of one country about the other. In a concluding essay Mushakōji Kinhide tries to develop a conceptual model to comprehend the nature of the mistrust that characterized Japanese-American mutual images before Pearl Harbor. These images were obviously distorted, but little effort was made to correct them. This was, according to Mushakōji, because Japanese and American leaders were fundamentally concerned with other apparently more urgent issues such as the war in Europe and the conflict in China. Unfortunately, the greater the lack of communication, the more distorted the images became, and the more probable grew chances of war. Richard W. Leopold, summing up the conference as its cochairman, notes that whatever one may say about the communication gap and distorted images in the 1930s, there was complete communication between Japanese and American scholars at Lake Kawaguchi. This was also the sentiment of the participants themselves. They were engaged in the common task of shedding light on the past, and the linguistic handicap, not ideological dogmas or national egoism, was the only obstacle to a fuller interchange of ideas.

The essays in this book are built on these historiographical achievements and aim further to explore aspects of Japanese-American mutual perceptions. They do not claim to enumerate all the important images or roles of images in Japanese-American relations. Nor are they chronologically comprehensive. Some topics and some years are stressed primarily because each author has tried to fill a gap in the existing literature. The result is a number of empirical essays, essentially case-studies of how Japanese and Americans have viewed one another. Nevertheless, each study in its own way contributes to raising further questions methodologically and conceptually. For instance, Neil Harris' study of fairs in the United States points to the question of sources of images. He considers the intriguing possibility that for the bulk of Americans in the nineteenth century going to a world's fair was an educational experience that helped them confirm or modify preconceptions about other peoples. Kamei Shunsuke's essay, in contrast, shows the crucial importance of a handful of Japanese visitors to the United States as the shapers of the initial images of America in the nineteenth century. The article also provides a link to the essays by Saeki Shōichi and Miwa Kimitada by mentioning Uchimura Kanzō as a transitional figure who could no longer believe in the simplistic image of the United States as "the sacred land of liberty." The question of why images change (or do not change) is one to which almost all the authors of these studies address themselves. For instance, the Harris and Iriye essays describe sharply different concerns Americans had when they thought about Japan. The former stresses an aesthetic aspect, and the latter the theme of competition. One is couched in universalistic language, while the other is more political and therefore more particularistic. In contrast, the essays by Saeki and Miwa overlap not only chronologically but also substantively. Although they cite different examples, both of them stress the psychological and intellectual readiness of the Japanese in the 1920s and 1930s to consider war with the United States. Are we to say that at this time there was a great deal of uniformity in Japanese perceptions of America, perhaps greater than in American images of Japan?

Interestingly enough, the essays that deal with postwar images come to the opposite conclusion. Katō Hidetoshi, Nagai Michio, and Nishijima Takeo stress diversity in Japanese images, whereas Nathan Glazer, Priscilla Clapp, and Morton Halperin point to some continuing themes in American perceptions of Japan. Katō's essay shows that even at the superficial level of tourists' impressions of the United States, there is a wide spectrum of images. Nagai and Nishijima deal with the policy level and discuss American influence on postwar Japanese education. They argue that an official's image of American education had much to do with postwar educational reforms in Japan, whereas for the teacher there was the added ambiguity of how to accommodate what he considered the merits of American-style education with the policies and practices of cold war diplomacy to which he objected. Katō, Nagai, and Nishijima all emphasize that for postwar Japanese the United States has been very much part of their lives and imply that the divergent images of America they hold may be approximating the reality of American life.

The two essays dealing with postwar American perceptions of Japan present a rather different picture. Glazer as well as Clapp and Halperin note the limited amount of knowledge about Japan in the United States. They concentrate on specialists, officials, and non-specialist writers, but even so these essays have found more continuity than variety in their images of Japan. In Glazer's view, American writings on Japan stress its instability and unpredictability, a contention that is disputed by the Clapp-Halperin essay which finds that most American officials consider Japan a stable ally, an image which represents the middle spectrum between the two extreme poles of unconditional affection and unconditional antipathy. In both instances, however, the essays seem to suggest that American images of Japan after the war have been a function of the reality of the political, military, and diplomatic relationship between the two countries. The essentially stable, continuous image of Japan may have reflected the official definition in Washington of America's role in Asia. Unfortunately, none of the essays speculate on the possibility that events since 1971—the "Nixon shocks" administered to Japan; the rapprochement of the People's Republic of China with both the United States and Japan; the oil crisis and the subsequent search for energy resources and foodstuffs—may have altered the reality of international relations in such a way as to transform Japanese-American mutual images. Nonetheless, it may be hoped that the conceptual and methodological frameworks used by these essays will be as helpful in forecasting the future as in analyzing the past.

Finally, the essay by Don Nakanishi is a genre in itself. The author, a Sansei (third-generation Japanese-American), presents the result of his interviews with various generations and groups of Japanese in Los Angeles. He asks them the kinds of questions Harold Isaacs asked in the 1950s to find in depth the sources and implications of one's images. Images held by Japanese-Americans are products of their experiences in the two countries, including their education and family life. Some of their ideas about Japan approximate general American views, while others are more closely related to images of America in Japan. Furthermore, the essay suggests that Americans sometimes form an opinion about Japan through their perception of Japanese-Americans and that, on the other hand, the Japanese-American view of Japan is often a perception held in common with other Americans.

Nakanishi's essay gets as deeply into the minds of certain individuals as one can. Ideally, the same approach should be used in any study of images. Even then, however, there will remain difficulties in establishing meaningful connections between separate individuals' images. For instance, Nakanishi shows the contrast between the images of Japan held by Nisei (second-generation) and Sansei Japanese. But is this contrast explainable in terms of the overall differences between the two generations? If so, one's images will be basically a function of one's existential conditions. There are divergent images because people who hold them are different. At the same time, some of the essays, for instance Harris', suggest that images may have a life and history of their own, quite independent of the image-holders. Otherwise it would be difficult to account for the persistence of certain stereotypes and idiosyncracies in the way men look at other countries. On the other hand, if Nagai and Glazer are right, images can be formed, utilized, or transformed by policy. Are some images, then, autonomous and some others susceptible of manipulation by state power? If by images we mean more than just a sum total of policy-makers' ideas, how do we analyze the relationship between image and policy? How are they in turn related to the social system?

The essays here printed point to but do not attempt to answer these problems. They do, however, serve one useful function. By juxtaposing mutual images between two countries, they enable the reader to maintain a comparative perspective. Much has been said about the "exceptionalist" tendency in American self-perception or about the particularism of Japanese world views. The essays help to dispel the notion that either of these, or any other commonly suggested themes such as moralism, sentimentalism, or selfishness, is a monopoly of Japanese or of Americans. Both peoples share these traits. The question, then, becomes one of devising a methodological framework in which both Japanese images of the United States and American images of Japan can be analyzed and compared.

It is beyond the scope of this Introduction to develop such a frame-work, but it will be useful to consider these essays as pieces of a puzzle which are all authentic but partial elements of the total picture. The totality of mutual images can be examined only when it is recognized that individual pieces do not represent the whole but only segments of the whole. One way of defining these segments would be to classify given images into various categories. Clapp and Halperin offer one device for classification; they categorize American images of Japan into three themes; inevitable harmony, partnership, and inevitable conflict. They rightly point out that quite often these seemingly contradictory images are entertained by the same individual on different occasions. It might also happen that he has all these images simultaneously, at different levels of consciousness or in response to various circumstances. It is conceivable, for instance, that a businessman may feel threatened by Japanese competition (inevitable conflict) but at the same time have an aesthetic appreciation of Japanese culture (harmony) and believe in the wisdom of continuing the Japanese alliance (partnership). These would all be genuine images and emotions, and it would be difficult to say that only one of them in particular represented his view of Japan.

Such a simplified model merely points up the basic truth that an individual relates himself to the world in a number of different contexts and from a combination of various motives and preconceived notions. The result is that his images and subimages of another country are likely to consist of several symbols that contain various connotations in different contexts. At the very least, it seems possible to identify five types of symbols: globalism, cosmopolitanism, nationalism, particularism, and provincialism.

An American's image of Japan can be said to have a globalistic connotation when he views that country in terms of world politics, an Asian balance of power, or the role of the United States in East Asia. The same is true of a Japanese view of the United States which stresses these considerations. Since power politics are by nature amoral, this component is devoid of moralism or sentimentalism. To the extent that the idea of Japanese-American partnership envisages the maintenance of close political and military ties between the two countries as the key to stability in Asia and the Pacific, such a notion, whether entertained by Japanese or by Americans, falls into this category. Another example from the essays in this volume would be the

American view of Japan during the 1910s which stressed "cooperation" between the two countries. The word implied recognition, tacit or explicit, by America of Japan's superior rights and interests on the Asian continent. It was a reflection of the power realities of the situation and had as its counterpart Japan's readiness to recognize the supremacy of the United States in the Caribbean.

Harris' essay shows that for most Americans these considerations of power politics may have been of only minor interest; for them Japan was what they saw in the fairs. This way of looking at another country may be called a cosmopolitan outlook. It represents the level of consciousness that is receptive to universalistic values and willing to deal with other peoples not as objects of global strategy but in the context of intercultural relations. The Meiji image of America as "the land of the free" is another good example. As Kamei describes them, Japanese visitors to the United States before the 1890s were eager to universalize their observations and see in American ideas and institutions something that transcended the United States. Somewhat different but nonetheless cosmopolitan in outlook were the efforts of Ruth Benedict and other Americans whom Glazer discusses who were genuinely interested in Japan and wanted to learn about the Japanese as a subject for scientific inquiry. Even at the turn of the century, when the theme of rivalry defined a distinct strand of American opinion about Japan, it never entirely replaced cosmopolitanism. For instance, *Japan and Japanese-American Relations* (1912), edited by George Blakeslee, contained many articles that stressed the importance of viewing Japan as a civilization and the Japanese as a people who were not inferior to Americans in aptitude and achievements.

Cosmopolitanism can be economic as well as cultural. "Peace, commerce, and friendship with all nations" was Thomas Jefferson's idea of America's foreign relations. Peace, commerce, and friendship were considered closely interrelated. The idea has had an enormous influence on American thinking. Thus Francis M. Huntington Wilson, whose hostility to Japan was of fundamental importance in Japanese-American relations during the administration of William Howard Taft, could write: "Commerce means contact; contact means understanding; and if one is worthy enough to be respected and liked, if understood, international commerce conduces powerfully to international sympathy."[9] From such a viewpoint, Japan can be seen not only as just another market for American goods and capital but also as a link in the developing network of commercial intercourse through which both Japan and the United States would promote interdependence and understanding among peoples of the world. Basic to such an attitude is appreciation of foreign manufactured goods and of opportunities to integrate a country's economy into the global economy. In a sense the postwar Japanese economic drive, promoted by men whom foreigners have called "economic animals," has the same cosmopolitan connotation. There is a universalistic belief that people everywhere would appreciate quality goods obtainable at lower cost. This was traditional American economic expansionism; it has characterized postwar Japanese expansionism.[10]

Yet trade is not wholly universalistic or cosmopolitan. It is very much part of the national interest for both the United States and Japan. The two governments have found it necessary to protect domestic industries from each other's competition and to devise tax and monetary policies to stimulate exports. Thus, when a Japanese and an American argue about the wisdom of devaluating or revaluing the dollar or the yen, their concern is with safeguarding their respective national interests. This type of pragmatic consideration most frequently characterizes official perceptions of other countries and may be called a nationalistic component of images. Not only in economic but in security, political, and other matters Americans and Japanese view one another at least in part from such an angle. As Miwa's paper shows, for professional military strategists this is often the basic mental framework, although there are always men like Ishihara Kanji who are concerned not only with immediate problems of national defense but also with trends in global politics.

Considerations of national interests do not always dictate that one view another country as a potential enemy. For many Japanese before the war, as Saeki argues, this was indeed the case. They felt that the nation's very existence was being menaced by the United States and worried how war with America could be waged. For other Japanese, however, avoidance of war with the United States was the cardinal objective of national policy. Here may be a case where policy dictates image; once it was decided either that war with the United States was inevitable or that it must be avoided at all cost, images of America could be correspondingly adjusted to buttress such a policy. In any event, a man's image of another country is at times determined by his perception of his own country's interests. This category of images should be distinguished from both the globalistic and cosmopolitan images, although it is possible for an individual to find complete rapport among the three. If there is no such harmony, then he must either establish some priorities among the conflicting images or merely ignore the fact and let them coexist in separate compartments.

Nationalism is particularistic at the collective level. An individual can also be particularistic when viewing another country in terms of his own interests, experiences, and prejudices. Nakanishi's paper gives twenty-eight particularistic entities, each developing his own world view derived from these factors. A Japanese-American's image of Japan is an extreme example of image-formation based on experience. But his is by no means an exceptional case. Consider a statement by a Californian made in 1896: "the industrial revolution now in progress in Japan is a menace to some of the most important interests of America, and . . . it is indeed time to act."[11] His view of Japan was derived from the protectionist sentiment in California, which was beginning to feel the impact of Japanese imports. Although they comprised a tiny fraction of total American imports, Japanese products posed a genuine threat to some groups of Americans. Similarly, Japanese immigration seemed a real menace to some Americans on the West coast. Exclusionists felt their own welfare and stability should take precedence over considerations of power politics, international understanding, or the national interest as defined in Washington. Here was racial particularism. One's image of Japan was largely determined by one's self-consciousness about racial differences.

In Japan particularistic images of the United States were often a function of domestic politics. In the 1920s as in the postwar period the elites in government and business tended to identify with a pro-American attitude, whereas those outside the establishment were prone to have a negative view of the United States. As Miwa's essay suggests, some in the Imperial army and navy advocated war with America in order to reconstruct the country; they were revolting against national leaders who seemed to have corrupted the spiritual essence of Japan by tying the country too closely to the United States. These men were viewing America, not directly, but indirectly as refracted through the lens of domestic politics. Similarly, after

1945, as Nagai and Nishijima note, left-wing teachers grew anti-American not only in response to cold war diplomacy but primarily because they identified the country's leadership (the conservative parties, the business establishment, and bureaucrats) with a pro-American orientation. More recently, the "Nixon shocks" of 1971 revealed that even the pro-Americanists who had staked their power and self-identity on close relations with the United States could be proved to have entertained a misconception about American policy and opinion. Their position domestically was undermined the moment it was shown that their image of the United States had been based on wishful thinking.

Particularism, then, defines the way one looks at other countries in terms of one's self-interest and prejudices. But it does not follow that everybody takes a particularistic view of another country. Quite often attitudes spring from ignorance or indifference. This was the case with an overwhelming majority of Americans during most of the nineteenth century when (if at all) they considered Japan. Japan was no different from Brazil or Samoa. Apart from those few who were affected by ideas about power politics, cultural concerns, nationalistic considerations, or specific personal interests, the attitude of most of the population was one of indifference. Such a response (or rather, lack of response) to a foreign country may be termed provincialism. For instance, throughout the nineteenth century it was customary for American politicians to twist the British lion's tail as an oratorical device. It was not so much that they were interested in British politics or American-British relations as that they thought Britain was irrelevant to the United States and that the latter could and should live a life of its own, independent of British (and world) influences. William Jennings Bryan best exemplified such an attitude. "I say Bryanism is Americanism," declared Senator Henry M. Teller during the presidential election campaign of 1900.[12] Insofar as foreign affairs were concerned, it would have been more correct to say that Bryanism was American provincialism. It represented an attitude of disdain, ignorance, or indifference toward things external to the United States (which were by definition considered un-American).

In terms of exposure and receptivity to foreign influences, the essays in this volume would seem to indicate that provincialism has been less noticeable in Japan than in the United States. This is in part due to the fact that there has generally been a higher rate of mass participation in politics in the United States and therefore provincialism has been more of a problem than in Japan. Equally fundamental has been the tradition of Western learning in Japan.[13] Since the mid-nineteenth century Japanese have been reading and learning from Western literature, history, and the sciences. Most of this learning has been conducted in Japanese; the number of translated works has been staggering. Certainly the average Japanese high school or college student has far more at his disposal (translations of American literature, textbooks of American history, or daily newspaper coverage of the United States) than is the case with his American counterpart. It may even be true that there are more Japanese than English translations of European literature, philosophy, and the social sciences. This does not necessarily mean that the average Japanese is more sophisticated about world affairs than the average American. The papers by Saeki and Katō show that the amount of translated knowledge about the United States does not always enable one to take a balanced view of the country. Japanese as much as Americans have experienced periods of extreme xenophobia. Moreover, while Japanese have been more receptive to foreign ideas and fashions, they have been less tolerant of foreigners residing and working in their midst. While American provincialism has often resulted in isolationism and retreat from overseas commitments, Japanese provincialism has been instrumental in providing an ideology of overseas expansionism.

Comparison of Japanese and American provincialism brings us back to the point of departure of this volume. All the essays seek to make a contribution to the study of images by examining the sources, ranges, uses, and constituencies of images. But they do so in a comparative framework. They are concerned with the issue of how we can come to a better understanding of Japanese history, American history, and Japanese-American relations by tracing the interaction between the two peoples' mutual images and self-images. One way of approaching the task would be to compare the Japanese and American varieties of globalism, cosmopolitanism, nationalism, particularism, and provincialism. Rather than talking about Japanese or American images as an abstract, monolithic entity, we would have to look at various levels of their consciousness and sources of their attitudes.

Japanese-American relations are after all a product of many interactions between individual Japanese, Americans, and Japanese-Americans who combine, in numerous proportions, considerations of global strategy, cosmopolitan concerns, pragmatic national interests, personal prejudices and idiosyncracies, and sheer ignorance and indifference.

Usually discussions of international relations tend to concentrate on global strategy, national security, and economic interests. In the final analysis, however, the bulk of Japanese and Americans would not be found viewing one another in these frameworks. Provincialism or, as its opposite, cosmopolitanism would appear to be a more pervasive force, and such existential conditions as one's race, age, and occupation would be as crucial determinants of one's attitude as considerations of power politics or national interests. If by Japanese-American relations we mean the sum total of all the ways in which the two peoples have responded to one another, then it is obvious that these relations depend ultimately on the attitudes of individuals as they develop a variety of symbols to cope with the perceived world. Ultimately, then, to study images is to engage in symbolic analysis, and to examine mutual images is to compare cultural symbols and philosophical constructs of individuals in several societies. Since international relations are at bottom intercultural relations, scholars of all countries should be able to make significant contributions in this inquiry. It is to be hoped that a volume such as this one will serve to demonstrate the feasibility of scholarly exchanges between different cultures and contribute, if indirectly, to the further refinement of analytical tools.

All the World a Melting Pot? Japan at American Fairs, 1876-1904

The great fairs of the nineteenth and twentieth centuries offer unusual opportunities for the study of international communications. In these controlled settings nation states set out their artistic and industrial achievements, before enormous audiences. Reactions varied, of course. But for certain cultures there was special meaning in these international displays.

The Japanese exhibits at American fairs attracted particularly strong attention. Some of the American interest was aroused by the inherent excellence of the Japanese displays, their novelty and ingenuity. Some was stimulated by the contrast between oriental design and the preponderantly European art and architecture at the fairs. But another reason for American interest had to do with a special feature of Japanese culture—its tension between the pull of modernization and the antiquity of native traditions. For reasons that are fundamental to the character of American civilization, this bifurcation of energy, between ancient arts and modern industry, echoed a different kind of bifurcation in American life. Examining American reactions to the Japanese exhibits we can find clues to the special place of Japan in the American mind of the nineteenth century.

Most Americans made their first contact with Japanese culture at one of the international expositions.[1] American contacts with China go back to the late eighteenth century and involved a variety of commercial, cultural, and missionary expressions. But Japanese exclusion meant that, except for a few sailors and shipwrecked civilians, there was absolutely no interaction between Japan and the United States before the mid-nineteenth century, and very little information about Japan diffused in this country before the Centennial Exhibition of 1876. In the post-Perry era of Japanese-American relations there had been one outstanding incident: the 1860 visit of the Japanese envoys. Their nationwide tour caused a brief sensation and a flurry of writing about Japanese customs. But the Civil War years quickly eclipsed this one experience. As a result, the various fairs made up the only concentrated encounter Americans had with Japanese life and whetted a taste for more information. This was serviced, in the late nineteenth century, by periodical articles and books of description written by travelers or Americans resident in Japan. The fairs not only acquired great importance for Japanese-American relations, they also gave the Japanese government an unparalleled opportunity (not shared by most foreign powers) to define the kind of impression they wished Americans to possess. Visitors to the fairs would have little with which to correct or supplement the official displays, for almost everything they saw or learned at the fairs was new. There is an element of control about these experiences that is quite novel and unusual in the study of mutual images.

International expositions must be considered one of the hallmarks of nineteenth century civilization. To many contemporaries they symbolized the world of peaceful progress that religion and technology seemed combining to establish. Although national expositions had developed in the eighteenth century, the first modern world's fair is generally accepted as the Crystal Palace Exposition held in London in 1851.[2]

Having made its point (and returned a profit), the international exposition was soon imitated in many countries. Americans erected a Crystal Palace in New York City in 1853, but their exhibition had much less impact than its British model. The French, however, took the institution and carried it to new heights of size and artistic elegance. The Paris world's fairs of 1855, 1867, 1878, 1889, and 1900 cost impressive sums of money and attracted millions of visitors. The 1900 fair, the largest of all, was viewed by almost 50 million people.[3] Instead of being placed within a single large building, the fairs of the late nineteenth century spread out over sites of many acres. The landscaped grounds were dotted with national pavilions and enormous palaces of agriculture, transportation, manufacturing, horticulture, and liberal arts. Here the latest achievements of industrial civilization could be viewed.

Although the Paris fairs were the most spectacular, major exhibitions were held in many other places. Vienna hosted one in 1873, on an area of parkland along the Danube. Brussels in 1883 and 1897, Antwerp in 1893, London in 1862, Dublin in 1853, Florence in 1861, Amsterdam in 1864, even far off Sydney in 1879 and Melbourne in 1880 sponsored important exhibitions. And, more to our point, in 1876 the United States got involved and began its own series of spectacular exhibitions.

Most of the major American fairs had as their justification some great national anniversary. However much the fairs turned into booster events for the host cities, the original themes were never forgotten. It was appropriate, therefore, that our first major exhibition celebrated national independence itself. It ran for six months in Philadelphia in the summer of 1876.[4] Planning for the festival began early. In March 1871 Congress passed an act to provide for celebrating the centennial, but it did not provide any funds. It did, however, establish the United States Centennial Commission to encourage foreign participation. One year later Congress established a Centennial Board of Finance to manage the budget of the exhibition, construct buildings, pay debts, and supervise the sale of stock to the public. After various delays, the officers of the fair were appointed in 1874, contracts were let out, and construction was begun on a site in Fairmount Park along the Schuylkill River. The exhibition was to cover some 236 acres, and the managers began with totally uncultivated grounds. All the details of drainage, sewerage, water supply, and plantings had to be undertaken upon this swamp, in addition to the construction. Some 249 buildings would be erected, many of them quite small but others among the largest in the world. The main building would cover twenty acres and Machinery Hall would cover fourteen. The centennial eventually cost several million dollars and recorded more than 10 million admissions. All in all an enormous undertaking, and the first of its scale to take place in the United States.

Because of the importance of the anniversary and the scale of the projected exposition, Americans were eager to learn the response of foreign states. The fair was designed to demonstrate that the United States now possessed the fruits of western civilization and could rival in splendor and elegance, as well as practicality, the great fairs that Europe had hosted. But without generous international participation, without the national pavilions, art collections, and examples of industry gathered from all over the world, the Centennial Exposition would be unable to make major claims.

As expected, the larger European powers responded. Great Britain appropriated $250,000 for its display (an amount supplemented and even surpassed by its private exhibitors); Germany followed close behind; France, Sweden, Austria-Hungary, Russia, and Italy also responded. Latin America made a good representation. All of this was very gratifying to Americans. "A unanimous, graceful and cordial bow of acceptance" swept "round the globe in response to the invitation of the youngest member of the family," wrote one contemporary historian, self-conscious about America's entry into the world of expositions. Many foreigners, he suggested, still had the impression that their host "was not yet fully out of the woods, that the chestnut-burs were still sticking in his hair, and that the wolf, the buffalo and the Indian were among his intimate daily chums."[5] But they would find something different. The "country cousin" would surprise his guests with "city hospitalities." It was not the American's habit "to aim too low."

Anxious to redeem themselves from the charge of boorishness and materialism, Americans were grateful for the scale of foreign participation. But there were other foreign powers, also new to the crowded stage of expositions, and as eager as the Americans to make a good impression. Foremost among these was Japan. The country had first been represented at the Paris fair of 1867, where the Shogunate and two provinces (Satsuma and Hizen han) had mounted small-scale displays. But the fair coincided with the turmoil of the Meiji Restoration, and it was not again until the Vienna fair of 1873 that the national government took charge of the Japanese effort. Preparations for the Vienna show were hurried. An official commission was not appointed until June 1872, barely one year before the fair opened. This did not allow enough time for the elaborate planning that was necessary. The American fair was another story. The Japanese learned about the centennial celebration as early as June 1873 and decided to participate in June 1874. They officially responded to the invitation six months later.[6]

Soon afterwards, Japanese carpenters traveled to Philadelphia to erect the national pavilion. Two structures were put up near the west gate of the grounds, one, a small bazaar and tea house, the other, a large, two-story building that contained, among other things, residential quarters for the Japanese commission. Besides this there were Japanese sections in Agricultural Hall and in the main exhibition building. The placing of the Japanese display in the main building revealed how literally Americans interpreted the power of national character and the peaceful competition of the fairs. Japan was placed in the western section of the building, next to China. This corresponded to its geographical location relative to the United States. "France and Colonies, representing the Latin races," reported the director general, "was given space adjacent to the northeast central tower. England and Colonies, representing the Anglo-Saxon races, were given spaces adjacent to the northwest central tower. The German Empire, and Austria and Hungary, representing the Teutonic races, were granted space adjacent to the southwest tower."[7] To make racial installation and identification complete, the commissioners tried to place around France those peoples of Latin extraction, and around Germany those of Teutonic extraction. Despite the optimistic environmentalism that dominated American thought, the careful racial classifications indicated that Americans were prepared for the hereditarianism that would become increasingly popular in the late nineteenth century.

More than thirty nations participated in the centennial. Japan's exhibit, however, stood out sharply. It had accepted early and the preparations were extensive. Japan shipped more than 7,000 packages to Philadelphia, exceeded only by Great Britain.[8] With 17,831 square feet in the main building and some 284 separate exhibitors, the Japanese were surpassed by only a few, countries much larger or much closer to the United States. And Japan had one of the nine foreign government buildings.

But the size and costliness of the display was not its chief characteristic. Rather, Americans reacted to its total novelty. The Japanese art wares were different from anything seen here before. The sense of newness spread even before the centennial opened. In February 1876 the *New York Times* described the Japanese workers building the official pavilion.[9] Crowds gathered daily to scrutinize the strange, "almond-eyed" carpenters and their bizarre methods. The tea house, constructed in Japan and put together in Philadelphia, resembled "an ingenious puzzle which was being connected." No nails were employed and the framework rested on posts, rather than the usual masonry foundations. The Japanese exuded an impression of neatness and precision. Their craftsmanship contrasted with that of the Chinese, the only Asians Americans knew. "Contrary to what has been observed of the Chinese in California and the mining regions," the *Times* continued, "the children of the Flowery Land do not burst into song when plying the implements of carpentry, but work away in absolute silence." Ignorance of Japan made any details welcome. The workers "wear a thick blue garment . . . and dark-blue pants, with some stout shoes apparently soled with paper. Their doublets are embroidered on the back with white, and have large loose sleeves." The *Times* declared that the people of Philadelphia were delighted and wished only for a bit more animation, distrusting "the cold reserve" of the Japanese workmen. "Some of the lookers-on certainly believe all Japs to be acrobats, and I overheard a young lady ask her mother if the Jap who was hammering one of the lengths of the upright post with the other would not climb up and balance himself on the top." Because he did not, the girl said she wouldn't have come "through all that mud and clay if she hadn't thought that they were real Japs, but now she saw that they were only imitation ones."

What articles like this revealed was the local thirst for exotica. Americans longed for the quaint and the different and were invariably disappointed at half-measures. In one of his pieces on the centennial, published in the *Atlantic Monthly*, William Dean Howells recorded his disappointment on seeing only one Japanese man in national costume. The others wore Western dress "which they had evidently but half subdued to their use." "It is a great pity not to see them in their own outlandish gear, for picturesqueness' sake," Howells went on; "the show loses vastly by it; and if it is true that the annoyances they suffered from the street crowds forced them to abandon it, we are all disgraced by the fact."[10] The Japanese example was imitated by many. "There is a lamentable lack of foreignness in the dress at the Centennial. The costumed peoples have all put on European wear." Americans expected foreigners to behave like foreigners; imitation seemed a form of cultural dilution, all the more objectionable in a land without much picturesque diversity. "In the cities of Europe," according to the *Atlantic,* "the spectacle of people from far-off countries in strange, picturesque garb is an every-day matter, and fails to raise the emotions it does with us."[11]

But if Americans could not encounter Japanese costume, there remained much that was strange and interesting in an exhibit "whose beauty has nothing to do with newness or utility." Americans seemed to take a special pleasure in the fact that Europe's boasted antiquity was dwarfed by this visitor from the East. The Orient could be used to strike back at the pretensions of the Old World, which for so long had reminded Americans of their youth and lack of cultivation. Compare Japanese antiques with the treasures of famous Christian shrines, one critic suggested. "What barbarous lumps of gold and silver stuck full of jewels of the rudest shape are the crowns." The very preciousness of the materials and the size of the diamonds and rubies only aggravated "the clumsiness of design and execution." But in Japanese handicrafts, 800 years old or more, one found "a grace and elegance of design and fabulous perfection of workmanship which rival or excel the marvels of Italian or ornamental art at its zenith." Moreover, there was "no decline nor degeneracy, no period of corruptness and coarseness, such as the Renaissance shows in its decay."[12]

The Japanese section in the main building featured porcelains, bronzes, silks, embroideries, and lacquered ware. With a frontage of some 100 feet, Japanese exhibitors arranged two large rectangular platforms, placed diagonally to the main avenue. In the middle of the triangle formed by the platforms stood a large bronze fountain, and flying above all was the flag of Japan.[13] According to James McCabe the display was "one of the great surprises of the fair." Visitors to the exhibition would have to amend their ideas about Japan, McCabe continued. "We have been accustomed to regard that country as uncivilized, or half-civilized at the best, but we found here abundant evidences that it outshines the most cultivated nations of Europe in arts which are their pride and glory, and which are regarded as among the proudest tokens of their high civilization."[14] Once again the theme of orientals beating Europeans at their own game appealed to Americans. "After the Japanese collection everything looks in a measure commonplace, almost vulgar," ran one comment.[15] The Japanese "have all the willing courtesy and readiness to show attention so often ascribed to the French people," went another observation, "but they have super-added thereto the same simplicity and artlessness in their manners which one cannot but recognize in the aesthetic work of the nation, and which crowns the knowledge and skill so conspicuous in it with a higher grade."[16] The fact that the most striking vase in the Japanese exhibit went to an English purchaser caused Edward Bruce to pause. "Think of such a concession from the conceit of Western civilization!" exulted Bruce. "It is content, at the first summons, to accept instruction in one of the highest walks of industrial art from what it has been wont to style the effete and mouldy civilizations of the extreme East."[17] American schools and museums were also heavy purchasers and in Bruce's account further testified to the new obeisance being paid the Orient.

A number of things can be generalized from reactions to the Japanese exhibit. First of all, despite occasional recognition of Japanese efforts at modernization, most attention was lavished on Japanese art and craftwork. Indeed, there was some criticism of the fact that the government decided to emphasize so heavily the aesthetic aspects of its culture. One Philadelphia newspaper, noting that "this veritable wonderland" was "constantly thronged by sightseers," took the Japanese commissioners to task. They should have remembered that the world wished to know more of Japan. Instead of turning their exhibit into a salesroom for bronzes and porcelain, it would have been better if "the commissioners had done more towards making us understand their country and the life of the people." The Japanese bazaar could have concentrated on selling and exhibiting. The public would have enjoyed learning more about Japanese schools, industries, and customs.[18]

But most observers did not criticize the concentration on art; they simply enjoyed it. Presuppositions that Eastern aesthetic principles were grotesque eroded as Americans reconsidered their faith in realism. The year following the centennial the *New York Times* insisted that "a correctly-drawn, much less a noble, human figure never came from the brain of a Japanese draughtsman," but it allowed the Japanese "delicacy of fancy, a thorough sympathy with a few aspects of nature, a fine sense of humor, and an intimate acquaintance with the use of the primitive colors."[19] Most other commentators were still more enthusiastic. One newspaper was impressed with "the subdued elegance, the subtle and delicate taste, the symbolism of art" that lay everywhere. There was nothing suggesting Greek or European plastic art, and no exaltation of the human body. But this could bear interesting interpretation. "The Japanese artist seems to sink the human personality in deference to the vast personality of nature, and oftener humbles the former by putting men and women into pantomime, comedy, grotesque, and ridiculous situations, than ministers to human pride by anything grandiose or dignified."[20] This may produce, the writer concluded, the "utter absence of conceit" that marked the Japanese character. The grotesque was rarely employed in depicting natural objects, such as trees or mountain ranges, which indicated that "the instinct of sublimity" remained part of the Japanese artist's sensibility.

A second and related aspect of the American reaction was not simply an interest in art but particular delight in certain aspects of it. Instead of praising Japanese restraint, harmony, and reticence (although occasional comments appeared), Americans enjoyed Japanese profusion, costliness, and adornment. Japan had escaped the domination of machine-made objects, "mouldings . . . run out for us by the mile, like iron from the rolling-mill or tunes from a musical box."[21] In place of hackneyed forms Japanese art used original and intricate designs. It was "gorgeous" and "delicate." "There is no repetition of parts on different sides or faces" of the objects being exhibited, marveled one reporter. "The variety, the patient originality, has no limit."[22] The fountain that dominated the entry to the Japanese section was "inlaid with silver, covered with raised figures, and more crowded with embellishment than a Gothic shrine. Beyond this is literally a forest of bronze, with interlacing stems, leafage and feathered, scaled and furry inhabitants. Penetrate it, and you find that like other forests it separates into individual members, vases of various hue and shape representing the trees." Even the gardens, as Americans described them, were profuse and lavish, rather than economical and restrained.[23]

Everything, in fact, gave an impression of patient work. In an America where labor was dear, this meant extreme costliness. Visitors and guidebooks alike emphasized how long it had taken to manufacture various items and how expensive it would be to purchase them. One vase on exhibition, reported J. S. Ingram, represented the equivalent of 2,250 days of steady labor for one man, and the $2,000 price did not seem excessive.[24] Marietta Holley, author of a series of books narrated by an American Mrs. Malaprop, Samantha, developed this theme. "Such nicety of work, such patience and long sufferin' as must have gone into their manufactorys," observed Samantha. "Why there was a buro, black and gold, with shelves and draws, and doors hung with gold and silver hinges, and every part of that buro clear to the backside of the bottom draw was nicer, and fixed off handsomer than any handkerchief pin. They asked four thousand five hundred dollars for it, and it was worth it." The vases stood higher than Samantha's husband, and the handles were "clear dragons . . . and a row of wimmen a dancin' round it, each one carryin' a rose in her hand bigger than her head, and up the side of it was foxes in men's clothes. And the handles of another vase was a flock of birds settlin' down on a rock, with a dragon on it, and on top of it a eagle aswoopin' down onto a snake."[25]

Creators of such delicate objects had to be sensitive themselves. The Japanese men at the exhibition ("though dark complexioned," complained Samantha) were so patient and polite answering questions, "not losin' their gentle ways and courtesy, not gettin' fractious or worrysome a mite."[26] Their art work seconded the impression of Japanese character that Americans had held since the Perry expedition. The 1860 visit, according to American commentators, showed how polite, disciplined, and imperturbable were the Japanese. "They are the sweetest-voice, gentlest-manner folk," said one visitor to the fair, "and it is impossible to look from their small forms to their exquisite productions without an uncomfortable misgiving that they may feel like so many Gullivers in Brobdingnag."[27] The *Atlantic* made the connection between art and national character most explicit, when it described the "doll-work" of the park and bazaar and noted that the railings around the lily garden were "about as stout as a sandalwood fan." If this served as protection in Japan, not only the men but the beasts themselves "must be as gentle as the lilies of the field."[28]

Thus Japanese screens, porcelain, silks, and bronzes were welcomed. American parlors and drawing rooms of the 1870s featured profusion and redundancy, cabinets filled with curios, carpets with complicated patterns and rugs over them, antimacassars, flowers, carvings, paintings hung from ceiling to floor. Although Japanese art was exotic it suited American tastes and fitted American expectations.[29] This combination accounted for the craze that succeeded the exposition, a popularity that permitted Tiffany's to make profits from Japanese imports and that prompted the Japanese government itself to open an agency in New York to distribute its native products. In the years that followed tens of thousands of fans, vases, and bronzes flooded middle-class households.

Although this exotica was popular because it fitted American taste, Americans had a third and paradoxical reaction to the Japanese exhibits: one of anxiety and concern. They feared that Western patronage might destroy the distinctive Japanese characteristics they claimed to admire, and substitute subservience to European and American taste and shoddiness of manufacture and design. Japanese art is excellent and honest, Charles Wyllys Elliott conceded in the *Atlantic*, but it would "certainly go down before the arrogant demands of trade. Already there is sufficient evidence that they are perceiving the desirableness of shoddy and the importance of cheapness; already they are making us pay 'through the nose.' "[30] The *New York Times*, in its critical report on Japanese art, suggested that the only changes it had undergone were "for the worse," from a foolish desire to please the West.[31] Oriental designs based on French or Dutch models were hideous. "Some travelers complain that the people of Eastern Europe and Asia are losing their old-time picturesqueness," noted the *Philadelphia Bulletin* in an article on Japanese preparations for the fair. "Many of these natives are fast adopting the manners and customs, as well as the costumes, of Western civilization. By and by they will cease to make the curious things with which we have always identified them." China and Japan will continue to export silk, tea, and carvings, but "we shall have no more cloisonné, jade-work, wonderful lacquer-ware, and eggshell porcelain, if the Asiatics do not get over their rabid eagerness for sewing-machines, planes, and self-raking reapers." It was fine, as Carlyle put it, to watch an oriental nation "getting tragically out of bed," but "sentimental and poetical people say that the world is losing an element of pictorial beauty which it cannot afford to spare."[32]

The *Bulletin* refused to despair. It admitted that the mikado in high hat and pantaloons might lose dignity, "but we are bound to believe that his subjects are to be better, by the moral and material changes which come in with that awkward garb." Despite its brave front, and Edward Bruce's denial of the charge that the Japanese were no longer independent of European artistic influences,[33] one finds in these comments a curious mixture of deference and unquiet. Almost without exception guidebooks, newspaper comments, and visitors' reactions were favorable. It was not simply novelty, for the Chinese exhibits were either ignored or downgraded. "China and Japan are both queer," Samantha reported, "but Japan's queerness has a imaginative artistic quirl to it that China's queerness don't have."[34] If Japan was China's student, wrote Edward Bruce, "the pupil has surpassed the teacher."[35] "We relegate the Chinese to the half-civilized class without hesitation," offered one Philadelphia paper, "or without feeling that any indignity has been offered, and this fact shows what an important difference there is between Japanese and Chinese civilization."[36] For various reasons Chinese art had deteriorated, while Japanese art had still maintained its purity. The Japanese artists and craftsmen exemplified discipline, patience, and quaintness.

But what at first glance seems love for the exotic was basically assimilatory. The Japanese did not present fundamental challenges in their first appearance. The sense that Japanese civilization was an alternative (and superior) mode of life to Western models would come later. Yet the Japanese were admired, paradoxically, both because they respected the West and because they resisted it. The fear that communication would bring homogeneity was a real one. Just as Japanese nationals at the fair had lost picturesqueness by donning Western dress, so cabinetmakers and potters might abandon native gifts in favor of client orientation. The *Bulletin*'s conviction that loss of picturesqueness would mean physical improvement was equivocal. The dilemma of how to accept the prospect of westernization crystallized American attitudes toward national difference generally: on the one hand, a tendency to see Americanization as a sign of progress; on the other, a desire to freeze national customs into a picturesque whole. One of the two effects produced on fair visitors was a feeling "that they are glad that they are Americans," wrote a visitor to another exposition. "And the other one is that they know, as they never knew before, that not by any means all of the world is in America, nor even all the best things."[37] The Japanese raised the problem graphically. "In view of the education, intelligence, and refinement of the Japanese," one newspaper argued during the centennial, "it seems hardly consistent to class them with the 'half-civilized' races, and yet the gulf between them and the highest civilization is hardly less than on the other hand is that between the American Indians and themselves." It might be allowed, the newspaper continued, "from a partial view that Japanese culture is the highest of its kind, and that the kind is one peculiar to the East," but we must have standards, "and Europe is that standard."[38] Confronting real difference, Americans drew back; confronting the uniformity that would come from westernization, they had their doubts as well. The paradox that would come to dominate mid-twentieth century reactions to industrial and technological change was thus demonstrated in this first experience with Japanese culture.

In the wake of the Philadelphia show knowledge about Japan increased among Americans. William Griffis' *Mikado's Empire* became a major source of information, supplemented by travel reminiscences and periodical articles about Japanese art, religion, and modernization. These pieces were designed for highly literate audiences and frequently took on an academic and scholarly tone. Ernest Fenollosa, Percival Lowell, Edward Morse, Lafcadio Hearn, and Sturgis Bigelow, collectors, architects, philosophers, and artists flocked to the East in greater numbers. They grew convinced that Japanese attitudes toward family life, rituals, and personal relationships were complex and worthy of study, if not emulation. More Americans than not, however, received information about Japan from occasional newspaper articles or pieces run in semipopular magazines like *Harper's Weekly*. But there were more fairs to come.

After the centennial the Japanese went on exhibiting in European expositions, but the government also paid attention to smaller American shows. In 1885, for example, New Orleans hosted a fair in which the Japanese participated. Lafcadio Hearn, later an influential com-

mentator on Japanese life, was working as a newspaperman in New
Orleans at the time. He gave extensive coverage to "The East at New
Orleans" for *Harper's Weekly*.[39] Japanese emphasis had changed
somewhat. Japan now featured its educational advances, universities,
scientific apparatus, and publishing industry. Hearn argued that the
scientific volumes he examined at New Orleans compared favorably
with the best French work. Moreover, the Japanese showed great
ingenuity in the design of scientific instruments for teaching, particularly when they were unable to purchase what they needed. Hearn
paid his respects to the bronzes, the ivories, the fans, and the animal
paintings, but unlike the commentators at Philadelphia he spent more
time describing Japan's response to the modern world and its rapid
strides in science and education.

The New Orleans exhibit, however, was just a taste of what would
come at Chicago in 1893. The World's Columbian Exposition, held in
Chicago to celebrate the four hundredth anniversary of Columbus'
landing, was probably the single most successful exposition held in
America. No other fair ever matched its reputation for beauty and
harmony, a brilliant technical display of what Victorian administrative genius and building ability could accomplish at their best.[40]

Everything about the Chicago fair was bigger than its predecessor.
The Jackson Park site was 686 acres, and the official expenditures on
the exposition came to more than $28 million. The number of foreign
buildings was doubled from Philadelphia to Chicago and the number
of exhibition palaces more than tripled. Around the palaces and
pavilions clustered hundreds of concessions that brought the fair
authorities thousands of dollars from various restaurants, foreign
villages, and amusements. All in all close to 30 million people visited
the fair, and its greatest single day, Chicago day, saw a crowd of
more than 600,000 struggle into the park grounds.

Like many other governments Japan sought to participate in this
great festival, which had so many more assurances of success than
the affair in Philadelphia two decades earlier. Indeed, Japanese participation revealed a special intensity of interest, because of the circumstances under which it was demonstrated. In March 1890 the
Imperial Diet was holding its first session, in Japan's initial attempt
at parliamentary government. Although an official invitation from
the Columbian Exposition had not yet been received and despite the

strain between the Diet and the executive concerning the national budget, the Diet voluntarily proposed that provision be made for Japanese participation in the Chicago fair and agreed to appropriate the funds when necessary. In November, six months later, a supplementary appropriation of 630,000 yen for participation was submitted to the Diet by the government and passed unanimously. Six months later the emperor appointed a commission to supervise preparations. It was placed directly under the government's control, the minister of agriculture and commerce becoming the ex officio president of the commission. To widen support and improve communication, an advisory council was appointed that included manufacturers and merchants.[41]

The care and self-consciousness that marked the creation of the commission also characterized its later works. The commission declared that the selection of Japanese artifacts and manufactured goods was to be representative of the country's actual production, not specially chosen for high quality nor given misleadingly false prices to attract international attention. The same items employed in domestic use were to be shown in Chicago. The one exception concerned art; here, stung by previous criticisms about the westernization of Japanese artists and already caught up in the revival of interest in Japanese traditions that succeeded the westernizing craze of the 1870s, the commission announced it would be carefully selective. In each Japanese prefecture local commissions were appointed to examine and advise potential exhibitors. As before, the government promised to pay the freight on exhibits, in addition to insurance and storage charges which the long trip inevitably would require.

This concerted national effort resulted in an enormous quantity of goods. Originally, Minister Tateno noted, the government had expected that 1,000 tons of material would be shipped to Chicago, three times the weight shipped to Philadelphia and triple even that sent to Paris for the great 1889 fair. When local commissions forwarded their proposals, however, the total amounted to 7,000 tons, and it was only after considerable effort that a final figure of 1,750 tons, more than five times the Philadelphia total, was arrived at.

With all these preparations it was of course vital that adequate space be obtained at Chicago. Here the authorities were under great pressure from exhibiting countries, each wishing better locations and larger sites than could be made available. The Chicago managers, after some early arguments, agreed to make available for the official Japanese display a 40,000 square foot site on the Wooded Island, a small piece of land located near the Fine Arts Building and a superb spot for visual relief from the overpowering classicism of the exposition. Originally Frederick Olmsted, who supervised the fair's landscaping, wanted to keep the island a refuge from all formal fair activities. But the Japanese, who promised to present their buildings as a gift to the people of Chicago, managed to change the commission's mind. In addition to this central display the Japanese were to have sections in the Palace of Manufactures and Liberal Arts (40,000 square feet), in the Fine Arts Palace (2,850 square feet), in Agriculture, Horticulture, Forestry, Mines, and Fisheries, and a large spot on the Midway Plaisance, where the amusement and refreshment concessions were located, for a tea house and bazaar. Although the Japanese building on the Wooded Island took up only a small part of the site, the rest being devoted to landscaped gardens, the Japanese building was still the seventh largest at the fair, exceeded only by the great powers and various Latin American countries.

As in Philadelphia, the preparations made by the Japanese attracted great attention. Everything about the national effort seemed praiseworthy. *Harper's Weekly* ran a little note in the spring of 1893 about Japanese skill at unpacking the delicate art works. Packers could learn much from "the patient and careful Japanese, who do this thing to perfection. Not only is each article put away so that there is no chance for breakage, but after the case is fastened tightly provision is made against mishaps from rough handling."[42] The Japanese indicated by marks the side to be placed uppermost, apparently an innovation, and placed handles on their cases so that stevedores could move them conveniently.

But the unpacking was trivial compared to the construction efforts. Even while the snow from Chicago's winter still covered the Wooded Island, Japanese joiners began to construct their pavilion, surrounded by curious crowds. "And what bright and nimble fellows these workmen were," reported *Harper's*. "It may be that they were picked men, selected for their skill and intelligence . . . It seems almost a pity that these carpenters could not be kept at work all during the fair."[43] The numbers gathering to watch the workmen were so great that ropes had to be put up to keep them from the construction site, and they plied the workmen with questions about the novel techniques they were employing. The carpenters, according to observers, retained their good humor and answered the inquiries.

What they were building represented an ambitious attempt to sum up important periods in the history of Japanese art and architecture. The pavilion actually consisted of three separate parts, designed to resemble the plan of the Hō-ōden or Phoenix Hall, built at Uji near Kyoto in the twelfth century. This new version of the Phoenix Hall was designed by a government architect, Kuru Masamichi. The north wing was set up to display the art of the Fujiwara era, with ornamental doors, paintings, and objects appropriate to the period. The south wing was done in the style of the Ashikaga period and contained several rooms including a library and a tea room. A central hall, which connected the two wings, was done in the elaborate style of the Tokugawa period and included an interior that duplicated one in Edo castle. The total supposedly cost the Japanese government more than $100,000, but if the delighted response of visitors was any test, the sum was a good investment. Moreover, portions of the building remained standing well into the twentieth century, and some years later, the Japan Society built a tea house on the Wooded Island which remained in use until the 1940s.

The Chicago building, argues Clay Lancaster, the best student of Japanese architectural influence in America, was both more significant and more elegant than the centennial effort. Its structural honesty and craftsmanship contrasted with the huge plaster palaces that stood nearby, a building that was "human in scale and appealing," showing that "architecture—real architecture—need make no apologies for its use of simple, everyday materials."[44]

Besides the building on the Wooded Island, the Japanese made extensive exhibits in the other buildings already mentioned. Their fine arts display was particularly impressive (270 of the 291 items of decorative art in the Palace of Fine Arts were Japanese, although they contributed only 24 of the 1,013 sculpture works and 55 of the 7,357 paintings), and unlike at Philadelphia the manufacturing and educational aspects of Japanese life were well treated also. There were 72 exhibits of rice, 215 exhibits of tea and tobacco, specimens of vermicelli, hemp, mineral waters, umbrella handles, artificial fruits, photographs of railroad lines and telegraph systems, surgical instruments, textbooks, statistics of life insurance and crime, razors, safes, buttons, silverware, toys, perfumes—in short, everything that any Western nation was producing could be found in the Japanese display.[45]

The response to the Japanese exhibits took note of both the objects of art and the objects of industry, but the art continued to attract the most attention. Again the carvings in wood, ivory, and bronze, the vases decorated with dragons, the incense boxes, metal screens, embroideries, cut velvets, portières, all attracted admiration because of their marvelous colors and elaborate detail. That it was different from Western art did not seem to matter to the visitors. "Having no lumps of Parian marble with all but speaking tongues, and no canvases that the royal palaces might covet," wrote H. D. Northrop, "Japan welcomes the nations to see gems in pounded brass and chiseled ivory and carved wood and inlaid gold." Their art presented "life as the people of the rising sun know it, muscles and bones and sinews as their athletes possess them, flowers and rivers and mountains such as their country affords. No foreign school of any age or any clime has warped the native taste."[46] Once again, as in Philadelphia, it was costliness and elaborateness that attracted Americans, things like the $30,000 tapestry displaying a festival procession with more than 1,000 separate pieces. That the strange animals and vegetable forms might be termed grotesque some admitted, but "there is no gainsaying the extreme delicacy of execution and design."[47]

Americans now felt it easier to generalize about the Japanese character and to couple their praise for art with admiration for Japanese modernization. The enormous Japanese school system, with its eight "higher schools" and tens of thousands of primary schools, was displayed in photographs and pamphlets. The Japanese ability to gain discipline without punishment was longingly described by Americans, who did not know how to accomplish it in their own land. One visitor reported on the reaction in Japan when the emperor published an address inculcating moral duties that was hung in all the schools. In America such a statement, issued by the president, "would have invited every mischievous boy in school to aim paper wads and bits of crayon. But in Japan the effect was tremendous. Children looked up to the address as a thing to remember and ponder.

Both they and the teachers made obeisance to the photograph before they began the school work of the day."[48]

Japanese courtesy provided an object lesson for *Harper's Weekly* while the fair was still on. Angry because the United States Senate refused to pass needed legislation during the financial panic of 1893 (senators insisted that the opposition be permitted to oppose aid to the unemployed for as long as they wished to talk), *Harper's* labeled this a false politeness. "What might have been the effect on American manners if the gentle Japanese had been held up to our childish eyes as our models of propriety," the magazine wondered. "For what the Japanese call politeness springs from the heart, and is the simple expression of kindly feelings. Think of cities where the potter places the still moist products of his wheel out in the middle of the street to dry in the sun, and where the children in their play step carefully around among the fragile wares lest they work injury to the trustful artisan."[49]

Politeness remained the overwhelming characteristic Americans associated with Japan. The ubiquitous Samantha also visited the Columbian Exposition, as she had the centennial, and reported that the Japanese temple was gorgeous but queer. "But then," Samantha theorized, "I spoze them Japans would call the Jonesville meetin'-house queer; for what is strange in one country is second nater in another."[50] "The Japans," she went on, "are the politest nation on the earth; they say cheatin' and lyin' haint polite, and so they don't want to foller 'em; they hitch principle and politeness right up in one team and ride after it."[51] Politeness was coupled with a childlike nature; the Japanese were invariably termed "little," and Samantha philosophized that "The Japanese are a child-like people easily pleased, easily pleased, easily grieved—laughin' and cryin' jest like children."[52] For Americans in the late nineteenth century docility and childlike behavior were often associated with laziness and backwardness. A favorite theme of southerners was the "childlike" character of the Negro. The Japanese, however, belied this image because they added to politeness and docility tremendous industry and discipline. Denton J. Snider, an American philosopher, found its unified excellence the most impressive feature of the Japanese displays. It was not only their art that pleased: their exhibit in the Liberal Arts Building was "large, very attractive, and well-ordered." "We meet them everywhere, and they are doing their best."[53]

So clear was Japanese energy and advancement that comparisons with China now flooded to the surface. "The Japanese," wrote H. G. Cutler, a visitor to the fair, "have not the staid, placid dispositions of the Chinese. They are more light-hearted, and even at table often enliven the simple courses with music upon the guitar."[54] For Mrs. D. C. Taylor, China was a "strange, cold, homeless, heartless, heathen land!" It was filled with "down-trodden women, priests, and tyrant-ridden men." A "strange depression of mind and sickness of heart" came over her when she thought of the Celestial Kingdom. Japan, however, was quite different, the "suave, smiling" Japanese just the opposite of the "pigtailed, avaricious Chinese."[55] Julian Hawthorne, son of the famous novelist, found Japanese art humorous and lively, but Chinese humor reminded him of a "weird grimace," and he assumed the Chinese were "without souls" in their worship of antiquity and their earthly everlastingness.[56]

The unexpected combination of industry and docility puzzled some commentators, who found other paradoxes to ponder. It is a wonder "how so mild and good-humored a people as they evidently are," commented H. G. Cutler, "can live under so sanguinary a code of laws. Death is the general penalty."[57] The combination of chrysanthemum and sword was noted early by American visitors.

The popularity of the Japanese displays was attested to by more than the comments on the official pavilion and the manufacturers' show. The Midway Plaisance featured a myriad of amusements. They grossed more than $4 million during the exposition, ten times what the concessions at the Philadelphia fair had taken in. There were such popular features as "Cairo Street" where "Little Egypt" danced, "Old Vienna," "Hagenbeck's Zoological Show," "Donegal Castle," and many others. Almost four hundred concessions competed for public favor. One of the most popular shows on the Midway, certainly within the top ten of the foreign exhibits, was the Japanese bazaar, operated by Y. Maurai. It was "dretful ornamental," said Samantha, who wandered about looking at Japanese spinners, weavers, dyers, and musicians, visiting houses made of bamboo without nails, and, of course, the tea house. The Japanese bazaar did a business of more than $200,000 in the six months of the fair, and the Nippon tea house took in an additional $23,000.[58]

For the second time, then, Japan had succeeded in making an enormous impact among the visitors. Everything Japanese excited interest. Wherever "the flag of Japan was displayed," wrote Tudor Jenks in a children's book about the fair, "the boys never grudged time for examination. That artistic little nation can always teach a lesson to natives of the young occident."[59] Even the grocery displays in the Manufactures Building revealed a special touch and elegance. The Japanese government seconded its exhibitions by large amounts of printed material, books, and pamphlets listing Japan's recent statistical triumphs, timetables, travel literature, and comprehensive catalogues. "I just made up my mind that if they were heathens," said the hero of Carl Western's novel about the exposition, "there were lots of things we could learn from them."[60] "I don't see," observed another visitor in similar terms, "the use of sending missionaries to Japan. I suppose they do worship all them things, but even if they do, I think that if they had as much pretty china to home as they've got here, I'd be inclined to worship it myself . . . I should think the Japanese would almost feel like sending missionaries over here."[61]

There remained, of course, some sense of the dangers of modernization. Hubert Bancroft complained that as a result of the great demand for Japanese articles "the simple characteristics of earlier Japanese work have become somewhat vulgarized, for the restless commercial spirit has seized upon Japanese and American alike, and lowered the former standard."[62] Nevertheless, the anxiety level seemed lower than at Philadelphia. "They have grown quite accustomed to our ways," proclaimed the official directory to the fair, "and do not surrender their methods in favor of ours unless the superiority of the new over the old is apparent."[63] Few commentators bothered to say much about the dangers of Japanese assimilation.

So impressive was the Japanese effort that some felt it needed to be explained. The energy put by Japan into the fair argued that it was demanding more respect than the world had paid it previously. The carvings, the ivory, the porcelain and lacquer work, "all arranged faultlessly and displayed with the peculiar smiling self-confidence which marks the race," wrote Joseph and Caroline Kirkland, "seemed to say 'We belong among you; we have something to teach as well as something to learn.' "[64] Denton Snider thought the Japanese exhibit so conspicuous that it demanded commentary. "The Japanese are plainly the vanguard in the Occidental movement toward the Orient," he argued. Historically, the movement of civilization had been east to west, coming from western Asia, through Europe, America, and now Japan. The Japanese were the bearers of the new order and stood confronting the Chinese, representing the old. "We are, therefore, inclined to read in this attempt of Japan the effort to put itself into line with the world-historical movement of the Occident. It allies itself with the nations of the West, especially does it appeal to the United States," Snider noted approvingly. "One cannot help noticing here the care with which the Japanese man explains that he is not a Chinaman."[65] Snider felt that Japan was preparing for an approaching struggle by winning the sympathy of the West. This was the reason for the many books and pamphlets reporting on Japanese progress that the government was distributing in Chicago. Snider agreed with the Kirklands. The Japanese message was "I am one of you."[66] Japan will remain Japan, he concluded, and would not lose its individuality, but it had nonetheless joined the march of Western civilization.

The Chicago exposition, then, had meaning both for the Americans and the Japanese. American visitors, still clinging to their image of the Japanese as a childlike, humorous, artistic people, now began to acknowledge that this oriental civilization had somehow managed to achieve a parity of sorts with the industrial West. The Japanese welcomed the tributes paid their arts and manufactures. Traveling in Japan in the 1890s William Elroy Curtis noted how the White City had advertised Chicago in Japan. "Everybody knows about it," he wrote. "Three or four years ago the ordinary Japanese tradesman and mechanic knew of the existence of London, Paris, and New York, and many of them were familiar with the name of San Francisco." Now, however, "every school-boy and girl, even the little tots in the kindergarten, are familiar with the name and the location of Chicago and with the appearance of the buildings of the exposition, and when an ordinary merchant or mechanic heard I was from that city he looked up with a gleam of gratified recognition—as if he had met an old friend." The Japanese, reported Curtis, called the exposition "Dai Bankoku Hakuran Kwai," or "the great place for seeing objects from all countries."[67]

Some years later an English visitor to Japan, A. Herbage Edwards, made a similar discovery. On a pilgrimage to Izumo in western

Japan, he visited a temple at Kizuki. The priests greeting him took him to a plaster statue of the sun goddess, who bore proudly on her wrist "a much-worn ticket, stating in printed Roman capitals, that 'This exhibit has won a Prize at the World's Fair at Chicago.' " Edwards recalled the "white sunlight filtering through the yellow matting" falling on "white-robed priests who serve a temple worshipped through two thousand years" and "on the faded ticket on the arm of the Sun-Goddess."[68]

The Japanese had specific hopes for Chicago. Describing the exhibition in the *North American Review,* Tateno Gōzō closed by hoping that Japanese efforts would entitle them to "full fellowship in the family of nations, no longer deserving to labor under the incubus which circumstances forced upon her." Tateno was referring to the treaties Japan had signed granting foreign powers certain extraterritorial rights. The restrictions may have been necessary originally, he admitted. But the Japanese felt the restrictions constituted an "unnecessary, incumbering vestige of the past" and hoped for their removal. They welcomed the Columbian Exposition "as one means of proving that they have attained a position worthy of the respect and confidence of other nations."[69] In fact, the centennial display had stimulated some Americans to demand the return of the Shimonoseki indemnity, some $750,000 paid to the United States as a result of an 1863 incident in which Samurai of Chōshū attacked foreign ships.[70] Obviously, the Japanese now hoped for similar rewards from Chicago.

At Philadelphia, the Japanese made their first entry into the popular consciousness as an exotic but artistic people whose ornamentation and aesthetic fantasies fit well the eclectic taste of Victorian America. At Chicago they broadened their claim on public attention by demonstrating their feats of modernization and their architectural skill. Japan was emerging as an alternative rather than a supplementary culture, worthy of understanding on its own terms. But something more was necessary to raise respect to veneration, and this came about in 1904, with the combined triumphs of the Japanese in the Russo-Japanese War and at the Louisiana Purchase Exposition in St. Louis.

St. Louis had been disappointed in its effort to host the Columbian Exposition. But it was the natural site for the fair held nine years later to celebrate the centennial of Thomas Jefferson's Louisiana Purchase. The area that Jefferson had purchased from France was now a thriving and well-populated region of twenty-three states, and St. Louis was its chief city. As with other American expositions, planning began several years in advance. Originally, it was supposed to take place in 1903. When Japan was invited, local attention was concentrated on a great exhibition in Osaka. The government thereupon declined. When the Louisiana Purchase Exposition was postponed until May 1904, the Japanese accepted the invitation, after sending several representatives to visit St. Louis, early in 1903.[71]

The Louisiana Purchase Exposition was constructed on a scale exceeding even that of the Columbian Exposition.[72] Located in Forest Park, the grounds of the fair totaled some 1,272 acres. As one historian has pointed out, this was nearly equal to the combined area of all previous expositions.[73] More than 1,500 separate buildings were put up, 15 of which were exhibition palaces. As in Chicago, classical themes predominated, but the total effect was more exuberant and more fanciful. The palaces themselves were constructed on a monumental scale; some were more than 1,500 feet long. Despite the attractions which the exposition authorities provided, including automobile and balloon races, the international Olympics, and visits by heads of state, the total attendance of about 19 million was considerably below that of Chicago. Nevertheless, foreign states were eager to participate. Twenty-one of them, more than at Chicago, had national buildings, and some put up more than one.

The Japanese had now participated in more than two dozen exhibitions and, as usual, their careful preparations stood out. The Japanese exhibit was the only foreign display ready when the fair opened, despite the fact that the government was fully involved in the war with Russia. It had appropriated $800,000, and Baron Matsudaira Masanao, the vice president of the imperial commission, supervised the actual preparations.[74] Japan received more than 150,000 square feet, making large displays in the palaces of Industry (27,000 square feet), Manufactures (54,000 square feet), Education (6,300 square feet), Transportation (14,000 square feet), Fine Arts (6,800 square feet), Mines (6,900 square feet), and Agriculture (8,600 square feet). Private exhibitors were better organized now than ever before. Every Japanese exhibitor was a member of the Japan Exhibit Association. One week after the government decided to participate in St. Louis, a meeting was held in Tokyo of the representatives of the various commercial associations throughout the country. A business organization was formed to consolidate the exhibits, and government appropriations helped them. A year before the fair opened representatives were sent to St. Louis to examine the site. Not only did individual firms such as the Japanese Mail and Steamship Company prepare displays, but associations of companies —the Kyoto Chamber of Commerce was one—also demonstrated the skills and resources of areas within the country. Ōtani Kahei, president of the Japanese Exhibitors Association, and other representatives of the association were in charge of installing all the exhibits, distributing information, handling sales, and shipping back what was left to Japan. The display was twice as large as the immense display at Chicago and three times as big as the important Paris exhibition of 1900. The fine arts collection was particularly noteworthy. So important did the Japanese government conceive it that before the art works left Japan 3,000 artists visited the collection in Tokyo, by government invitation.

Besides the industrial and artistic objects scattered through the exhibition palaces, there were two other displays of the Japanese effort at St. Louis. One was the official government exhibit, the Imperial Japanese Garden. In a setting of landscaped gardens, water, and bridges, a group of buildings was put up. The major building was a replica of the Kinkaku, the Golden Pavilion built for the Shogun near Kyoto at the end of the fourteenth century. Uncannily, as Clay Lancaster has pointed out, the Kinkaku shared some features with indigenous design in the lower Mississippi Valley: the hipped roof, the open galleries resting on slender supports—both characteristic of Creole architecture in the eighteenth century. That the Japanese building made such an impact in St. Louis, Lancaster concludes, was due in part "to their own aesthetic and structural merits, in part to their affinities to pre-existing building forms . . . The design of the Kinkaku mirrored a local type in the deep South, and in turn itself was reflected in the New Orleans suburbs in combination with belated Mississippi steamboat and contemporary bungalow elements."[75] Along with the Kinkaku there was a bamboo tea house, representing newly acquired Formosa, a commissioners' residence, a reproduction of a reception hall from an imperial palace at Kyoto, and, of course, the gardens. "A visit to the Japanese pavilion on the hill is one of the pleasantest experiences of the whole fair," a writer reported in *The World's Work*.[76]

Aside from the displays scattered through the palace and the official pavilion, an unofficial group of buildings called the Japanese Village took up a spot on the Pike, the fair's amusement area and its counterpart to Chicago's Midway. These included several gateways, a tea house, a bazaar, and a Japanese theater. One of the gateways, a replica of a gateway to the tomb of Ieyasu at Nikko, rose 100 feet above the Pike. The Japanese Village attested to the public's interest in Japanese curiosities. There were 540 separate concessions in St. Louis, including 60 restaurants, 53 amusements, 11 transportation companies, and 153 souvenir and novelty centers. The Village, which took in $205,000 proved to be the tenth most popular concession, exceeded only by the largest and most elaborate displays such as the Tyrolean Alps and the Transvaal Military Spectacle. The Japanese bazaar produced an additional income of $85,937.[77]

The three separate areas permitted Japanese exhibitors to satisfy a wide variety of tastes. Connoisseurs of art could linger in the Fine Arts Building; businessmen and educators could examine displays in the Manufactures and Education buildings; casual sightseers could stop in the Japanese Village; and lovers of Japanese gardening and architecture could wander through the official pavilion and its landscaped grounds. The latter were opened with a reception, on June 1, with more than 200 guests served tea by geisha girls. Baron Takahira Kogorō, the minister at Washington, along with Matsudaira Masanao, stood at the head of the receiving line. The guest of honor was the president's daughter, Alice Roosevelt. During the six months the fair ran, other celebrations—the Mikado's birthday, for example—were held as well.

The comments made about the various Japanese displays continued the trend of earlier observations. That is, they were extremely favorable. Perhaps the most overwhelming effort at the fair was made by Germany, enticed by the large number of German-Americans in the St. Louis area, but after Germany there was no question that Japan created the most excitement. The ever-present Samantha, also a visitor to St. Louis, felt the Japanese had outdone everyone. On the one hand, Samantha was still impressed by the ornateness of the Japanese objects and their expense. In the Temple of Nikko, in the official pavilion, she saw one pair of vases "worth ten thousand dollars. . . . There is one spring room in it that holds the very atmosphere of spring. The tapestry and crape hangings are embroidered with cheery blossoms . . . And there wuz an autumn room, autumn leaves of rich colors wuz woven in the matting and embroidered in the hangings, the screens and walls white with yellow crysanthemums."[78] Still another room, with walls of carved wood and rich silk hangings, cost $45,000 and was therefore even more impressive. Thus the tradition of delight in Japanese profusion, established at Philadelphia, continued.

On the other hand, even Samantha was impressed now by other things, including efficiency, modernization, and cleanliness. "In cleanin' house time, now I have fairly begreched the ease and comfort of them Japanese housewives who jest take up their mat and sweep out, move their paper walls and little mebby and there it is done. No heavy, dirt-laden carpets to clean, no papered walls and ceilings to break their back over . . . Kind hearted, reverent to equals and superiors, trained to kindness and courtesy and reverence in childhood when American mothers are ruled and badgered by short skirted and roundabout clad tyrants." Japan was becoming more of a total civilization to be studied, not merely on antiquarian grounds but because it had accomplished things westerners seemed unable to do. "I set store by the Japans and am glad to hear how fast they're pressin' forwards in every path civilization has opened," Samantha concluded. "They could give Uncle Sam a good many lessons if he wuz willin' to take 'em."[79]

Particularly interesting, from the American view, was the display of the Red Cross in the official pavilion. "This is the only hint this courteous country gives of the great war going on at home that would stop the exhibit of most any other country."[80] The Red Cross seemed to symbolize not only Japan's new military power but also its commitment to obey the rules governing international relations, its assumption of a "civilized" role, even when fighting a "Western" country, Russia.

Reactions to the fair exhibit could not be separated from the loud American admiration for Japanese military prowess. While the exposition was in progress, American magazines were dominated by detailed news of the conflict in the Far East and by overwhelmingly favorable reports on the morale, abilities, and restraint of the Japanese armed forces. Military success, more than any fair exhibits, demonstrated what the Japanese government had been trying to show: that Japan had managed the adjustment to modern industrial conditions with great skill. The St. Louis fair concentrated American attention on achievements such as the Japanese telegraph system, only thirty years old but with 60,000 miles of wire; the railroad network, more than 4,000 miles, constructed in twenty years; the elaborate postal system, which in 1903 handled 902 million pieces of mail; the Japanese textile industry, which was employing more than 700,000 persons; and so on. More than 80,000 exhibits in the name of some 2,000 firms and individuals represented Japan at St. Louis, and the displays skillfully used photographs, topographical maps made of rice paper, mechanical models, and carefully prepared handbooks. In the electricity palace a map thirty feet high and twenty-five feet wide showed the Lake Biwa Canal connecting Lake Biwa with Kyoto; a mine was reproduced in its entirety, along with a first-class salon on a ship of the Japanese Mail Steamship Company. "In arrangement and detail," wrote Isaac Marcosson, "the national pavilion shows that, to the achievement of commerce and industry, the Japanese have brought the perfection of landscape beauty, another expression of the genius of a people who, in the art of war and the pursuits of peace, are steadily making their way to a large place in world power. For this is the real significance of the Japanese exhibit at St. Louis."[81]

But beneath this praise, and more explicitly in articles dealing with Japanese power generally, Americans revealed concern about what was happening to Japan's distinctiveness in its mad zeal to imitate the West. The anxiety penetrated comments on Japanese art. *The Nation* reported that although the Japanese exhibit in the Varied Arts Building was large, "table after table is crowded with common ceramic ware (it is a shame to apply such a term to it) and poor modern bronzes." "A few dealers gain by selling the trash, but the public estimate of Japanese technical skill suffers."[82] Mabel Loomis Todd described the Japanese paintings by artists trained in foreign

substance of a noble national life."[89] This led, in time, to a growing
interest in immigration restriction and an increasing set of pressures
on public schools to "Americanize" newcomers and melt them down
into an approved mold. But other Americans favored individuality
and variety; traditions of diversity would fulfill rather than subvert
the national genius.[90]

Japan presented an analogous problem. Americans were fascinated
by the rapidity and completeness of Japanese modernization; they
approved of the new school systems, railroads, telegraphs, and military skill. At the same time, the only reason the Japanese were special
lay in their distinctive preindustrial arts, habits, and mores. If the
Japanese modernized, would they lose their special contribution to
world civilization? If they did not modernize, could they survive as
an independent state and resist the blandishments and intimidations
of Western powers? Different Americans arrived at different conclusions concerning both the actual and the normative aspects of
Japanese development. But the above comments on expositions may
suggest that this problem underlay the fascination Japan held for
Americans. The gradual appreciation of the fact that pottery,
bronzes, and silks were products not of unconnected and incidental
craft skills but of a civilization with special emphases and loyalties
can be found in the decennial revivals of concern with foreign cultures that expositions sponsored. At just the same time in American
cities, settlement workers like Jane Addams were finding in immigrant craft skills and family organization a rich social texture capable
of resisting the oppressive features of urban life and preserving human
dignity and diversity. The trend toward larger generalization and
increased concern with Japan that reached its apogee in St. Louis in
1904 reflected more than American efforts to understand the Japanese. It was also an attempt to examine the future shape of their own
civilization, one in which modernization itself would soon form the
only tradition.

The Sacred Land of Liberty: Images of America in Nineteenth Century Japan

The image of America as the "sacred land of liberty" prevailed in Japan throughout the latter part of the nineteenth century, although some Japanese objected to it and others denied its reality. As the century drew to a close, however, the ideal became increasingly difficult to maintain, particularly when, at the beginning of the new century, the possibility of war between the United States and Japan began to be discussed.

In 1853, when Commodore Matthew C. Perry knocked at the door of what Herman Melville in *Moby Dick* called the "double-bolted land," some Japanese intellectuals were already fairly well acquainted with aspects of the history, geography, and contemporary situation of the United States. The narrator of Perry's expedition related the Americans' astonishment at the knowledge that the supposed governor of Uraga, Kayama Eizaemon, and his interpreters demonstrated on board Perry's flagship, the *Susquehanna*:

When a terrestrial globe was placed before them, and their attention was called to the delineation on it of the United States, they immediately placed their fingers on Washington and New York, as if perfectly familiar with the fact that one was the capital, and the other the commercial metropolis of our country . . . Their inquiries in reference to the United States showed them not to be entirely ignorant of the facts connected with the material progress of our country; thus, when they asked if roads were not cut through our mountains, they were referring (as was supposed) to tunnels on our railroads.[1]

Indeed, as Perry's company learned, the Japanese had been acquiring knowledge of the West from imported Dutch magazines and newspapers as well as from Dutch residents in Nagasaki. In 1826, for instance, a Japanese scholar of Dutch, Takahashi Sakuzaemon, learned from Philipp Franz von Siebold that General George Washington had led the American people to independence from Britain. In 1845 another famous scholar, Mizukuri Gempo, published *Konyo zushiki* (Information about the countries of the world), in which forty-six pages were devoted to North America. He mentioned Washington and Benjamin Franklin as respectively the "military" and "civil" leaders of the struggle for American independence and explained the political and social system of the United States as follows: "There is no king in this country. Each state nominates several wise men to the government. Inhabitants are of several stocks, and manners and customs vary in different localities. There is, however, no distinction of rank among them."

Although Perry's company did not know it, the Japanese also had learned about America from Chinese books. One of the most popular sources was *Rempō shiryaku* (an outline history of the United States), written by E. C. Bridgeman, an American missionary in China, and published about 1840. Incorporated into Kai Gen's widely read *Kaikoku zushi* (Information about the maritime countries, 1842), the book itself was imported into Japan about 1853 and was eagerly read by Sakuma Shōzan, Yokoi Shōnan, Hashimoto Sanai, Yoshida Shōin, and other forerunners of the Meiji Restoration of 1868. Translated into Japanese by Masaki Atsushi, it was published in 1854 under the title *Mirikakoku sōki wage* (Outline of America: A translation).

To the Japanese, however, the idea of liberty and the practices of republicanism were difficult to comprehend. Masaki, for example, was unable to grasp the meaning of the Declaration of Independence as presented in Chinese by Bridgeman. His Japanese version, therefore, did not express the spirit of independence at all. "Government" was rendered by a Japanese word meaning "king," and the right to change the government was given to the "Supreme Being," not to the people.

Before long Japanese with direct experience of the United States began to impart a more accurate picture of American institutions and liberties to their countrymen. The first group to do so were shipwrecked sailors who published their observations on the United States when they returned to Japan. The two most famous were Nakahama Manjirō (who was given the English name John Mung) and Hamada Hikozō (Joseph Heco), later nicknamed Amerika Hikozō. In 1853 Nakahama published *Manjirō hyōryūki* (Narrative of Manjirō's drifting). The information it contained, however, was scanty and questionable, perhaps because the author feared suppression by the Tokugawa authorities, always suspicious of Japanese who brought intelligence of foreign affairs. But his unpublished affidavit, "Hyōryū Manjirō kichōdan" (Castaway Manjirō's homecoming story), contained substantial information about the United States.[2] He said, for example:

The king is selected from among the wisest men of the nation. He keeps his throne for four years; if he is especially wise, for eight years. On the road he takes only one or two servants with him; he does not give himself airs . . .

Even to commoners, such as peasants, all careers are open, according to one's education and abilities . . .

America is a country in the midst of development. The sciences are advancing year by year.

Hamada acquired American citizenship while in the United States, so he was not as afraid of the Tokugawa authorities as was Nakahama. In his *Hyōryūki* (Narrative of drifting), published in 1863, he explained America's history, politics, laws, religion, education, and manners and openly praised its spirit and its institutions. Recording the story of Washington's rejection of a crown, he commented:

In this country all men are to be equal. No fiefs and ranks are to be hereditary, able men whom others willingly obey are to be selected for government offices, and the most prominent of them is to be appointed Grand Leader of the nation. The Grand Leader's term of office is to be four years, because a man is apt to become complacent when he holds high rank for too long a time.

Such information was a revelation to Japanese political leaders, for most Japanese still regarded the United States as a "barbarian" country. But according to Hamada's English autobiography, *The*

Narrative of a Japanese (1892–95?), a considerable number of progressive daimyo and samurai came to hear from him about American affairs. Kido Takayoshi, one of the greatest leaders of the 1868 restoration, and Itō Hirobumi, the most influential prime minister of the Meiji era, repeatedly visited him and heard him explain the constitution of the United States.[3]

The first Japanese embassy to the United States, consisting of seventy-seven samurai who crossed the Pacific in 1860, also brought back with them a similar image of the United States. To judge from their travel diaries, the higher ranking and older officials did not like American democracy. Vice Ambassador Muragaki Norimasa, for instance, despised President James Buchanan's plain clothes and manners and compared congressional debates to fish sellers shouting loudly in the fish market of Edo. But younger and lower ranking officials generally appreciated the liberty and equality they observed. To cite one example, Fukushima Keisaburō, who was nineteen years old, wrote in his diary:

Western people show kindness to foreigners just as they do to their relatives. Americans especially, because they are from a new country, are gentle . . . And in that country high officials do not arbitrarily despise commoners, nor do they abuse their power. Commoners, therefore, do not flatter high officials. The nation is rich and the people are peaceful, finding themselves in a position of perfect security . . . Most of the seventy-seven samurai of the Japanese embassy had felt displeasure and hatred toward them, but now that they know the truth, they are repenting their past error.[4]

Japanese respect for American ideals of liberty and equality was undoubtedly strengthened by discontent at the arrogance they observed in European, especially British, attitudes toward Japan. Fukushima's praise of Americans was coupled with an expression of antipathy toward the British, whom he called "cunning and . . . untruthful." Japanese intellectuals condemned the British as unjust to China during the Opium War and resented the high-handed diplomacy of British ministers Rutherford Alcock and Harry Parkes. The United States, in contrast, had had no career as a conquerer in Asia, and Minister Townsend Harris' diplomacy seemed peaceful and friendly. Expressions of gratitude were conveyed to Harris by many contemporary and later Japanese. To quote a later example, Tōkai Sanshi wrote in his 1885 novel *Kajin no kigū* (Strange encounters with beauties): "In the first place, the British usually act according to treacherous designs. If at such times the American minister, Mr. Harris, had not exercised his influence in accordance with his just and unselfish spirit, Japan would by now be another Annam, if not another India."

Those members of the 1860 embassy on board the escort ship *Kanrin-maru*, who saw only the San Francisco area, were similarly impressed. Katsu Rintarō (Kaishū) and Fukuzawa Yukichi, both great leaders of modern Japan, in particular praised the liberal and republican United States, and their impressions had a lasting impact in Japan. According to *Kaishū zadan* (Informal talks with Kaishū, 1930; new edition, 1937), Katsu told his friend Yokoi Shōnan the story of Washington's rejection of a throne. Yokoi, one of the most enlightened political scholars and a respected mentor of the revolutionaries of the time, at once realized what Katsu meant by the story. "America," he said, "is just like the reign of Yao and Shun," recalling the mythical regime of ancient China that Chinese and Japanese have always held up as an ideal. To Yokoi the United States became a modern utopia, and Washington an ideal statesman. In "Numayama taiwa" (Talks at Numayama), recorded by one of his disciples in 1864, Yokoi is quoted as saying: "In the modern age only Washington of America has ever acted in a spirit of justice on the basis of Heaven's rule . . . and has gotten rid of sectionalism."[5] Sakamoto Ryōma, a disciple of Katsu and another contributor to the tumultuous events of the 1860s, also heard the story from Katsu and determined to overthrow the Tokugawa feudal system. His friend Nakaoka Shintarō was likewise a great admirer of Washington. Yokoi, Sakamoto, and Nakaoka were all assassinated because of their radical progressivism, but their disciples drafted the "Gokajō no goseimon" (Charter Oath) which in 1868 laid down the fundamental policy of the Meiji government. Although the Oath was not always translated into practice, it contained articles corresponding closely to the idea that "all men are created equal" and that "able men whom others willingly obey are to be selected for government office." It may not be inexact to say that the image of America as the modern incarnation of the rule of Yao and Shun had a deep, if not immediately apparent, influence on the spirit of the revolution of 1868.

The first decade of the Meiji era (1868–77) is called by historians the age of "civilization and enlightenment" (*bummei kaika*). The new central government and the people tried to become enlightened

through studying Western civilization. Fukuzawa Yukichi, who remained outside the government but was leader of this movement,
considered the United States the foremost nation of "civilization
and enlightenment," and it was primarily he who popularized the
image of America as the sacred land of liberty. His visits to the
United States in 1860 and to Europe in 1862 as a member of another
embassy enabled him to gain direct knowledge of social, political, and
economic affairs in the West. In 1866 Fukuzawa published his *Seiyō
jijō* (Conditions in the West), which was an immediate success and
was followed by sequels in 1868 and 1870. In this "bible of overseas
information" Fukuzawa presented American history and institutions
as admirable incarnations of liberty.

The United States of America is republican in the best sense of the word.
This is the country in which real representatives of the people meet and discuss national politics without any private interests. Although nearly a century has passed since it was established, the laws of the country have never
been thrown into confusion.

Fukuzawa also gave a translation of the Declaration of Independence.
Unlike Masaki's secondhand translation, Fukuzawa's was fresh, clear,
and complete—and, according to one authority, it inspired several
leaders of the revolution to work for the overthrow of the Tokugawa
regime.[6]

In 1867 Fukuzawa went to the United States for a second time and
bought as many books as he could bring back to be used as textbooks
at Keiō Gijuku (the present Keiō University), which he had founded.
Under this impetus, American books became widely used in Japanese
schools during the first decade of Meiji. Two years later he published
another very popular book, *Sekai kuni zukushi* (All the countries of
the world), written for juvenile readers. In it, Fukuzawa again expressed an almost uncritical admiration for America's liberty, justice,
republicanism, and prosperity. After narrating, in a melodious style
easy to recite and memorize, the history and the spirit of independence of the American people, he said of the situation at the time:

The government keeps its word, and since there is no tyrannical king, the
land belongs wholly to the people . . . Laws are made through open discussion and are never enforced severely. Thus the nation has become rich . . .
and nothing necessary is wanting there.

As his knowledge of the United States deepened and as the political and social situation in Japan stabilized, Fukuzawa's admiration for the United States became more reserved. In *Bummeiron no gairyaku* (Outline of civilization, 1875), his philosophical masterpiece, Fukuzawa ranked American republicanism above French and Mexican, but he also enumerated its defects and denounced its tendency toward mobocracy. His respect for Britain, in contrast, was heightened.

Like Fukuzawa, many other exponents of "civilization and enlightenment" at first expressed almost unqualified admiration for the United States as the land of liberty. But as the revolution of 1868 developed into a restoration and the establishment of an emperor system became the aim of the new political leaders, praise of republicanism was virtually tabooed in Japanese politics, and toward the end of the first decade of Meiji, the "civilization and enlightenment" leaders began to be muted in their respect for the United States, if not critical of American liberty itself. A good example is Mori Arinori, the first Japanese minister resident in the United States (1870–73). He was one of the foremost westernizers and a great admirer of American civilization. In 1871 he published *Life and Resources in America*, an English book of more than 400 pages. In this comprehensive study, he emphasized the virtues of liberty, especially of freedom of the press, which he considered one of the foundations of American civilization. He wrote:

With regard to what is called the liberty of the press, in time of peace, it is quite unbounded . . . Notwithstanding its many drawbacks, the conclusion is inevitable that the press of America is the leading civilizer of its multivarious population, and is the particular engine which has brought about the present prosperous condition of the Republic.[7]

Mori, however, was opposed to the adoption of republicanism in Japan and was cautious about introducing American liberty to the Japanese. "The evils resulting from the misuse of freedom in America," he warned, "are among the most difficult to correct or reform, and ought to be carefully avoided."[8]

While Mori was in Washington, an embassy headed by Vice Premier Iwakura Tomomi and composed of nearly half of the leading figures in the government, including Kido Takayoshi, Ōkubo Toshimichi, and Itō Hirobumi, made an inspection tour to the West. This in itself demonstrates how eager the Meiji government was to learn and promote "civilization and enlightenment." The first country the embassy visited was the United States, where they stayed for almost seven months. In 1878 Kume Kunitake, the recorder of the mission, later professor of history at Tokyo Imperial University, published his *Tokumei zenken taishi Bei-Ō kairan jikki* (Authentic record of the embassy to the United States and Europe), the only published record of the embassy's travels. Kume, like Mori, praised American liberty but opposed its importation into Japan. Concerning the fundamental character of the United States, he wrote:

America has been the reclaimed land of European peoples. Those who were strong and independent in nature and who wanted to start a great enterprise in the spirit of liberty and independence found a place across the Atlantic; they went to the vast land of America and reclaimed it. This was the beginning of the country's civilization . . . The United States of America is composed of the purely independent and is truly republican.

At the same time he cautioned that in the democratic society of America "people persist in their private rights, bribery is practiced among officials, and political parties collide with each other." It was Kume's view that "when these practices flow into other countries, they estrange subject from sovereign . . . they first brought calamity upon France and later disaster to Spain."

In 1873 Mori Arinori, returning home, mustered the leaders of the "civilization and enlightenment" movement and founded the influential Meirokusha (Meiji Six Society). Most of its members regarded the United States in much the same way as did Mori and Kume. Even Nishimura Shigeki, a nationalistic moralist and the most conservative of the group, respected Americans as "a people possessing a large measure of independence and liberty." In an essay of 1876 entitled "Tōzai seiji no idō" (Political differences between East and West),[9] however, he opposed imitating American liberties for the reason that the "American people are, figuratively speaking, like an adult over twenty years old who can take care of himself, but the Japanese people are just like a child of about ten who cannot take care of himself."

American books used in schools also served to diffuse and reinforce the image of the United States as the land of the free. In particular, books on American and world history by such authors as George

Payne Quackenbos, Samuel Griswold Goodrich (alias Peter Parley), and William Swinton, who all idealized America in one way or another, were not only read in English in many schools but also translated into Japanese for the general reader. A portion of Alexis de Tocqueville's *Democracy in America* was translated and published in 1873 by Obata Tokujirō (one of Fukuzawa's proteges and later president of Keiō University) under the title *Jōboku jiyū ron* (On freedom of the press). A more complete, though still abridged, translation by Hizuka Ryū, a future mayor of Tokyo, appeared in 1881–82, entitled *Jiyū genron* (Principles of liberty). The Japanese titles show that the translators were mainly concerned with "liberty" in the United States. Francis Lieber's *On Civil Liberty and Self-Government* (1853), which was used as a textbook at the college level, was translated and published in 1876 by Katō Hiroyuki, the future president of Tokyo Imperial University, and in 1880 by Hayashi Tadasu, a future foreign minister.

These publications demonstrate that the Japanese people, or at least Japanese intellectuals, were generally aware of the values of liberty and were unstinting in their praise of the United States. But they grew increasingly skeptical of the adaptability of the system of American liberties to Japan. Indeed, they came to prefer British civilization to American because Britain was an ancient monarchy much like Japan. Ishii Nankyō's *Meiji no hikari* (The light of Meiji), published in 1875, rejected America's disdain for royalty and praised Britain as "the champion of the West." Similar opinions were expressed in numerous other books.

The second decade of the Meiji era (1878–87) is generally called the age of "liberty and the people's rights" (*jiyū minken*). Opponents of the increasingly oppressive, absolutist Meiji government rallied to the flag of "liberty and the people's rights" and demanded the establishment of a national assembly. Led largely by discontented ex-samurai and gentlemen farmers, the movement was not as powerful as they made it appear; nonetheless, their cry for reform was heard throughout Japan. Under their pressure the government in 1881 promised that a national assembly would be established in ten years; but at the same time it tried to strengthen itself by eagerly learning from and adopting the political and cultural system of Germany, regarded as a model of centralized power.

The movement for "liberty and the people's rights" was inspired by Fukuzawa and other promoters of "civilization and enlightenment," most of whom looked to the constitutional monarchy of Britain as a model for Japan and ranked American democracy as second to it. Yano Fumio (Ryūkei), a famous politician-novelist, for instance, wrote in an 1888 essay entitled "Nipponjin ga mottomo fuchūinaru seijijō no yōketsu" (The essential points of politics of which Japanese are most ignorant): "What is the country in which the constitutional system is enforced in the best way? It is Britain, the originator of this system, and second best is the United States."[10] Radicals within the movement, however, idealized the history of the American Revolution and the American spirit of liberty. The more they were suppressed by the government, the more they looked to American institutions as a model for Japan. The United States thus came to represent a utopia for a small minority who disdained both the authoritarian government and the Japanese masses, whom they considered subservient to authority.

The attitude toward the United States among the proponents of "liberty and the people's rights" is well illustrated by Baba Tatsui, one of their most competent theorists. A disciple of Fukuzawa, he studied law in Britain for several years. After returning home in 1878, he was active in politics as well as the press on behalf of the movement. Moderate at first, looking to British parliamentarianism as an ideal, governmental oppression drove him to radicalism. In 1881 he took part in the formation of the Jiyūtō (Liberal party) by the radical wing of the movement but was soon expelled from the party for criticizing its president Itagaki Taisuke for vacillation. Now completely alone, Baba apparently began secretly to entertain republican thoughts and to put forward the political structure of the United States as an ideal. In 1886 he went to America, a voluntary exile, and died the following year in Philadelphia, the birthplace of American liberty.

Nor was Baba alone in seeking refuge in the United States. A number of likeminded radicals settled in California in the late 1880s, and in 1887 a group in Oakland published the first Japanese newspaper in the United States, *Shin Nippon* (The new Japan). Exiles in San Francisco formed the Aikoku Dōmei (Patriotic league) and started their own organ, *Jūkyū seiki* (The Nineteenth century) the following year. *Jūkyū seiki* soon incorporated the *Shin Nippon* and gained influence among the Japanese in the United States. The editors printed radical viewpoints that could not be published in Japan and reprinted articles that had been banned at home. The Tokyo government was irritated by the newspaper and prohibited its importation into Japan, but the editors changed its name repeatedly—calling it *Jiyū* (Liberty), *Kakumei* (Revolution), *Aikoku* (Patriotism), and so forth—to circumvent the government's ban. To those radicals the United States was truly a blessed political asylum.

Of interest with respect to the image of the United States within the "liberty and the people's rights" movement are the literary works of Ueki Emori, a radical poet-politician who chose to remain in Japan to work as a close associate of Itagaki Taisuke. In his popular political pamphlets, *Minken jiyū ron* (On the people's rights and liberty, 1879) and *Tempu jinken ben* (In defense of the people's natural rights, 1883), Ueki referred repeatedly to the United States as the exemplification of liberty and the people's rights. But his admiration was best expressed in his poems. He was not the first writer to express such admiration in verse. In Tosa, the birthplace of Japanese liberty from which Itagaki, Baba, and Ueki came, a verse of the favorite "Minken kazoe uta" (The people's rights counting song) went: "America above all other countries of the world is the forerunner of liberty. Ah, how grateful we are to her." In Komuro Kutsuzan's famous "Jiyū no uta" (Song of liberty) published in his *Shintai shiika* (Poems and songs in the new style, 1882), America's struggle for liberty and independence was eulogized. But it was Ueki, in his *Jiyū shirin* (Poems on liberty, 1887), who extolled the United States most extravagantly.

Jiyū shirin was a small book of six poems in the "new style," imitative of Western poetry, that had begun to be used in Japan in the early 1880s. In the first poem, "Beikoku dokuritsu" (American independence), Ueki praised the "fragrant" civilization of the contemporary United States and then sang in heroic words of the history of the American Revolution. Referring to the Liberty Bell, he recalled those who rang it and "loudly called for liberty and liberty." He described the battles in which "Ah, the greatest heroes that ever lived and the fairest of the fair ended their days, evanescent as the dews, in the battlefields." And he expressed admiration for the nation that had created "a new country of republican liberty." Ueki, like Baba, seems to have inclined toward republicanism. In the second and third poems he praised the independence of Switzerland and the republican spirit of Brutus. The last three poems were all entitled "Jiyū no uta" (Song of liberty), and again he referred repeatedly to America's history and its people. In particular he glorified Patrick Henry, over whose challenge "Give me liberty or death," he said, "even God himself weeps."

In the 1880s political novels became popular, and most of them were written in the cause of "liberty and the people's rights." It was natural that the United States as the sacred land of liberty should have provided a favorite setting. A novel that is regarded as the forerunner of this genre, *Minken engi: jōkai haran* (The idea of the people's rights: Tempestuous seas of human feelings, 1880), was written by Toda Kindō, a nobleman who had been to the United States where he had come to be a social reformer. The novel itself is a rather poor allegory in which the hero Wakokuya Minji (that is, the Japanese people), after undergoing many difficulties, happily weds the heroine Sakigakeya O-Ken ("forerunner of rights"). While the story makes no direct reference to the United States, the preface by Miwa Shinjirō is wholly devoted to emphasizing the American people's love of liberty. They love liberty, he says, just as they do a beautiful woman. He is, of course, trying to say that the love between Minji and O-ken corresponds to the American love of liberty. Likewise, Sudō Nansui's *Ryokusa-dan* (Tale of a green straw raincoat, 1886–88), a novel that deals with the problem of local autonomy, is a fictitious adaptation of Francis Lieber's *On Civil Liberty and Self-Government* and of course refers frequently to American liberty.

One of the best works of this type and the one that had the closest connection with the United States, however, was Tōkai Sanshi's *Kajin no kigū*. Tōkai Sanshi (meaning "exile wanderer of the eastern sea") was the pen name of Shiba Shirō who, as a samurai of a clan defeated in the uprisings in 1868, went to the United States in 1879 and became infatuated with the spirit of liberty. Soon after returning to Japan, he published the first volume of *Kajin no kigū*. It was enthusiastically received, and he wrote and published sequels to it for over a decade, during which his views changed as did the theme of the novel. By far the most interesting are the first several chapters, which are set in the United States and revolve around the theme of liberty.

The story begins with the hero Tōkai Sanshi's visit to Independence Hall in Philadelphia. Here he encounters two beauties from Spain and Ireland and later an old gentleman from China, all of whom have taken refuge in America. At a riverside arbor they exchange their stories and opinions and express admiration for American liberty. In a pithy style that makes abundant use of vivid Chinese words and phrases, Tōkai says:

Outside the country, while Europeans have aggressively invaded neighboring states, Americans have made it a rule to side with the weak and crush the strong; and within the country they have produced schools instead of arms, encouraged industry and commerce, fostered agriculture, and established this rich, strong, and civilized nation for themselves. They are thus now enjoying liberty and singing the praises of peace.

In the protagonist's opinion, American politicians are especially praiseworthy for their public spirit. Comparing Japanese politicians with them, he notes:

Our people are too myopic . . . Out of personal grudges they ignore public duties, and out of personal friendship they employ mediocre persons. When we compare them with Americans, who abandon personal feelings, follow public opinion, and serve their country, we see between the two a gap as vast as the gap between heaven and earth.

Obviously Tōkai Sanshi's image of the United States was, like Ueki's, idealized. In one section, however, he points to one defect in American liberty—racial discrimination. He lets the Chinese gentleman express it in terms of his resentment against prevailing anti-Chinese attitudes. Though first mentioned only in passing, this blemish seems to have been important to the author. In later chapters of the novel he came to advocate the necessity of emphasizing national rights rather than insisting on individual liberties, in part because of discrimination against Orientals in the United States. This shift was a common phenomenon. Even the radical Aikoku Dōmei in San Francisco was disillusioned when anti-Japanese incidents occurred in the city. Receiving its report, the Liberal party's organ *Tōhō* in September 1892 denounced the United States as passionately as it had praised it before.

We have been maltreated, abused, and ejected, as if we were homeless pigs or stray dogs. Ah, how are the Japanese people to endure this? It is they that break friendship and it is we that suffer disgrace. Can our government overlook this in silence? It should certainly lodge a proper protest with the American government and look after our national rights.

Noguchi Yonejirō (English name, Yone Noguchi), who went to the United States in 1893 at the age of eighteen and sympathized with the Aikoku Dōmei, hoped to overcome American contempt for the Japanese through "singing highly of our spiritual life." He turned to poetry, writing in English, and in 1896 published in San Francisco a collection of poems entitled *Seen and Unseen*. It was a strange mixture of Whitman's free spirit, Poe's aestheticism, and the Japanese *haiku* poet Bashō's nature worship; but most important, it was strongly nationalistic.[11]

A drastic shift in their attitude toward the United States also occurred among the advocates of "liberty and the people's rights." Eventually the movement declined, in part because of governmental oppression, but partly because of conflicts within the movement itself. Its doctrine was too idealistic and its policies too unrealistic to cope with national and international events. In the end many of its leaders turned easily and willingly to the absolutist government.

The third decade of Meiji (1888-97) might be called the age of "national rights." Both the government and the people, having gained self-confidence from the preceding twenty years of progress and development, wanted acknowledgment of Japan's equality with the Western powers. The Sino-Japanese War (1894-95) also enhanced their sense of national pride. Even "people's rights" advocates tended to speak out more strongly for national than for popular rights. Political novels in this period were written mostly in the cause of national rights, and in philosophy the traditionalists became influential under the leadership of the Seikyōsha (Society for political education), a nationalistic organization composed largely of graduates of the now firmly established Tokyo Imperial University who were critical of the West-worshiping "civilization and enlightenment" movement and of the sentimentalism of those who advocated "liberty and the people's rights." In the world of religion Buddhists and Shintoists regained their influence. Under the circumstances, although America's image as the land of liberty persisted, its magic power was greatly dissipated. A good indication of this change is the transformation that took place in Japanese attitudes toward Christianity and its relationship to the United States.

When in 1858 Consul General Townsend Harris negotiated the U.S.-Japan treaty of friendship with Hotta Masayoshi, the representative of the Tokugawa regime, he repeatedly stressed that "in America religious belief is solely a matter for each person to decide and no particular sects are prohibited or promoted. Anyone is free to believe in any religion he pleases."[12] Hotta was convinced that America was not like those Catholic countries that had once "invaded" Japan with religious forces. Soon after the treaty was concluded, Christian missionaries, of whom an overwhelming majority were American, were permitted to enter Japan. Many exhibited great nobility of character and were good transmitters not only of religion but also of Western civilization. They emphasized freedom of religion. It was natural, then, that many Japanese, both Christian and non-Christian, came to view the United States as an ideal Christian nation. In 1888 Kitamura Tōkoku, one of the most prominent literary critics of the time, admitted that he looked to the Christian United States as his model. He confessed in a love letter that he had been "too arrogant" in thinking that the "people's rights" group would be able to reform Japan politically and declared that from then on he would try to serve society by means of "Christian power."

Ah, God's help is absolutely necessary . . . Look at the Christian country. American independence was achieved by simple-minded farmers who never discussed politics. Patrick Henry said, "Besides, Sir, we shall not fight our battles alone. There is a just God who presides over the destinies of nations."[13]

During the age of "national rights," however, an anti-Christian and anti-American attitude arose. A travelogue entitled *Ō-Bei kakkoku seikyō nikki* (A political-religious diary of travels in America and Europe, 1889) by Inoue Enryō, a Buddhist scholar and leader of the Seikyōsha, is a good example. Inoue understood, and even praised, the principles of republicanism and freedom of religion in the United States, but he was convinced they would be harmful if applied to Japan. A society's religious and political systems were interrelated, he believed, and America's Christianity had produced its republicanism. "If the American religion is brought to Japan . . . and captures the minds of the people," he concluded, "liberal thought and republicanism will seize them unawares, and in the end political republicanism will become influential in this country."

The most dramatic example of the changing image of the United States may be found in the writings of Uchimura Kanzō, the most influential Christian of the Meiji era. While in college Uchimura was converted from Shintoism to Christianity under the strong though indirect influence of an American teacher, William Clark. In 1884 he crossed the Pacific to learn directly about the country he had come to idolize. In his spiritual autobiography, *How I Became a Christian* (1895), he described the image of America he held before visiting the country:

My idea of the Christian America was lofty, religious, Puritanic. I dreamed of its templed hills, and rocks that rang with hymns and praises. Hebraisms, I thought, to be the prevailing speech of the American commonality, and cherub and cherubim, halleluyahs and amens, the common language of its street . . . The land of Patrick Henry and Abraham Lincoln, of Dorothy Dix and Stephen Girard . . . Indeed the image of America as pictured upon my mind was that of a Holy Land. [14]

His image was not completely shattered in the course of his four years in the United States. In *Columbus kōseki* (Columbus' achievement, 1893), for instance, he applauded America as a "new Eden," and in *Chirigaku kō* (Thoughts on geography, 1894) he eulogized it as the land of liberty, "the hope of civilized nations for the past two thousand years." Nevertheless, while he was there another image of the country had emerged. In *How I Became a Christian* he wrote of his disappointment upon landing when he heard blasphemous words and phrases, found "pick-pocketing in Christendom as in Pagandom," and, upon being asked for tips, realized the existence of "that mammonism in the highest spiritual sense." He was particularly angered by the "strong racial prejudice" against Indians, Negroes, and especially Chinese and was likewise incensed at the hypocritical "mission show." His denunciation of the United States was often bitter:

Time fails me to speak of other unchristian features of Christendom. What about legalized lottery which can depend for its stability upon its millions in gold and silver, right in the face of simple morality clear even to the understanding of a child; of widespread gambling propensities, as witnessed in scenes of cockfights, horseraces, and football matches; of pugilism, more inhuman than Spanish bullfights; of lynching, fitted more for Hottentots than for the people of a free Republic; of rum-traffic, whose magnitude can find no parallel in the trade of the whole world; of demagogism in politics; of denominational jealousies in religion; of capitalists' tyranny and laborers' insolence; of millionaires' fooleries; of men's hypocritical love toward their wives; etc., etc., etc.? Is this the civilization we were taught by missionaries to accept as an evidence of the superiority of Christian religion over other religions?[15]

It was as a result of his disappointment with the "Holy Land" that Uchimura decided to start a new and independent "Japanese Christianity." But torn between admiration for the "past" America and disillusionment with the "present" one, he nonetheless continued to love, or at least to try to love, that country. In the July 1897 issue of the *Fukuin shimpō* (Gospel magazine) he published a short article, "Beikoku shijin" (American poets), in which he made the astonishing statement that "American poets are far better than English poets." This assertion was further elaborated in a longer article in the January 1898 issue, where he praised the United States as "the land of liberty, unparalleled in the world," and expressed his admiration for such poets as Bryant, Whittier, and Whitman for voicing the "great ideas" that were fostered by republicanism and America's "great nature." But he implied that these poets were not properly respected in their own country. In his *Rakurin-shū* (Essays in the oak wood, 1909) he extolled Whitman in a long essay as a poet sent by heaven to save Americans blinded by their desire for earthly comforts and money instead of God, liberty, and humanity.

By the end of the nineteenth century, as the United States entered a difficult and realistic age, the Japanese could no longer sustain their earlier romantic image of America. In the next decade of the Meiji era (1898-1907), and particularly after the Russo-Japanese War, Japanese and Americans came face to face as serious problems arose between them. One of these was the treatment of Japanese immigrants in California. A typical reaction to American racial prejudice was shown by Uchimura. In an English essay entitled "The Passing of America" published when the anti-alien land law was enacted in California, he lamented, "The voice of Lowell and Bryant and Whittier is heard no more in the land, and the spirit of Lincoln and Sumner and Garrison rules it no more; in that sense, America is no more."[16] The United States as the sacred land of liberty was no more, and the America Japanese now saw was not what it should have been. Criticism of contemporary America became widespread in Japan in the early years of the twentieth century. But the criticism, like that of Uchimura, betrayed nostalgia for the past, for an image of America that had been deeply held in Japan. The nostalgia itself gives eloquent testimony to the depth and seriousness of that earlier image of the United States as the sacred land of liberty.

Japan as a Competitor, 1895-1917

"The peoples of the Occident," wrote an author for the *Arena* magazine in November 1898, "are face to face with a powerful Oriental competitor in the arts of war, diplomacy, industry and commerce."[1] Here were summed up many of the themes that were to characterize American images of Japan in the decades to come. The key word was "competitor." Of all the epithets descriptive of Japan in the period between the Sino-Japanese War (1894-95) and World War I, probably none was used more often than this one, and none better expressed a central theme in Japanese-American relations.

Competition requires at least two parties. To describe Japan as a competitor is tantamount to viewing the United States also as a competitor. Japanese-American relations are thus defined as those between rivals. This in turn implies certain assumptions about America's position, interests, and role in the world, as well as about the structure of international relations in those areas in which the two countries engage in competition. What impact Japanese competition has on the United States depends on the nature of the competition—whether it takes the form of war, diplomacy, industry, or commerce. Moreover, as the above quote reveals, Japan is not merely another competitor. It is "powerful" and it is "Oriental." The former adjective is related to the concept of power, as this word came to be redefined during the 1890s in American thinking. To describe a country as powerful was to recognize its status as a power in the international arena, just as the United States was emerging as a power after the Spanish-American War. But it was an occidental nation, whereas Japan was the only oriental power. The dichotomy between Orient and Occident, too, was a prevailing idea of that period, and these words evoked a whole range of images and sentiments. To call a country an oriental competitor was to make a statement full of symbolism and value judgment. Thus the idea of Japan as a competitor serves as a thematic framework within which one may examine historical forces in the United States and Japan that created dimensions of their intellectual and psychological encounter.

Americans saw Japanese as competitors not in the abstract but in specific circumstances. It will be useful to look at the phenomenon in different parts of the world.

First of all, Americans became aware of Japanese competition on their home grounds. In 1896 the *North American Review* was featuring an article entitled "Is Japanese Competition a Myth?" The writer, Robert A. Porter, was a congressman who argued for protective tariffs to cope with the expanding Japanese trade. "It is not so much the quantities . . . exported to the United States that has given alarm," he said, "but the sudden manner in which the Japanese have . . . thrown their hats into the American market, and challenged our labor and capital with goods which, for excellence and cheapness, seem for the moment to defy competition." As yet Japanese technology was behind Western, but "when Japan is fully equipped with the latest machinery, it will . . . be the most potent industrial force in the markets of the world."[2]

Concern with Japanese commercial competition was especially strong in the western states. According to a January 1897 article in the *Contemporary Review*, "A spectacle so unique [that is, the rise of Japan] seems to have inspired Western manufacturers with a feeling closely allied to fear. The United States are so apprehensive of danger that one of the planks in the Republican platform is a protective tariff to secure immunity to the States on the Pacific Coast from the invasion of Japanese productions."[3] The *Overland Monthly*, published in San Francisco, harped on the theme of Japanese competition throughout 1896. One author declared, "It would be a waste of space to repeat all the details which have led the writer to the conclusion that the Japanese are destined to become formidable competitors of Western peoples."[4] Another agreed, saying, "Competition with American and European manufacturers in goods of the same class which they [the Japanese] make is to be entered into even in American and European home markets. This policy appears to have been definitely settled upon, and to be national in its character." The Japanese, according to this article, were not simply producing manufactured goods for home consumption, although this alone would be a matter of serious concern for foreign suppliers of goods to Japan. "Manufacturing goods for Japanese consumption is clearly not the strongest incentive in the movement which has astonished and alarmed the industrial nations." The writer concluded: "Japan has entered upon a commercial war against the great industrial nations of the world with the same energy, earnestness, determination, and foresight, which characterized the war with China . . . The industrial revolution now in progress in Japan is a real menace to some of the most important interests of America, and . . . it is indeed time to act."[5]

The overall trends in Japanese-American trade belied such fears. Between 1894 and 1899 Japanese exports to the United States remained more or less stationary, amounting to about $25 million. Since total Japanese exports were expanding rapidly, this meant the declining importance of the United States as a market. On the other hand, Japanese purchases of American goods increased from a little over $5 million in 1894 to $20 million in 1898, and the ratio of imports from the United States in the total Japanese import trade increased from 9.3 percent to 14.4 percent in those five years.[6] By far the bulk of Japanese exports to the United States consisted of teas and silks, and there was little justification as yet for the fear that Japan would compete with goods produced in America or Europe.

Yet the appearance of an image of Japan as a commercial rival is significant. It reflects the neomercantilist thinking of the 1890s which saw commercial rivalry in the world as a key to national growth. Unless the nation stayed in "the race for supremacy," as a writer noted, it would be doomed to fall behind others and eventually be forced into stationary existence. Japan looming as a competitor was considered a threat because it meant the addition of a potential winner to the race, implying that the United States could not take for granted its own superiority.[7]

The anticipated inundation of American markets with Japanese commodities never took place, but the fear was soon transferred to what was considered an even more ominous phenomenon: the coming of Japanese to the United States. Already in 1895 there were 6,000 Japanese, mostly on the west coast, some of whom were merchants and travelers temporarily in the country; but others were agricultural workers, laborers, and domestic servants who had come to make a living in American society.

There had, since the 1860s, been persistent agitation against Chinese immigration in the western states, but to some Americans the menace presented by Japanese in the United States was even more serious because of the power that stood behind them. By 1899 the *San Francisco Chronicle* was arguing that Japanese immigration was more serious than Chinese because Japan had attained the status of a great power, whereas China had not.[8] Such fears seemed justified as the number of Japanese coming to the United States began to increase spectacularly after the American annexation of Hawaii. The incorporation of Hawaii into the United States enabled thousands of Japanese laborers in the islands to enter the continental United States, and the number of Japanese in the continental United States increased from 6,000 in 1895 to 35,000 in 1899. More were to come after the turn of the century, and especially right after the Russo-Japanese War.

This war, like the Sino-Japanese War, gave an impetus to alarmist thinking on the part of those Americans who were concerned about Japanese competition. More than ever before the idea of competition symbolized the fear that Japanese, self-confident and cocky as a result of their victory over Russia, would settle en masse in the United States, driving Americans out of their jobs. The image of a Japanese immigrant as a potential rival and threat provided the intellectual framework in which the immigration dispute, reaching its climax during 1906–8, was viewed. As Archibald Cary Coolidge noted in *The United States as a World Power* (1909), Japan's victory over Russia "may have given a rude blow to the complacent assumption of the peoples of Europe and America that they were called upon to rule the world; but this has not altered a whit the determination of the Californian or the Australian to keep his land, at any cost, 'a white man's country.' " Japanese immigrants, Coolidge believed, "form the vanguard of an army of hundreds of millions, who, far from retreating before the white man, thrive and multiply in competition with him. It is not they, but he, who retires from the field." All evidence, he went on, proved that "white men, as a working class, cannot maintain themselves, in the long run against the competition of Chinese, Japanese, Hindus, and perhaps others." Because Japan was the most advanced of the Asian countries, the influx of Japanese immigrants to America was an indication of the East's counterexpansion toward the West. As Coolidge wrote, "were the Japanese coming over in small numbers only, it would be invidious and wrong to impose restrictions on them, even if we might regret the addition to the American population of another ethnic element, which, whatever may be its own virtues, would not, in the opinion of many, blend well with the rest. But the question at issue is different; it is that of checking such an influx of the yellow race as will swamp the whites on the Pacific coast . . . [We] may accept it as beyond doubt that, if Japanese immigration to the United States were to keep on growing at its recent rate, some means would be found to stop it, treaty or no treaty, peacefully or by force, at any risk and at all cost."[9]

Clearly, here was an image of the Japanese immigrant as a competitor who represented a different life-style, an alien civilization, and a threat to American society. As Senator Francis G. Newlands of Nevada wrote in 1909, the United States must exclude Japanese immigration in order "to maintain this country as the home of the white race free from such racial competition and antagonism on our own soil as will surely breed domestic violence and international hatred." Once Japanese were freely admitted, they "would quickly settle upon and take possession of our entire coast and mountain region." Newlands reflected the growing sentiment in America at that time which distinguished Japanese and Chinese when he said, "The presence of the Chinese, who are patient and submissive, would not create as many complications as the presence of the Japanese, whose strong and virile qualities would constitute an additional factor of difficulty. Our friendship . . . demands that [it] should not be put to the test by bringing two such powerful races of such differing views and standards into industrial competition upon the same soil."[10]

By the time these thoughts were penned, steps were being taken by the governments in Washington and Tokyo to restrict and eventually stop the flow of the immigration of Japanese laborers into the United States. The number of Japanese in America, reaching an all-time high of 103,000 in 1908, began to level off. Yet the fear of them did not entirely subside. This was because the Japanese in America came to be seen not simply as economic rivals but as a threat, not only social and cultural but even military, to American society. What made Japanese immigration seem more serious than Chinese immigration was the fear that it might lead to diplomatic crisis and even war between the two countries. The image of Japan as a power implied that should such an eventuality occur the United States would be faced with a formidable enemy. An essential ingredient of this fear was the notion that the Japanese would fight with all means at their disposal, including their nationals in the United States. Indeed, to some Americans it seemed axiomatic that the Japanese in America were ready, at a moment's notice, to rise and fight for their mother country. An extreme view held that this was the purpose of their coming to America to begin with, that Japanese workers and visitors in the United States were in fact disguised soldiers.

Among the many handwritten letters President Theodore Roosevelt received during the Japanese immigration dispute was one from a resident of Los Angeles. His letter, dated December 1907, is fairly representative of the above type of thinking and deserves to be quoted at length.

[The Japanese] are and have been seeking employment in every public and semi-public building. They are employed on all railroads and most of the avenues of approach. They are familiar with every one of the landing places within 60 miles of Los Angeles by the observation obtained as navigators, fishermen, etc. and from, I firmly believe, different motives than any white man, mainly gaining information of strategic nature and value . . . They are silent, sly, inquisitive, and toward America inclined to be sullen . . . They are undoubtedly under some form of general organization and control, which seems to be military in its ability to command and dominate them by the hundreds in a body . . . They are educated observers of every "foot of ground" so to speak, from Alaska to South Dakota . . . [Most] of them are spying, and are here with disguised motives.[11]

Another correspondent, from Spokane, used even more extreme language and talked of the "Jap invasion of this country," spearheaded by immigrant laborers. Unless the tide were checked, "the United States will in a few years be as yellow a country as Japan or China. Is it not true that self preservation is the first law of nature?"[12]

Not only Japanese laborers but students and visitors came under suspicion. A Methodist minister from Murrayville, Illinois, wrote the War Department: "I met a Japanese soldier and student on one of the Alton trains going to Kansas City . . . I saw one of his maps of Kansas City . . . I am perfectly satisfied this Jap is here getting notes for his Government."[13] From New Haven a man relayed what he had heard from a stenographer; she had told him that she had been typing a paper for a Japanese student at Yale and that the "subject is about a war between the two nations which is supposed [to] take place about the year 1941."[14] A man wrote from Maine: "I was in Bucksport Maine yesterday and learned that a strange Japanese without any apparent business has been a guest at the Robinson House several days. It is common talk that he is spying on Fort Knox."[15]

These communications, mostly handwritten and often illiterate, were addressed to the White House, the War Department, or the army forts scattered throughout the country. Ordinarily they would have been dismissed as daydreams of paranoiac men. High officials in the government, however, shared one assumption with them: that war with Japan was a possibility. As Secretary of State Elihu Root wrote in October 1906, "Japan is ready for war, with probably the most effective equipment and personnel now existing in the world. We are not ready for war and we could not be ready to meet Japan on anything like equal terms for a long period."[16] Japan was thus seen as a formidable military rival, an image that accounted for the extraordinary interest taken by President Roosevelt, Secretary Root, and others in reports of Japanese activities in the United States. The military intelligence division of the War Department regularly instructed the army forts to check out suspicious-looking Japanese, and their reports were usually given careful attention by the higher authorities in the department. The Military Intelligence Division, for instance, instructed the commanding officer of Fort Worden, Washington, to forward information on Japanese residents in the area: "the number of Japanese (males and females), the average age and height of the males, how long they have been there, what occupations they are engaged in, and whether or not they have seen service in the Japanese army." These instructions yielded a series of reports, some of them merely reproducing hearsay, which provided basic material usable in the event of conflict with Japan. As Hunter Liggett, chief of the War College Division of the War Department, wrote in 1911, "Reports from various sources would seem to indicate that certain Japanese have been occupying themselves with obtaining information regarding the bridges, tunnels, rolling stock, etc., of the railway lines leading to the Pacific Coast. Two confidential reports just received from the Treasury Department indicate that preparations by stealing powder and learning to use explosives, are being made by certain Japanese in Montana, Colorado and other places to blow up tunnels and bridges on the different railway lines leading to the Pacific Coast in the event of trouble between the United States and Japan." Liggett recommended that the railroads running to the coast be requested to supply data on "the number of Japanese in the employ of the western lines, especially those employed along the lines as members of section gangs, construction gangs, etc."[17]

Not only Japanese in the United States but also those elsewhere in the western hemisphere were objects of interest and fear on the part of Americans who were convinced of a crisis in relations between the two countries. In December 1910 the chief of staff of the army directed military attachés in the Latin American countries to report on Japanese activities in those countries. From Peru the attaché responded that Japanese in Peru and Ecuador were "showing unusual activity," sketching military points of interest. The Mexican chief of secret service was said to have remarked, "Wait until Mexico and Japan get together; with Japan to attend to naval work, we will attend to land attack and make short work of Gringos."[18]

Mexico particularly was considered vulnerable to Japanese overtures, because of the Diaz regime's cooling relations with the United States and the common racial antagonism of Mexicans and Japanese toward white Americans. A federal official in Phoenix relayed information that "a number of corps of Japanese engineers have been making a study of the topography of the country at many points along the international boundary line."[19] A man wrote from Virginia that "it seems quite certain . . . or at least very probable that the Japs have arranged to attack us through and with the assistance of our friends the Mexicans."[20] Such suspicions were often given official recognition, as, for instance, when in 1910 the military attaché in Mexico City reported to the army general staff that he had examined "cartographically the territory of this Republic as a stepping-stone for a Japanese invasion of the United States." He was convinced that there already was a secret military alliance between Japan and Mexico under the guise of a commercial agreement. "Considering the strained though friendly relations between Japan and the United States and the advantages of commercial treaties between Mexico and Japan, why not have a lot of Japanese come to Mexico for commercial reasons, and incidentally finish the business by forming a secret alliance? To look into the commerce Japan would have to examine the harbors, and thus gain important military knowledge. I have a lurking suspicion that this is what has actually happened."[21]

These memoranda and reports indicate that preoccupation with the Japanese crisis was not confined to the immigration dispute. This came more and more to be seen as but one aspect of the Japanese-American struggle for greater power. Japan, said a War College paper entitled "Preparedness of Japan to Wage an Aggressive War against a Trans-Pacific Power" (1913–14), "has several open diplomatic questions [with the United States] which she can raise at any time, such as immigration, school and land laws, etc."[22] They were serious issues only because Japan made them so. The two countries were involved not simply in competition in the United States or the western hemisphere but throughout the Pacific Ocean. After the United States emerged as a Pacific power in 1898, having annexed Hawaii, Guam, and the Philippines, an image of Japanese-American rivalry in the ocean began to emerge. It became widespread after Japan's victory over Russia in 1905. "Japan is ambitious," wrote Minister William H. Calhoun from Peking in 1911. "She is already a world power. Japan aspires to be mistress of the Pacific."[23] Such a view was modest compared with that expressed by Major General J. P. Story in 1909: "Japan now has sea supremacy in the Pacific."[24]

Whether Japanese supremacy in the Pacific had already been achieved or not, these ideas had immediate implications for Japanese-American relations. According to Homer Lea's *The Valor of Ignorance* (1909), "At present, and for some time to come, there are only two powers, that can . . . enter into a war for the supremacy of the Pacific." America's acquisition of Pacific possessions and the elimination of Russia "from any immediate future struggle for power in the Pacific" had left only the United States and Japan as competitors in the ocean. Since Japan aspired to dominion in the Pacific, it was bound to seek to obtain "such naval bases as will in the future prevent the establishment of a Pacific naval power by any other nation."[25] In the event of a Japanese-American war, Secretary of State Root said in the above-quoted memorandum of 1906, "the loss of the Philippines, Hawaii, and probably the Pacific Coast, with the complete destruction of our commerce on the Pacific, would occur before we were ready for a real fight."

The vision of the struggle for supremacy in the Pacific was related to specific situations in Hawaii and the Philippines, where Japanese residents were pictured as doing their part for their country's ambitious expansionism. What Francis M. Huntington Wilson, third assistant secretary of state, referred to as "the numerical and economic preponderance of the Japanese in the Hawaiian Islands"[26] was becoming more and more visible after the Russo-Japanese War. In 1906 nearly 18,000 Japanese entered Hawaii and the total Japanese population of the islands reached 60,000. When coupled with the view, as W. R. Castle, a prominent lawyer in Honolulu, expressed it, that the Japanese in Hawaii since the war "have gotten the swell head and are literally trying to run things out here,"[27] the presence of so many thousands of Japanese could easily give rise to suspicion and fear on the part of Americans. The above-cited War College study of Japanese preparedness, 1913–14, noted that the Japanese population in Hawaii would be readily available to serve their home country in the event of war with the United States. This was because "the Japanese retain their allegiance to Japan and . . . Japanese children born in Hawaii are taught to retain allegiance to the Mikado." It was widely rumored in the islands that there was a secret military organization in Hawaii organized through the Japanese consulate general. Because of "their clannish disposition and secretiveness," it was pointed out, it was "comparatively easy for the Japanese government to carry out and perfect an organization of the Japanese in Hawaii Islands."

In 1916 the War Department's War College Division noted that the Japanese population in Hawaii had increased from 79,674 to 93,136 in the preceding five years. This was an increase of 5.78 percent, in contrast to the number of whites, who had gained by only 1.29 percent in the same period. "The time may therefore come," the division's memorandum to the chief of staff warned, "when the Oriental races may get control of the legislature, and the laws may assume a form not compatible with the Constitution and interests of the United States." The Japanese in the islands presented a problem since "the Japanese national spirit is so strong that they do not amalgamate with the Anglo-Saxon or European races and their connection with their mother country is never broken and . . . the sympathies of the Japanese born in Hawaii will be greater for Japan than for the United States." Hawaii, however, was still part of the United States, and "its retention is absolutely essential to the defense of the Pacific Coast." Under the circumstances, steps must be taken to defend the islands against the possible danger arising from their activities. The War Department's chief of the Bureau of Insular Affairs suggested a military form of government to prevent Japanese control of the Hawaiian legislature. General H. C. Scott, chief of staff, wrote to Secretary of State Robert Lansing that "every effort should be made to prevent the ownership of locations necessary for the defense of the Hawaiian Islands from falling into the hands of aliens. The very large proportion of such people already in those Islands, especially on the Island of Oahu, constitutes a real danger."[28]

The danger, if anything, seemed even greater for a time in the Philippines, where American authorities were never completely satisfied that they had obtained the support or even acquiescence of the native populace in the new colonial regime. It was widely believed, and quite correctly, that Emilio Aguinaldo had tried to solicit Japanese assistance in his cause. After the suppression of the rebels the fear persisted that they might continue to turn to Japan for help. The coming of Japanese diplomats, officers, and businessmen to the Philippines was closely watched and their activities scrupulously followed. The Philippine Constabulary, whose headquarters was in Manila, employed Filipinos as intelligence agents to infiltrate meetings

On the part of Orange the war will be offensive during the first period." Japan was likely to attack Hawaii "to deprive the United States of the naval base there, and to establish one for her own use." Japan would also attack the Pacific end of the Panama Canal and seize part or all of Guam and the Philippines. Under the circumstances, it was considered all but impossible to defend the Pacific possessions except Hawaii against Japanese assault. The Orange plan called for strengthening of the defenses of the Panama Canal Zone, Alaska, Hawaii, and above all the west coast of the United States. Should war become imminent, the commanding general in Hawaii was to be sent the following telegram: "War with Japan is imminent. Be prepared to resist the enemy with all the forces under your command. Three regiments of infantry, one field hospital, and one ambulance company, all under Naval convoy, will leave San Francisco for Honolulu immediately upon declaration of war. Muster into the service and organize all the recruits available in the Islands. Intern and put under surveillance all the subjects of Japan. Put into effect the plans, now on file in your Department, for the land defense of the seacoast forts of Oahu."[32] Such strategic concepts, a product of the image of Japanese-American rivalry in the Pacific, remained the guiding principles for another quarter century.

China was another area in which rivalry and competition came to provide the vocabulary of Japanese-American relations. As early as 1897 an observer noted, in an article entitled "The Commercial Expansion of Japan," that Japan "is a Power that must be reckoned with in the Pacific, and in some industries she will probably defy competition in the Asiatic markets."[33] For several years after the Spanish-American War, however, Russia rather than Japan appeared as the major competitor in Asia, especially in the China market. The image of international commercial rivalry over the prized market of China became popular after 1898, now that public attention had turned to events in that part of the world. The "commerce of the world," wrote Alfred Thayer Mahan in 1900, "has become the prize for which all the great states of the world are in competition." They were no longer content to engage in free commercial competition but were exercising military force and political influence to obtain advantageous positions. The result was that "competition becomes conflict, the instrument of which is not commercial emulation, but

military power—land or sea.''[34] Russia was the archexample of imperialistic expansion, and Mahan hoped that the United States would
be able to meet the challenge in cooperation with Britain and Japan.
This was the general American attitude before the Russo-Japanese
War. On the whole, Japanese policy of opposition to Russian pene-
tration of Manchuria seemed to accord with American interests.

It was after the Japanese victory over Russia that Japan replaced
Russia in American thinking as America's chief opponent in China.
The idea of Japanese-American rivalry in China emerged as a basic
theme in American images of Japan. Japanese began to loom large
as serious rivals of Americans in China. But they were not simply
vying with Americans in conditions of free and fair competition.
They came to be pictured as engaging in devious tactics and unfair
methods to drive out competitors and entrench their own influence
on the Asian continent. "I really cannot see any evidence," wrote
Willard Straight, consul general in Mukden, "that the Japanese in
this part of the world are willing to play the game fairly, except in
those cases where a discovery of their real intentions might be noised
abroad and injure their position in the 'eyes of the world.' ''[35] Huntington Wilson likewise commented, "Japan's present policy in
Manchuria, if continued, must result in grave impairment to America's policy for the preservation of the territorial integrity of China,
and in serious detriment to the accepted principles of the 'open door'
and equality of opportunity in China."[36] Thomas F. Millard, the most
untiring critic of Japanese policy, wrote, "Japan's goal is commercial
supremacy in the whole East, and this means that she must meet
competitors in regions where she has not yet secured the advantages
of political control. So she is devising ways and means to defeat this
competition" through methods in violation of the Open Door.[37]

The efforts of Straight, Wilson, Millard, and others to reinvigorate
American policy in East Asia in conscious opposition to Japan have
been well described by historians and need not be repeated here. In
the context of Japanese-American mutual images, what is interesting
is a perception of Chinese-American friendship that is often consciously proposed as an antithesis of and in conflict with Japanese
policy toward China. "Our interests in China are identical with the
interests of the Chinese themselves," said the *Memphis Commercial
Appeal* in June 1900, in the middle of the Boxer crisis.[38] A month

later, as the foreign powers, including the United States, prepared to launch an international expedition to Peking, a commentator wrote in the *Independent*, "If China maintains her independence through our support, the United States in another decade will have greater material and moral influence than all other nations combined."[39] From this time on, despite the continuing chaos in China and despite America's official policy that did little actively to support Chinese independence, the belief that the two countries stood for the same objectives became deeply implanted in the American consciousness. China and the United States seemed to be united by some special bonds of friendship, and this intimate relationship came to define the framework of America's presence in East Asia.

From such a perspective, it is not surprising that as suspicion of and opposition to Japanese continental policy grew after 1905, Americans came to view Chinese-American friendship as part of the developing rivalry between Japan and the United States for greater influence in Asia. It was as if these two were competing for the attention and affection of China. Those trying to cultivate Chinese friendship naturally supposed that they were supporting China against Japanese ambitions and preventing Japanese hegemony over China. "China is looking to us to help her out of her difficulties," wrote William Phillips in 1908. "Shall the United States use its influence to preserve the integrity of China or shall we let Manchuria go to Russian and Japanese influences?"[40] The Chinese, said Thomas F. Millard in 1909, "are as averse to being ruled by Japanese as by westerners; indeed, it may be that brought to a choice between these alternatives China would choose a western master." Given China's hostility toward Japan, the United States could readily offer its help. "Between the United States and China is a genuine community of interests, which has no proportionate parallel with the relations of our nation and any other Oriental state." The author asserted that Japanese expansionism was "causing China to turn to the United States." It was as if Japan and the United States stood for two opposite principles in Asia. Comparing the two countries, Millard wrote, it was obvious that the United States was in the right since its interests coincided with China's. "The political and commercial forces now operating in the East are steadily inclining China toward closer contact with America, and it requires only circumspect diplomatic activity for the United States to become the most influential foreign power in the Empire."[41]

The Japanese, wrote Joseph King Goodrich in *The Coming China* (1911), seemed to see "in our friendliness towards China a sordid motive." This was an error derived from an inability to perceive that the United States was not like Japan and other powers. "It is undeniably this lamentable mistake of judging the future by the past that makes Japan disapprove so vehemently America's growing popularity with the Chinese and America's frank championing of China's interests on every reasonable occasion." But actually the United States was presenting an entirely new alternative to the Chinese as they struggled to be free and independent. Since "the Chinese and the Japanese have hated each other cordially for many centuries," it was only natural that the former should turn to America in opposition to the latter. Goodrich was sure that the Chinese had always wanted to do so. That was why they "welcomed" the coming of Americans to the Philippines after 1898. "That welcome was thoroughly sincere . . . because the Chinese Government had never had any reason to doubt the friendliness of our own; and it was assumed that if there were American officials so close to their own shores as just across the narrow sea, which separates Luzon from the China coast, it would necessarily mean a closer acquaintance on our part with events in the Far East than had ever been known before, and the comforting assurance of having a good friend where the hand could be laid upon him in case of need." The Japanese, on the other hand, resented America's intrusion in the Orient and expressed the view "that it might become necessary for Japan to give the United States a lesson in manners." Such dichotomizing, totally unrelated to fact, reveals what the symbolism of the triangular relationship did to one's view of the past.[42]

Since the United States was not in a position to use armed forces on the continent of Asia to vie with Japan and since commercially, too, America was behind Japan in China, it is easy to see why many Americans stressed education as one area in which their country could compete successfully with Japan. As Goodrich wrote, "probably the most pernicious influence exerted by Japan has been in educational matters, because the defects in ability and the false notions imparted affect so many of the common people of China." Floods of Japanese school teachers had gone to China to take care of the rising needs of modern education, but "nearly all of these low-grade Japanese teachers were soon found to be incompetent to teach anything, they could not talk Chinese, and they were slow and stupid in learning the language; they either knew no English at all or their pronunciation, grammar, locution were so atrocious as to make it impossible for them to use that language as a medium of instruction."[43]

Here was an opportunity for America to step in. As an editorial in the *Journal of the American Association of China* noted in 1908, "The people of the nation acting as teachers to China will win a popularity which will help to advance all relations between the two peoples—diplomatic, commercial, industrial, and social." The Chinese, it declared, "naturally came to look to the United States as the best place to send their young men for study."[44] Millard reported that Yuan Shih-k'ai once told him that "experience has demonstrated that Chinese who were educated in America have shown better results." Officials like Yuan, trying to combat increasing Japanese influence in Chinese affairs, were surrounding themselves with men who had studied in the United States or in schools in China founded and run by American missionaries and educators.[45] Such thought was behind the campaign, ultimately successful, to use part of the Boxer indemnity money for educating Chinese youths in the United States. A. W. Bash of the China Development Company was convinced, he wrote Taft in 1905, that the Japanese had "won the native press and have instigated animosity against the Americans." A good way to turn Chinese opinion toward friendship with America would be through educational programs sponsored by the United States.[46] President Edmund J. James of the University of Illinois asserted that although more Chinese students were going to Japan than elsewhere, "the Chinese are in many points jealous of the Japanese, and, other things being equal, would often prefer to send their young people to other countries. Among all these countries the United States would be the most natural one to choose, if it had not been for our anti-Chinese legislation."[47] Arthur H. Smith, a missionary of long residence in China, agreed. Was it not, he asked, "the part of wisdom for us to put forth our best exertions to deflect this stream of students [going to Japan] to our shores, not for the good of China alone, but also for the welfare of America and of the world?"[48]

The remission of the Boxer indemnity, wrote Captain William Mitchell in 1912, upon his return from a two-month tour of East Asia, "created a very favorable impression among the Chinese. They are convinced that we do not want any of their territory, and that we are the greatest guarantee of their territorial integrity. Before many years pass they will be able to take care of themselves, but at present, they would be an easy prey for Japan, providing the latter were allowed to go in by other powers." For this reason, the Chinese seemed solicitous of American support. Whenever Chinese officials and officers found out that Mitchell had come from the United States, he reported, "they did all in their power to show their friendliness, and in an entirely different way from the superficial suavity of the Japanese. I believe that China would be very willing to accept American officers for the training of her army at this time. If this were done it would lead to a great strengthening of our prestige in many ways; this is suffering at the hands of Japan and Germany in Asia today." It seemed most desirable to reciprocate Chinese friendship and bring about closer American-Chinese cooperation. Since the two wars had left Japan "mistress of the East," such steps were bound to increase friction between Japan and the United States. Mitchell was convinced that "this will eventually lead to war sooner or later." But this was the inevitable outcome of the two nations' ambitions to expand their interests and influence in Asia.[49]

These were some of the representative views expressed by Americans concerning their rivalry with Japanese in the western hemisphere, the Pacific, and on the Asian continent. Their statements make it clear that ultimately they were concerned with the global and historical implications of Japanese-American confrontation, not merely with specific instances of their economic, political, or military competition.

The "ultimate issue of any war between America and Japan," wrote Thomas F. Millard, "will be whether the ideas and genius of the white or yellow races will dominate the future of civilization." The basic question the Western nations faced in China, he went on, was "whether the institutions and ethical standards of East or West shall shape the course of civilization there."[50] One must remember, said an officer of the War Department in 1911, that "at last Western man in his great migration around the world has met the East and if the said East is to take on the benefits of Western Civilization, the great task is one that the United States and the United States only can assume."[51] If, wrote Joseph King Goodrich, "Japan were to convince China that an alliance . . . with her is a wise thing; and if then she could persuade her ally to join in the aggressive measures, there might well be good grounds to apprehend all manner of disasters from a revised and strengthened 'Yellow Peril.' That there is no such probability is our comfort."[52] "If England can unite a victorious Japanese nation with her own," Murrat Halstead wrote to Taft in a private letter in 1905, "and bully France out of the way, and assist in getting up a Chinese army of a million Chinamen, grilled on the Japanese style, the yellow peril would rise up in Europe, sure enough, and England would be at fault about it."[53] "Will Japan," asked Huntington Wilson, "really use her . . . political potentiality with China for the maintenance of the principle and spirit of equal opportunity and the policies advocated by the United States, or will she be at work beneath the surface only for herself, and for the Orient against the West? As this is a government with all the Oriental talent for inscrutability and talent for intrigue, shrewd and calculating, there may be grounds for such fears."[54]

The vocabulary used by these men reveals the kinds of images that are evoked when they discuss America's role in Asia and its relationship with China and Japan. The theme of Japan as a competitor is fitted into symbolic frameworks of intercultural and international relations. In such a context the rivalry between the two countries is not simply one between the United States and another power. It involves two different cultures and ways of life. For, as William Graham Sumner wrote in *Folkways* (1906), even after their victory over Russia, "the mores of the Japanese masses have not been touched . . . It is idle to imagine that the masses of an oriental society . . . could, in a thousand years, assimilate the mores of the Occident." Such a prognosis gave comfort to some. The fact that a Japanese-American war, should it come, will determine the future of world civilization, Millard wrote, "assures to America the moral support of greater European powers should such a conflict ever come."[55]

Or did it? During the first years of the twentieth century, as Americans became aware of the complexities of international affairs, some of them thought they found a stabilizing factor in the idea of

Anglo-American collaboration. In a world of rapid changes and bewildering subtleties, it was reassuring to think that at least one could take the unity and friendship of the English-speaking peoples for granted. In Asia and the Pacific, no less than in Europe and the western hemisphere, the United States and Britain seemed to pursue similar goals and be guided by the same principles.[56] All the more disconcerting, therefore, was the existence of the Anglo-Japanese alliance, which was renewed once in 1905 and again in 1911. So long as it continued in force, it did damage, psychologically and intellectually, to the idea of Anglo-Saxon unity standing against alien forces. Gallant efforts were made to believe that despite the Anglo-Japanese alliance there was a deeper moral union of the Anglo-American countries. Henry Hoyt, counselor of the State Department, advocated cooperation with Britain in Manchuria in opposition to Japanese expansionism. If such collaboration could take place, he wrote, "We would thus materially but inevitably weaken the force of the Anglo-Japanese alliance . . . [The] natural alliance in the East in many cases is between America and England."[57]

In an imaginary novel about a Japanese-American war, *The Coming Conflict of Nations* (1909), Ernest Hugh Fitzpatrick depicted how the British people, despite the Anglo-Japanese alliance, sympathized with the Americans. They "longed for a just and proper excuse to join hands across the seas to help to expel the invaders from American soil. Were not the United States but an expansion of Great Britain? An expansion of Anglo-Saxon civilization?" Upon the Japanese invasion of the Panama Canal, in this novel, Britain severed its alliance with Japan and formed a new one with the United States. "In one day a hundred and fifty years of misunderstanding was swept away forever. George Washington belonged equally to the two great sections of the Anglo-Saxon race." The fate of the war now hinged on a sea battle between the erstwhile allies. The British navy won, and throughout Britain and the United States "the people congregated in churches and halls to return thanks to Providence for the victory and deliverance from the yoke of an oriental civilization." Even so, they were willing to make further sacrifices "and to go to any length to remove, for all time, any apprehension of a doubtful issue in a conflict between the civilizations of the East and the West."[58]

The reality of British foreign policy belied such a romantic notion of Anglo-American mutuality and friendship. The Anglo-Japanese alliance remained in force, obstructing on more than one occasion efforts by the United States government to break up the imperialistic hold on China. As Under Secretary of State Huntington Wilson complained, "Britain sacrifices everything to the Japanese alliance. [Such] an attitude makes our cooperation difficult . . . [and] tends to force Germany and the United States into special relations in the Far East."[59]

Theoretically, however, Britain did seek a framework of basic understanding with the United States. Edward Grey, upon entering the Foreign Office in 1905, expressed the hope "that a bond of union between ourselves and the United States will be found . . . in our tendency to take the same view of events in the world generally. If the two countries think alike about public events, they will be found acting together in foreign countries where they have mutual interests; and even where only one of them is interested, its policy and action will be understood by the other."[60] Unfortunately, such understanding was not easily found in matters concerning Japan. In reporting the American uneasiness about the Japanese, "who they say are suffering from the 'swollen head' and are likely to give trouble in the future," Grey's representative in Washington, H. M. Durand, commented: "For a well educated and intelligent people they [Americans] are curiously ignorant of foreign countries. Many of them seem to think the world practically began with the Declaration of Independence."[61]

In China, Minister John Jordan wrote, "American hostility to Japan is very pronounced in China and the Chinese rely to a certain extent upon American advice and sympathy in their dealings with Japan in Manchuria." But he predicted, "American participation in railway construction in China Proper will probably widen American interests in the country, bring them into closer contact with the hard realities of the Chinese problem, and make them less indulgent of Chinese methods." Jordan had little sympathy with American policy in Asia which, he wrote, "is always one of ostentatious bluster with little or no performance."[62] Responding to such thoughts, Grey wrote back that while cooperation with the United States in China was desirable, "I am afraid that their anti-Japanese tendency may lead them to lend their influence to the Chinese in anti-Japanese projects." In such an event, Britain was bound to stand with its ally.[63]

In light of these circumstances, there was no simple way in which Americans could comprehend their relationship with Japan in the overall framework of world politics. Slogans such as Anglo-American cooperation and Chinese-American friendship did not contribute to clearer understanding of international affairs of which Japanese-American relations were one aspect. International relations were becoming more and more complex and the United States more and more deeply drawn to them in the years preceding and during World War I. This perhaps explains why American images of Japan after 1912 were no longer as simplistic as earlier. As the United States became involved in world politics, Japan was only one of the many countries it had to be concerned with. Few now discussed Japanese-American relations in isolation, and few accepted without some modification the earlier theme of competition between the two countries, whether economic, racial, or military.

To be sure, as *Outlook* pointed out in 1915, it was still difficult to discuss Asian questions rationally since "the anti-Japanese propaganda in this country has been so urgent and aggressive that many Americans have come to suspect all statements regarding Japanese intentions and all interpretations of Japanese purposes."[64] But the European war, fought among the civilized powers of the West, complicated the matter. Some were convinced that Japan would take advantage of the opportunity to expand further in China. "Japan is bent upon having her way in China in spite of the Anglo-Saxon world," said *Current History*, referring to the Twenty-One Demands episode. "Japan is now convinced that if she is to have her way in China she must be prepared to go to war."[65] Others advocated American neutrality to prevent Japanese aggression. The *Richmond Palladium* (Indiana) asserted in August 1914, "Japan's entry into the field of international complications and war through her ultimatum to Germany has arrested the on-sweeping flood of public opinion in this country favorable to the Allies in their struggle with Germany . . . What power Japan gains at the expense of Germany now will later be used against this country in the great struggle that is inevitably coming between that nation and this."[66] When Foreign Secretary Arthur Balfour visited Washington in 1917 he wrote, "I found that the State Department took a profoundly gloomy view of Japanese policy. I did what I could to combat suspicions which seemed to me, on the evidence, somewhat excessive."[67]

Yet the war years forced some rethinking concerning Japanese-American relations. For one thing, the possibility that the United States might become involved in the European war made it desirable to maintain the status quo in Asia. But no stability in Asia would be realistic unless it recognized Japan's position there. On the other hand, the rhetoric of Wilsonian internationalism, which began to be heard more and more loudly after 1916, implied that the United States and Japan, as two great powers not yet involved in the war in Europe, should cooperate to redefine international politics so as to put an end to the Old Diplomacy. Quite symbolically, the Lansing-Ishii agreement, signed just after the United States and Japan became allies against Germany in 1917, had both these elements. It recognized Japan's special position in China, but it also contained the signatories' pledge not to take advantage of the war for selfish ends. Indeed, the very signing of such an agreement was evidence that events in Japanese-American relations had not quite progressed in accordance with images. In the old image of competition and rivalry there had been no room for a compromise agreement, let alone a political understanding, between the two countries. But the exigencies of the war necessitated it, and American opinion on the whole welcomed it.

Outlook, the most outspoken exponent of power politics, asserted, "We have over and over again . . . expressed the belief that Japan's leadership in the East was not a source of danger, either to the United States or to the world at large."[68] Mildred A. Clarke, writing for *Independent,* argued, "If only the American Government will seize the opportunity of the visit of the Japanese Mission now in Washington to take up the whole American-Japanese problem it will find that the Japanese are more than responsive and that there is nothing in the problem which cannot be settled in accordance with the principles of right and justice."[69] *Asia* magazine, the organ of the American Asiatic Association, said in its editorial that the Lansing-Ishii agreement "is the most valuable piece of constructive diplomacy in the Far Eastern policy of the United States" since the Open Door Doctrine.[70] The *Nation* and the *New Republic,* supporting Wilsonian internationalism, stressed the importance of trusting in "Japanese good faith instead of hunting for Machiavellian conspiracies" and accepting Japan's adherence to the principles of "the territorial integrity and political independence of China."[71]

The most revealing commentary on the Lansing-Ishii agreement was penned by Huntington Wilson, who had done perhaps more than anyone else in the government to emphasize the theme of Japanese-American incompatibility, economically and politically as well as culturally, and to bring about Chinese-American and Anglo-American cooperation against Japan. Now a private citizen, he jotted down his private thoughts, completely at variance with his earlier position. He wrote:

America is not China's keeper. If geographical, racial, and economic circumstances . . . have given the Empire of Japan a special position in certain parts of China, and, through them, a special interest in China, that is a fact. And if it is a fact, it is merely irritating and useless for the United States to hold back from recognizing that fact. With guarantees of equality of opportunity and the "open door" for our trade, industry and enterprise, our real interest in China ends. Cooperation with Japan, not obstruction, is clearly our proper part.

Nevertheless, he was not forgetting the underlying friction with Japan on account of the immigration dispute. On this matter he emphasized, in 1917 as he had ten years earlier, the desirability of forming an Anglo-American alliance. "The alliance would make . . . unassailable the common position of all the English-speaking peoples in regard to any future immigration questions," he wrote earlier in the year. But the Ishii mission induced him to accept the view that there would be no crisis with Japan on the racial question so long as the United States recognized that country's special interests in China. "Japan is far more sensitive about her Chinese interests than about the immigration and land-ownership difficulties, which are local, are more fanciful than real, and can easily enough be overcome when they are taken out of unscrupulous and unpatriotic state politics and are approached with tact and skill."[72] This was a pragmatic solution of the many difficulties that had arisen between the two countries, and in accepting such an approach Huntington Wilson, no less than Robert Lansing, was putting an end to one chapter in the history of Japanese-American relations.

The Japanese, wrote an American official in Tokyo in 1909, "undeniably crave our friendship, and only regret that it is not reconcilable with what they believe, wrongly or rightly, to be the just demands of their national destiny in Manchuria and Korea . . . While they resent our interference in Manchuria and are grieved at our treatment of their immigrants, down deep in their hearts they cherish our friendship. They appreciate that the maintenance of this friendship is beset with racial and political obstacles, and many of them sorrowfully apprehend that this friendship will some day be broken off by inevitable causes."[73]

Theoretically, "friendship" should have been reconciled, even compatible, with competition. After all, diplomacy is a device for regulating competition among nations so as to keep it peaceful. It is no accident that during the first years of the century, when Americans became accustomed to the sight of their country's involvement in international affairs, they were fascinated by ideas of arbitration and international organization as means to maintain peace among potential rivals in the world arena. The search for a world order in which nations engaged in friendly competition characterized a predominant strain of American thinking about foreign affairs.[74] Japanese-American relations, however, could not always be fitted into such a scheme. There was a distinct body of opinion in the United States that considered Japanese as competitors and rivals. Once the theme of competition was introduced, it was difficult for some to develop a vocabulary of mutual association in which Japanese would remain friends while becoming competitors.

That this was so was related to American self-perceptions—in the western hemisphere, the Pacific, the Orient, and the entire world. To the traditional axiom of predominance in the western hemisphere, the Spanish-American War added the theme of American expansion in the Pacific and East Asia. Japanese activities in these regions, both actual and imagined, could not easily be reconciled with such perceptions. Because Japan, just like the United States, was emerging as a world power, its emigration to the American continent, naval increases in the Pacific, and aggressive commercial policy in China could only be regarded as a challenge to and an obstruction in the way of American interests, power, and prestige. Resolutions of potential conflict seemed particularly difficult in view of the racial and cultural differences between the two peoples. From such a perspective, it was all but impossible to visualize a situation in which Americans and Japanese would engage in friendly competition in various parts of the world.

Fortunately, the United States and Japan managed to avoid collision and, in fact, became military allies in 1917. But what brought this about was the war in Europe, and it symbolized the fact that Japanese-American relations never developed in a vacuum. Indeed it was the multilateral nature of these relations that saved them from treading the rigid path leading to the final reckoning, as was so often predicted. Subsequent history was to show how dependent on the international environment was the amity between the two countries.

Images of the United States as a Hypothetical Enemy

For pleasure reading during the past few years I have become interested in delving into war-scare books published well before 1941 that portray the United States as a future enemy with whom Japan would inevitably have to do battle. It was amusing to read the foresight their authors believed they had, but after reading a number of these books, I began to notice a general pattern of seeming significance. Soon I began searching for images of the United States as a "hypothetical enemy" in the minds of these second- or third-rate hack-journalists who churned out sensationalist literature for the Japanese public. Most of the works take the form of a fictional narrative, trying to evoke scenes of a future war between Japan and the United States with more or less verisimilitude. Naturally the literary quality of these works is generally very poor, catering to the general public's taste for sensationalism and melodrama. Most are obviously books of the moment, works of subliterature, and having served their transitory function, whatever it may have been, they are deservedly forgotten and look dead enough for us today.

But although the jingoistic sensationalism expressed in most of these futuristic war stories is not only uninteresting but positively unpleasant, their predictions and warnings proved after all to be true. Deliberate exaggerations and unintentional miscalculations of various kinds are easy to detect, nonetheless the course of events proceeded almost as the authors predicted. So far as the basic theme is concerned, we must admit that these mediocre writers were somehow uncannily accurate, to a certain extent actually prophetic.

The relationship between image and reality—popular image and historical reality—is highly complicated and ambiguous. It is an open question whether the striking, sensational images communicated through war-scare books affect the emotions of general readers in a positive or a negative way—whether the images really stimulate the reader to some overt action or whether they tend to restrain him, having served as a means of "catharsis" by providing him with a substitute emotional outlet. It is even more difficult to know whether literary quality has anything to do with the impact of a literary work on its readers.

In any event, it would obviously be wrong to postulate any simple relationship between these musty third-rate works and the coming of the Pacific War. They should rather be taken as a very minor aspect of prewar history. But while they may have been no more than insignificant bubbles rising to the surface of the mounting waves, they may well have served as indicators of the drift of the general current underneath.

So far as group emotions and impulses are concerned, these cheap thrillers could be taken as more reliable reflectors or symptoms than the serious fiction of first-rate authors. In some cases the popular novels might be even more revealing as expressions of unconscious, blind, mass emotion in naked, raw form. Because of their very insignificance as literature, they could signify something quasi-literary. In spite of their naiveté as literary expression, they could serve as an outlet for popular emotions. They are not to be taken too seriously or too literally; neither are they to be dismissed too lightly or too contemptuously.

In the history of popular images, specifically images of the United States as presented in novels about a future war, three periods may be identified. The first was from the turn of the century to about 1911, when the first such novels were published. The second period followed immediately after World War I. The most important period, however, was 1932-33, when an enormous quantity of literature was published.

The first story of a future war between Japan and the United States to appear in Japan seems to have been *Nichi-Bei kaisen miraiki*

(Narrative of a future war between Japan and the United States), published in 1897 as a special issue of the literary magazine *Bungei kurabu,* together with a similar story of a war between Britain and France.[1] Both were translations, the former having been written by an American navy lieutenant named Hamilton and first published in the *San Francisco Examiner,* according to the translator's preface. The story was received as nothing more than an exotic romance of military adventure, not as a harbinger of future events.

The first work that could be considered as dealing with more or less realistic events and directly concerned with actual issues was *The Valor of Ignorance* by Homer Lea, two rival translations of which were published in Japan in 1911: *Nichi-Bei hissen ron* (The inevitable war between Japan and the United States) by Mochizuki Kotarō, and *Nichi-Bei sensō* (The war between Japan and the United States) by Ike Kyōkichi. Ike may have been the authorized translator, since he claimed to have been given the Japanese copyright by the author through the good offices of Sun Yat-sen, who was a close friend of Lea. In any event, the publication of two translations in the same year and the fact that it proved to be one of the most widely read, most frequently quoted works of this genre in Japan are indicative of Japanese responsiveness to the book's subject matter. As Lea wrote from the point of view of an American patriot, aiming his book at an American audience, and furthermore was exclusively concerned with Japan as a potential enemy and engrossed in the technical problems involved in the defense of the United States, it would appear at first rather strange that the work should have been so favorably received in Japan. One reason for this was probably Lea's patriotism. An archconservative, worried about the dilution and consequent deterioration of the traditional American spirit as a result of the influx of foreign-born immigrants, he put emphasis upon a fighting spirit and the necessity of a standing army. While he discussed Japan as potentially a dangerous enemy, he spoke highly of "bushido" and the valor of the Japanese. His motivation was neither hatred nor enmity but rather attachment to the military way of life. Many Japanese readers must have felt flattered rather than repulsed or angered, for Lea saw in Japan a worthy, honorable enemy. His attitude must have impressed Japanese readers as similar to the samurai spirit of old. Even Lea's dubious pretension to the rank of general was apparently accepted in Japan; I know of no Japanese who ever called it into question.

Another reason for the favorable reception of Lea's book was that the idea of a future war between the two countries was seen in terms of a distant, romantic military adventure with little likelihood that it would be actualized. At that time it was American journalism that took a serious and sensational view of the prospects for such a war. In *Nichi-Bei no shin kankei* (The new relationship between Japan and the United States, 1910), Takahashi Sakue, professor of international law at Tokyo Imperial University, expressed amazement at the hostile tone of some American papers, especially on the west coast, which he had encountered in the United States in 1907.

In the same year the two translations of *The Valor of Ignorance* were published, a curious and enigmatic book appeared on a similar topic: *Mōjin no honyaku—Eijin yori mitaru Nichi-Bei sensō kan* (The war between Japan and the United States, as viewed by an Englishman—Translated by a blind man). The author or translator, Sugiyama Shigematsu, claimed it was a free translation of an English book. He could not read English—which was why he called himself "blind"—but when a friend happened to tell him about it, he was so interested that he wrote it down from memory. It was a clumsy, naive adventure story of secret agents, in which a Japanese agent, trying to intercept a message he suspects relates to a secret American plan for war against Japan, kills an American agent in England. In the end, the Japanese agent confesses to murder and kills himself. Although set in England, the book does not impress one as British at all. Most likely the author wanted to give it an exotic flavor and literary prestige by pretending it was a translation. Nonetheless, the book reflects the fact that the idea of a future war between Japan and the United States still had an exotic, Western tinge.

Although Oshikawa Shunrō, widely known for a number of future war stories, wrote a novel on the theme of "a duel between Japan and the United States" in 1912, the book most comparable to *The Valor of Ignorance* was *Tsugi no issen* (The next war), written by an anonymous naval officer and published in 1913. It later turned out that the anonymous author was Mizuno Hironori, who had written the well-known *Kono issen* (This war), a lively report on the naval battle in the Japan Sea during the Russo-Japanese War. In his second book Mizuno made several references to Homer Lea and Alfred Thayer Mahan, seemingly with the aim of making a counter-statement to their writings. Although written in a fictionalized form, *Tsugi no issen* was as serious and technical as *The Valor of Ignorance*. Mizuno was still a regular navy officer when he published the book, and his expertise well qualified him for analyzing in detail naval strategies and tactics. In addition, Mizuno was an accomplished stylist, and his description of the anti-Japanese movements in California and the political situation in Japan formed a carefully constructed and readable story.

One interesting parallel between Mizuno's and Lea's books was their pessimism. Both were far more concerned with the weaknesses of their own countries than with those of their hypothetical enemy. Both made technical comparisons and analyses with detachment and concluded that their own nation's prospects in the future war were poor. Mizuno predicted the defeat of the Japanese navy, and Lea that of the American army. Mizuno closed his fictionalized narrative with the almost complete annihilation of the Japanese Combined Fleet, "more heroic but more miserable than when the Baltic Fleet was defeated in the Japan Sea or when the Invincible Armada was defeated in the English Channel." Lea ended with the prediction that the entire Pacific coast would be occupied by the Japanese army. Both perceived the urgent necessity of military and naval expansion and believed their own country must be better equipped in a military or naval way.

Mizuno's actual contact with the United States was slight. On his first voyage abroad as a naval cadet in 1899 his ship sailed along the Pacific coast and docked at several ports. In *Tsugi no issen* he recalled having observed in San Francisco "white urchins catching the passing Chinese, calling them monkeys, pulling at their pigtails." He felt "irrepressible anger as an Oriental."[2] This was the only reference in the book to his personal experiences in the United States, but the theme of resentment toward the arrogance and insults of white men and his self-assertion as an Oriental were magnified and woven into the whole fabric of his narrative. It was not that Mizuno conceived of his imaginary war as a racial conflict, nonetheless the theme of Orientals against whites pervaded the entire novel. This was true as well of Lea's book, which contained several references to the "yellow peril." While he did not put too much emphasis upon this aspect of the conflict, he tended to interpret the future war with Japan in such a framework.

The next major Japanese writer of war-scare novels was Lieutenant General Satō Kōjirō, who published the best-selling *Nichi-Bei tata-kawaba* (If Japan and America fight) in 1920 and *Nichi-Bei sensō yumemonogatari* (Dream tale of a Japanese-American war) in 1921. By then relations between the two countries had become so strained that talk of a crisis across the Pacific was commonplace. Professor Payson J. Treat of Stanford University summed up his observations on a visit to Japan in 1921 as follows:

> By the summer of 1921 a very dangerous state of mind had developed on both sides of the Pacific. The daily press, and even the more thoughtful publications, of both America and Japan, had indulged in such reckless criticism of the conduct and policies of the other country that the traditional friendship of Japan and the United States seemed to have completely vanished. When an attempt was made to sift out the firm facts from the chaff of suspicion and foreboding it was soon found out that there was little to excite alarm, except this state of mind, but in these days when public opinion can influence chancelleries, an unwholesome state of mind is something to be feared by statesmen.[3]

While in Japan, Treat gave a series of lectures on Japanese-American relations at Tokyo, Waseda, and Keiō universities. His lectures were translated into Japanese by Professor Murakawa Kengo of Tokyo Imperial University and published in Japan prior to publication in the United States. A chapter entitled "Peace and Friendship," which was the first chapter of the Japanese edition,[4] begins:

> Diplomatic relations between the United States and Japan cover a period of just 75 years—a brief span in the history of international intercourse . . . And finally [after the friendly phase lasting from 1868 to 1905] comes the phase since the Russian war, from which Japan emerged as a world power with enlarged interests and responsibilities on the continent of Asia; a period in which contacts increased, and with contact, friction; a period in which popular opinion was moulded by more or less reliable information; and a period in which wise statesmanship has been in demand on both sides of the Pacific.[5]

In his preface to the Japanese edition Murakawa expressed deep concern over recent strains in relations between the two countries.

There is no doubt about the urgent need to deepen mutual understanding between the two peoples on the Pacific, to brush away the "trace of dark clouds" between the two nations, and to secure world peace through mutual friendship. Mutual understanding can be reached only by maintaining an impartial perspective on the historical relations between both countries. I became convinced of this when I visited the United States four years ago.[6]

Although rhetorical but subdued phrases such as *ichimatsu no an'un* ("a trace of dark clouds") were characteristic in the writings of Japanese scholars at the time, Murakawa's sincere, deep-rooted sense of anxiety is easily discerned. He even added, referring to anti-Japanese sentiment in the United States, "If some Japanese still hold to the illusion that all Americans are anti-Japanese, I should like to tell them that it is their obligation to listen to Professor Treat."[7]

It was in such circumstances that Satō's books appeared. First published on April 10, 1921, the second went through five printings in a week. Its author was a clever, sophisticated storyteller who placed his story within a framework of fantastic dreams, as its title suggests, that ominously foretold a bloody conflict between Japan and the United States. The setting was a small provincial town along the Tōkaidō line, where a General Genkai was invited to speak on the vital issue of Japanese-American relations. The town hall was packed with an eager audience, to whom Genkai urged the importance of "spiritual mobilization" of the Japanese people in preparation for the approaching emergency. The main action of the story took place the next day, when some of his listeners came to talk with him. They had been so stimulated and excited by his speech that all had had dreams related to the coming crisis, and each one was asked to relate his or her dream.

The first and most impressive talker was Miss Fuyue, "a nervous spinster, graduate of a women's teachers' college who had taught at several schools in Nagoya and Nara." Satō thus skillfully provided the framework and atmosphere for her "dream story," with a touch of humor in his depiction of this female character. Nothing could be more natural than for a nervous spinster to be possessed of hysterical fantasies. In her dream she had had a sudden premonition that some upheaval was about to take place. She could not bear remaining in the countryside, so she went to Tokyo. The city was unusually full of excitement, with newsboys running about the streets crying, "Extra edition!" Diplomatic relations were to be severed with the United States, which was expected to present an ultimatum to Japan at any moment. The United States had already assembled a large fleet at Port Petropavlovsk in Siberia, while at Vladivostok some 30 carriers and 6,000 airplanes were in readiness for an attack that would burn down Tokyo. Once war was declared, "the American fleet from Petropavlovsk will arrive in Tokyo Bay within six or seven hours, and airplanes from Vladivostok will be over the city within two or three hours." A woman who appeared to be a military expert was explaining the situation to people on the streets, and she was pale with fear. Wittily, the author has Miss Fuyue end with a description of Tokyo ruled by women:

Although the whole city was in an uproar, not a man could be seen working actively. All the men just cowered in corners, and all the soldiers and policemen on the streets were women. Besides, most of the women were muscular and stout, while the men looked so weak and feminine.

Anticipating women's liberation, the author turned Tokyo into a city ruled by Amazons in which men were completely subjugated! His intention was, of course, satirical. In his mind Japan in the 1920s had grown feminine and weak, lacking in masculine vigor, a criticism commonly made by traditionalists at that time against young men attracted by cosmopolitan culture and "decadent" Western literature. The implied condemnation was developed in a long, eloquent speech given at a rally by the chief Amazon, who was chairman of the House of Representatives. Most of the audience were again women, and they listened as if hypnotized to her eloquent words, accusing male statesmen of "mean-spirited passivity" toward the United States.

Even when the United States government tried to interfere with Japanese efforts at economic expansion in China and Siberia, all our male statesmen could do was make concessions, again and again . . . Now Japan is on the brink of national collapse. Once the fingertips of the United States touch our country, Japan will certainly go to pieces. The only salvation is for us women to rouse ourselves, warn and encourage our weak males, and be determined to fight at any cost.

Satō's story may have been humorous, but his aim was serious: to warn his readers of the dangers involved in Japan's fundamental weakness vis-à-vis the United States.

The dreams related by the other characters in the novel were equally pessimistic. A veteran of the Russo-Japanese War told of a "horrible dream" in which the Japanese army and navy both suffered so many repeated defeats that utter collapse was inevitable. The air force did its best, but the disparity in power and numbers was so great that the Japanese planes fled "like sardines chased away by a big whale." The sky over Tokyo was covered by "hundreds of American planes that overwhelmed us with a terrible buzzing."

The book ended with the dream of another female character, "not exactly a Christian but with an idealistic desire somehow to contribute to world peace." The author was clearly quite sympathetic toward her, describing her as modest, soft-spoken, and reserved—the traditional ideal of Japanese womanhood. She talked of a dream in which "the dawn of peace could be perceived." It was to be a "peace of women," based upon the cooperative efforts of women on both shores of the Pacific. Referring to Satō's earlier book, *Nichi-Bei tatakawaba*, she commented: "Some critics accused Satō of being a warmonger [in writing such a book], but this was a gross misunderstanding. His real hope was that world peace might be maintained through cooperation among the three big powers, Japan, Britain, and the United States." World peace might be the ultimate ideal, but she rejected disarmament and arms limitation as unrealistic. The balance of power among the three major nations was the realistic means of achieving peace.

Many other books published during the 1920s dealt with a future war between Japan and the United States. Higuchi Reiyō published *Nichi-Bei sensō miraiki* (Narrative of the coming war between Japan and the United States) and *Nichi-Bei mondai rimenshi* (Inside story of Japanese-American problems) in 1920, *Kazen Nichi-Bei* (Japan and the United States—What next?) in 1921, and *Nihon kiki—Beika kitaru* (The American peril—Crisis for Japan) in 1924. A typical hack author who had written two books about Kaiser Wilhelm in 1915, Higuchi was a prolific writer with an inflated and sensational style. His concentration upon Japanese-American relations at this time is evidence of the popular appeal of the subject. Other examples include Hiramoto Heigo's *Nichi-Bei tatakau bekika* (Japan and America: Must they fight?) in 1920; a translation of Walter B. Pitkin's *Must We Fight against Japan?* with critical comments by Satō Kōjirō in 1921; and a translation of *The Pacific Problem of the Twentieth Century* by General Nicolai Golovin of the White Russian army, also in 1921. Five years later Satō published, again with critical comments, a translation of *The Great Pacific War, 1931–33* by Hector C. Bywater, one of the most influential writers on this subject.

The future war stories of the 1930s contrasted sharply in many respects with those of the 1920s and are vividly remembered by Japanese who grew up during the 1930s. For many, these popular accounts contributed to their initial images of the United States. One book in particular, Hirata Shinsaku's *Ware moshi tatakawaba* (If we fight, 1933), seems to have provided them with one of the most exciting and important reading experiences of their childhood.

Hirata was a writer for juvenile magazines who wrote many works of this kind, both nonfiction and fiction. His attitude, however, was never jingoistic, and in the introduction to his book he wrote: "I am going to write about the possibility of a war in which Japan is attacked by a foreign country. But, dear friends, I never mean to agitate for war. War is the last measure one should use to settle a dispute. If possible, we should avoid it."[8]

The book consists of three sections. The first, entitled "If We Fight in the Pacific," begins:

I will describe a supposed Pacific war to indicate our defense of the sea. Friends, if you have a chance, stand on the rocks of Inubō Point. You will see the tide coming in from distant seas. It is the Japan current, called the "Mother of the Pacific." Look! There is the tide, of deep blue sea water. Listen! That is the roaring of the sea. How thrilling the ocean current is!

Later he states:

The enthusiasm of American naval planners for military strategy is striking. They have been doing research on battles in the Pacific, on how they might embark on an expedition to the Orient. They say, without really meaning it, that their supposed enemy is not Japan but Britain, and yet they concentrate 90 per cent of their naval power in the Pacific. There are more than 250 battleships off the coast of California. Captain Organ [?], an officer who once lived in Japan, keeps saying their target is the British navy and that it would be foolish to fight the Japanese navy. But if he really means what he says, well then, why have they kept the Atlantic free of warships? It is not at all likely that the British navy would come from the Atlantic and the Mediterranean to Singapore across the Pacific. Dear Mr. Organ, your excuses are of no use. What the United States navy aims at has never been the British navy. It is the Japanese navy. Your target for attack is the Eastern ocean.[9]

Part 2, "My Strategy for the Far East," and Part 3, "Japan under National Mobilization," are both an introduction to national defense written for boys. The Soviet Union plays a leading role in Part 2, and themes such as "Russian ambitions and Red power" and "the possibility of war in the Far East" are developed. Part 3 deals realistically with several subjects: "An Alliance of Nations in the Far East," which outlines the East Asia Coprosperity Sphere, "The Possibility of an Air Raid," and "Japan's War Potential." For a children's book it covers much ground in over 400 pages, with pictures and illustrations. And more than half the book is devoted to a discussion of the prospects for war with the United States in the Pacific. In a section entitled "If We Fight in the Pacific," Hirata refers to the British as well as the French and Dutch fleets in the East Indies as only incidental to the impending showdown between the United States and Japan.

One feature of the book is an objective comparison of the two countries' military strengths. There is a careful emphasis on such quantitative comparisons. For example, in an imaginary confrontation of battleships, he analyzes the likely result: "Our nine battleships, like the *Mutsu* and the *Nagato*, are stronger in single combat. But, I am sorry to say, 16 40-centimeter guns and 72 36-centimeter guns make only 88 guns, which are somewhat less powerful than their 160 guns." He notes regretfully, "I know the United States navy is the biggest in the world. I also know that they are never lax. If they maintain their defenses around the Panama Canal, they will never be defeated. The American navy would be best in a defensive war." He also expresses his worries about "defeat in war":

If the strength of our Combined Fleet is weakened, we don't know what will happen. If they begin to give up, they will become very weak; but if they begin winning, they will suddenly become strong. Japan could have all its overseas territories taken by the enemy. Japan could go back to its miserable situation in the Kamakura period when, with no navy, Tsushima and Iki islands were taken by the enemy.[10]

Despite all the disadvantages Japan faces, he concludes, such a thing would not happen, for the training and fighting spirit of the Japanese would outweigh their disadvantages.

Various differences can be perceived between Hirata's book of 1933 and Satō's of 1921. Hirata is optimistic about Japan's chances, while Satō is generally pessimistic. Hirata's basic self-confidence is obvious despite his cool, detached style, whereas Satō, behind his touch of sophisticated humor, tends to emphasize the bleaker aspects of Japan's situation. The individual temperament of each author doubtless had something to do with this difference, and Satō's concern in particular might be interpreted as strategic. He wanted to warn the "indifferent, unprepared" public: "If you do not wake up and face reality, you are sure to come to miserable defeat." That was what he implied in his pessimistic dream-stories. What motivated him was a passive sense of crisis rather than an active desire for expansion: "I will tell you how terrible an enemy the United States could be. You had better understand their power, their strategy, their intentions. But don't be timid. If you are determined to be well-prepared, you need not be afraid. Your determination, your preparations, will save you." This was his message to the Japanese public.

Even before Hirata's book appeared, other writers of the 1930s were developing images of the United States in accounts of trips to that country, in essays on America, and in books on a future war with it. In 1932 Ishimaru Tōta, a naval officer, published his *Nichi-Bei hatashite tatakau ka* (Will Japan and the United States fight?). The tone of the book can be seen in the opening sentence: "Over the past twenty years, like angry waves beating upon their shores, the devil's voice has been continually speaking to Japan and the United States, two countries set apart by the Pacific."[11] The same year two other navy officers published similar books: Hakosa Taneji's *Fukam-ariyuku Nichi-Bei no kiki* (The deepening crisis between Japan and the United States) and Nakajima Takeshi's *Nihon ayaushi* (Japan threatened!).

Periodicals, too, picked up the theme. A special issue of *Sekai chishiki* (World knowledge) in 1932 dealt with the possibility of a Japanese-American war. In one article a professor at Tokyo Imperial University discussed "The History of America's Pacific Invasion"; a reporter for the *Asahi shimbum* wrote on "American Policy in China and the Possibility of War with Japan"; and an anonymous contributor asked, "Will the United States Advance and Will Japan Retreat?" Common to all the articles was the accusation of "U.S. imperialism." The Tokyo professor, a specialist on Western history, concluded by tracing the historical development of American imperialism since the nineteenth century. The westward expansion of the United States, he stated, which had been going on since the nation was founded, had at last reached Asia, where the United States, through its great wealth, had begun to oppress the peoples of the Far East. Another writer noted that the United States was no longer to be looked upon as representing justice, freedom, and equality; on the contrary, it was simply another imperialist country.

Thus, the idea of the United States as a potential enemy was widespread in Japan in the 1930s. Hirata had merely formulated it for children.

Writings of the decade were obviously influenced by the Great Depression in the United States, as indicated by titles such as *Naked America, America in Distress*, and *America in Decline*.[12] The author of the second, the well-known writer Kimura Ki, wrote:

America in distress! There are more than 322 million bushels of wheat on the market, yet there are long bread lines in front of distributing stations in every city. There is George F. Baker, who left more than $100 million and donated nearly $1 million to charity, yet there are six million unemployed who have not had a single silver dollar for twelve years. Twenty-five negroes were sentenced to death last year, and six publications that had something to do with the Communist Party were banned. Even such an almighty power is as completely powerless as guinea pigs in front of a scientist . . . In 1929 36 people each paid $5 million in taxes, but a year later 1,300 banks went bankrupt.[13]

Yamauchi Kazuo, an analyst in the research department of Mitsui Gōmei, divided his report on the American economy under such headings as: "The Collapse of Prosperity," "Bankrupt Rural Communities," "The Collapse of the Business World," and "The Gap between Rich and Poor." He discussed the "Defects of the Universities," "A Society of Calamity," and "Evil and Crime" and concluded with "The Inevitable Fall." His introduction pointed to the sudden change that had occurred in foreigners' images of the United States and the dramatic fall of American prestige abroad.

When the first forces of the United States army under General Pershing landed in France, it was as though a messiah had arrived. World opinion of the United States reached its zenith when President Wilson swaggered into Europe. The praise lasted for about ten years . . . Then everything changed. We hear praise no longer. What attracts our attention now are the judgments of newspapers in every country. The attitude of intellectuals toward the United States has changed. Those who had never spoken a word of criticism of America have begun to attack it. America's prosperity and success have been lost in stumbling panic. But this is only a temporary fall. The fatal fall has yet to come.[14]

Many stereotyped commentaries appeared in magazines at this time arguing that the collapse of American capitalism was inevitable. Kiyosawa Kiyoshi, a leading journalist and the author of *Amerika o hadaka ni su* (Naked America), criticized this tendency: "There are too many things that are impossible for us to understand when we read articles about the United States that are published in Japan. That is, they are too ready to use tinted glasses made in Moscow." Pointing to an article in *Chūō kōron,* he went on: "There are no articles that do not have this tone, even in first-rate magazines. From the articles we read in Japanese magazines, it seems as if the United States had fallen to the bottom of hell."[15] Rather than arguing that the concept of America's collapse was wrong, Kiyosawa described his reactions to the United States on a visit ten years earlier. America had stumbled on its road to prosperity, he wrote, and had begun to have doubts about itself for the first time in its history. This was unsettling for Americans, who had never had any doubt about the value and perfection of Americanism. "Americans are facing adversity with the determination of an automaton. What lie in front of them are nothing but broken machines. It is not philosophy but techniques to repair broken machines that occupy them. They are in their work clothes now, trying hard to repair themselves without reference to any complicated theories."[16]

The effect of such writings about the United States was to create an image of America as gigantic yet feeble, a huge but fragile country beset by fatal weaknesses. Inevitably the images of America as a potential enemy in a hypothetical future war and of its unexpected but obvious fragility in the face of adversity came together. Did this fusion of the two images provide a psychological driving force for the war that was to erupt a few years later? Strangely enough, the prognosticators of war never wrote of the weaknesses of other countries. What could be better to arouse the spirit of the nation than a hypothetical enemy that was weak and beset by contradictions? Given the objective evidence of America's fragility, the image of a hypothetical enemy might easily have evolved to the level of actual perception. But on the unconscious level, Japan was psychologically prepared for war with the United States when this synthesis was made.

Japanese Images of War with the United States

It has been said that a profound psychological tension among the Japanese was relieved when they heard the news of the Pearl Harbor attack.[1] This sudden release of tension was apparently caused by the realization that the "inevitable war" had at last broken out and had erupted with great initial success. It seemed that the years of forbearance and watchful waiting were giving way abruptly but purposefully to a period in which vengeance would be taken against an old foe.

The train of events that culminated at Pearl Harbor may be said to have been set in motion in 1924 when the United States Congress passed the anti-Japanese immigration bill. The Japanese reacted violently, declaring that the United States no longer merited the designation "land of the free." Nationalistic organizations took up the refrain "Chastise the Americans,"[2] a song whose spirit represented popular sentiment throughout Japan. This widespread feeling that America's contribution to human history had ended marked the beginning of a new era in Japanese-American relations. In principle, the conflict between Japan and the United States had already begun.

Typical of this type of thinking was the influential journalist Tokutomi Sohō (1863–1957). Tokutomi considered the dictates of biological evolution to be a major principle of international politics. Only those nation-states that continued to grow could preserve their

existence and assure their survival. Constant expansion was the key to success in the international struggle for survival. The history of the American people, he believed, was a case in point. Successful in their movement westward, by the end of the nineteenth century their expansive energy had carried them beyond the western shores of the North American continent. In one direction expansion led to acquisition of the Philippines; in the other, bypassing Japan, they began to enlarge American commercial interests on the Chinese sub-continent. If Japan was to survive in this international struggle, it too had to enlarge its circle of influence, starting from the center of the Japanese empire and expanding that circle outward. These aggrandizing Japanese and American circles soon came to press against each other, producing international tensions. What was expected to arise out of such a situation was a conflict of physical forces.

When Tokutomi formulated this argument, he was not particularly concerned with the moral aspects of international conflict, which he considered an inevitable product of biological evolution. Morality or spiritual strength became relevant only when he began to consider how Japan might emerge victorious from an "inevitable war." It seemed obvious that spiritual strength would be a decisive ingredient for success. Moreover, national self-assurance and confidence would be far easier to maintain if the Japanese could unhesitatingly declare that justice resided with them.

Tokutomi at this time was engaged in writing what was eventually to become the hundred-volume *Kinsei Nihon kokumin shi* (History of the Japanese people in recent times). At the core of his historical view, as expressed in this work, was the notion that the Japanese were members of a family-nation whose history grew out of the unbroken line of the Imperial House. It may appear contradictory that Tokutomi predicted on the basis solely of biological determinism rather than any moralistic appraisal of the situation that the Japanese exclusion law would lead inevitably to a Japanese-American war while at the same time he held to an ethnocentric image of his own country that was built upon a highly moralistic concept of the national polity and the Imperial family. But the very stratified patterns of thought that frequently resulted in this type of contradiction were in fact peculiarly Japanese.[3]

In dealing with international relations, where it was thought an exceptionally objective assessment was in order, the Japanese tendency was to consider only the naked power of the nations involved. Yet in respect to problems relating to the political culture of his country, the same person would readily apply a uniquely Japanese notion of the national polity. Such an attitude may be observed frequently in Japanese intellectual leaders, such as Inoue Tetsujirō (1856–1944), an ideologue of statism who interpreted the Imperial Rescript on Education almost literally, or Nitobe Inazō (1862–1933), who was regarded as one of the foremost liberals of prewar Japan.[4] But it would be foolish to expect that a rational attitude in dealing with international politics could function completely independently of beliefs, transcending logic, that concerned the divine origins of the Imperial House and the national polity. Especially in a situation of mounting international crisis, the ethnocentric system of values must have begun to surpass the limits of the self-contained political culture and to demand that they be applied defensively in the realm of international politics as well.

A good example of this is the Japanese navy's image of the United States. A U.S.-Japanese war would be fought essentially on the high seas, a war between the navies of the two states. Unless control of the seas (and the air) was won, petroleum from Indonesia and the tin and rubber of Malaya could not be turned into material fighting strength for the successful prosecution of the war. That fact was well known to the Japanese, and no matter how much the army wanted a southern path of expansion, it would have been out of the question to declare war against the United States if a go-ahead signal were not forthcoming from the navy.[5]

The first Japanese naval plan that posited the United States as an enemy nation was formulated in 1907.[6] But this was rather a difficult proposition for Japanese naval officers, who had long held the British and the Americans as their teachers and very naturally acted as if the Anglo-Japanese alliance were an inalienable part of Japanese policy.[7] As a result, in 1921, when a naval disarmament treaty was proposed at the Washington Conference, Katō Tomosaburō (1861–1923), the Japanese plenipotentiary representing the Imperial Navy, made it a point to engage in negotiations with the conviction that it would be

unwise to insist on Japanese interests to the detriment of mutual trust and friendship between Japan and the United States.[8]

Some naval officers, however, held an image of history similar to Tokutomi's and prepared themselves for the eventuality of war between Japan and the United States.[9] They believed that the U.S.-Japanese antagonism of their time had begun with the historic visit of Perry's squadron to Japan. It has been said that Admiral Yamamoto Isoroku (1884–1943), who drew up the plans for the Pearl Harbor attack, actually had applied for admission to the Japanese Naval Academy at Edajima in order one day "to return Commodore Perry's visit."[10] That was in 1901, six years after the conclusion of the Sino-Japanese War and three years before the beginning of the Russo-Japanese War. This was the same Yamamoto who told Prime Minister Konoe Fumimaro: "If you insist that we should really do it, you may trust us for the perfect execution of a breath-taking show of naval victories for the first half-year or full year. But if the war should be prolonged into a second or third year, I am not confident at all."[11]

The first sentence of this passage points to the conclusion that Yamamoto must have been somewhat responsible for the Japanese government's final decision for war. Ordinarily, when Yamamoto's part in the decision for war is appraised, greater significance is attached to the second sentence, and he is pictured as a strong voice against the general trend toward war. I would incline to the former view, however, for no matter how Yamamoto may have qualified his words, he confidently stated a fair chance for spectacular initial success in a war against the United States. The issue of war or peace at one time or another must have been completely predicated upon such a statement concerning the capability of the Japanese navy.

This interpretation may invite fierce disagreement from those who argue that, as commander-in-chief of the Imperial Navy, Yamamoto had to speak with confidence. Indeed, from about 1937 on grandiose naval expansion plans were conceived and put into effect with the United States and Britain in mind as possible enemy countries, and expenditures were made even at the cost of slowing down the modernization of the army's mechanized equipment. In such a situation, Yamamoto's defenders say, he could not possibly admit that the navy was unprepared to fight a war with the United States.

To argue thus, however, is to say that Yamamoto was a man of so little caliber and such frail integrity that he could not stand firm simply because of the part he had played in increasing naval expenditures. Yamamoto did represent a large segment of antiwar opinion within the navy, and he fully recognized the implications of an American war. When he opposed war, he did so mostly because in his opinion Japan's chances of winning ultimately were very slim. Yet he too held many of the views shared by the general public at that time, views based upon a common system of ethnocentric values that gave meaning to such an unwanted war. If Yamamoto, unlike most chauvinists of the age, did not advance a completely self-righteous argument for opening hostilities against the United States, it must have been largely because he happened to possess sufficient information concerning the enormous discrepancy in war potential between Japan and the United States.

Apart from those like Yamamoto charged with planning for actual combat, there were other views held by high navy officials who sat at the conference tables where decisions for war were made. Nagano Osami (1880–1947), chief of the Navy General Staff, may be taken as representative of this group. Nagano expounded his ideas at the Imperial Conference of September 6, 1941, where the fundamental decision for war with the United States was made.

Representing the Navy High Command, I would like to express our views. According to the statements made by the government a little while ago, to capitulate to American demands would mean destruction of our country as a nation. But it may well be just as destructive to wage war against the United States. In other words, whether Japan remains pacifist or goes to war, before even attempting to wage war it is bound for self-destruction and is destined to national extinction. But if we are determined to be true to the spirit of defending the nation in a war, even if we might not win the war, this noble spirit of defending the fatherland will be perpetuated and our posterity will rise again and again.[12]

Nagano argued that Japan should wage war against the United States even if it was simply for the sake of remaining true to the spirit of national defense. What was most important was the spirit of defending the fatherland. It was of minor consequence whether the enemy happened to be the United States or the Soviet Union. His argument for war with the United States had little if anything to do with

images of that country. Nagano was concerned with the defense of
Japan in the sense of perpetuating the national polity for posterity.
In fact, a contemporary has stated that Nagano seriously feared an
imminent rebellion might destroy Japan from within unless it were
averted by a major war.[13]

Yamamoto and Nagano represent two different types of thinking
within the navy that supported Japan's decision for war. Nagano's
argument could have arisen from an exclusive consideration of internal problems. In contrast, Yamamoto viewed a war with the
United States as the inevitable product of the history of Japanese-
American relations. To Nagano the very act of waging war, even if
there were no chance of victory, was fraught with significance.
Yamamoto acquiesced in a declaration of war in the belief that at
least in the initial stages he could bring about spectacular victories,
then leave the ultimate outcome to the government's ability to negotiate an advantageous peace.[14]

Even after the decision to wage war against the United States had
been made, both these high-ranking officers of the Imperial Navy
continued to hope that a settlement might evolve from diplomatic
negotiations. But once the officers and men were mobilized and the
countdown had started, it would have been practically impossible
for Yamamoto, who as commander-in-chief of the Combined Fleet
had ultimate responsibility for actual combat, to call a halt. To do
so would have destroyed the morale of those under him who had gone
through so much hard training in preparation for the zero hour.
Moreover, a peace obtained with humiliating concessions would have
caused resentment and agitation.

To understand more fully the outlook of Japanese naval leaders, it
would be useful to examine the social classes from which they were
recruited, the kind of education they were given at the Naval Academy, and their responses to the United States on their first visits
there on cadet cruises.

In December 1928 Nagano was appointed principal of the Naval
Academy, where he had been a member of the twenty-eighth gradu-
ating class, remaining in that post until June 1930. The student body
was composed of approximately 300 men recruited through competitive examinations. Socially most were from the lower middle class,
but academically they were usually the top students in their respec-

tive middle schools. In 1927 a major curricular reform had extended the three-year program by eight months in order to modify the hitherto almost exclusive emphasis upon the military arts and those natural sciences directly related to navigation and warfare. Courses in languages and the humanities were introduced, and students were required to study both English and German, whereas formerly only one of the two had been required. A course in the history of the Western world was also added.[15] Nonetheless, the school retained its elitist orientation, for the Academy had to produce all the officers for the Imperial Navy. The isolated location of the school on Edajima, a small island off the coast of Hiroshima, helped foster cohesion within classes and unity of purpose. Just as in medieval monastic life, devotion to a higher cause and asceticism could thrive there. Such an environment reinforced the students' patriotic ideas concerning the state and their belief in the unique national polity of Japan derived from the mythical divine origins of the country and the Imperial family. If some came from a lower social class drawn to certain socialistic ideas, they soon found a commitment to values of a "higher order," the nationalism centered on the Imperial House. Even on Sundays it was customary for students to recite the Imperial Rescript of 1882 for the army and navy before leaving for a holiday outing. Commitment to the fatherland was strong before students were admitted to the Academy. Now the elitist career opening before them would turn nationalism into a means as well as an end. Their future lay with their nation, independent and strong.

In March 1929 the fifty-seventh class of 122 students was graduated from the Academy, the first class to finish school since Nagano had become principal. These cadets made an overseas cruise under the command of Nomura Kichisaburō (1877–1964), a member of the Japanese delegation to the Washington Conference. Nomura, who later was to engage in negotiations for reconciliation and peace with the United States until the moment of the Pearl Harbor attack, was already becoming something of an internationalist seeking mutual understanding among nations rather than ethnocentric self-righteousness.[16] The practice fleet with these cadets aboard sailed across the Pacific via Hawaii to Seattle, Tacoma, San Francisco, and Los Angeles. After visiting Manzanillo and Acapulco in Mexico, it traversed the Panama Canal into the Caribbean, stopping at Havana.

Sailing north, the cadets visited the naval academy at Annapolis. But the climax of their first voyage abroad came with their arrival at the port of New York City.

Before landing at New York, Nomura instructed them: "While on land, be sure to observe with your own eyes what America really is. See how materially great the United States is."[17] His intention was to cool the chauvinistic enthusiasm that characterized the cadets, who tended to talk at times of a war of "justice" against the United States, especially since the anti-Japanese immigration legislation had become law and was being vigorously enforced.

Despite Nomura's "materialistic" concern about Japanese-American relations, his words were not always heeded. Takuma Rikihei (1903–   ), the chief instructor on board one practice warship, engaged his cadets, who were five years his juniors, in a kind of Zen dialogue in the presence of the Statue of Liberty:

What do you see over there?
That is the Statue of Liberty, a symbol of the United States. It was given to the American people as a gift from the French people in token of their gratitude for the friendly attitude the United States had maintained during the course of the French Revolution. Standing 47 meters, it is the tallest statue in the world.
What about the Great Buddha of Nara?

To this, the same cadet responded accurately:

It is only 15 meters tall. The Statue of Liberty is of course far taller.
Are you sure your answer is correct? The Great Buddha is seated on his own legs. In addition, he is a buddha! Once he stands up, you cannot tell how tall he can become. Until the moment he does stand up, you cannot tell which is taller.[18]

The import of this type of psychological instruction was grave, for to "stand up" could signify Japan's determination to rise up against the United States. In "until the moment he does stand up, you cannot tell," one senses an indefinable yet profound trust in one's own spiritual potential. This type of spiritualism was common, not at all exceptional. In fact it was a product of the prewar education of all Japanese. The course of instruction at the Academy, which both cadets and Takuma had undergone, likewise imparted a nationalistic spiritualism reinforcing that which they already possessed.

With this frame of mind they landed in the great city of New York, the hub of the material wealth and prosperity of the United States, the archenemy of the Imperial Navy. It is easy to imagine how their youthful minds were fired with chauvinistic spirit.

As they landed, what they saw seemed to confirm the validity of what they believed. They were especially appalled at the policemen who not only drank freely with them, though they were off duty and aboard a Japanese warship on which the Eighteenth Amendment did not apply, but who even asked the cadets to give them some bottles of liquor to take home. America was a democracy. But if people did not abide by the law, what would happen to law and order? And these policemen were expected to enforce the law. Perhaps it was a consequence of "liberty" wantonly applied. Here liberty, the fundamental principle of American civilization, became identified with the source of American degeneration and America, it seemed, had no further contribution to make to human progress.[19] If this was where American-type modernization was leading, Japan must change its course of national development and intrinsically Japanese institutions should be valued anew and used to effect a remedial antithesis in Japanese modernization.

If the cadets sailed away from New York with the impression that the era in which America was at the forefront of human progress was fast coming to a close, the Great Depression that started soon afterward must have appeared to signal the end of American capitalism and, with it, the end of American materialism. And if this ailing civilization were destined to perish, it would be a fitting task for the Japanese people to help bring about its death as quickly as possible. The concept that a war against the United States was a "holy war" may have been born in this way.

The Japanese army in the meantime was developing its own conceptions of the United States. A critical point came in 1939 when the Nazi-Soviet Pact, combined with the Nomonhan fiasco, compelled the army to turn its attention southward to seek raw materials in Southeast Asia. Expansion in this direction would provoke American intervention, and thus for the first time in the history of the Japanese army it began the study of the United States as a probable enemy. Within the War Ministry, Colonel Iwakuro Hideo (1896–1970), chief of the Military Section, was concerned for the future of Japanese expansion and sensed the need for a detailed assessment of American strength. No sooner had the Nomonhan Incident ended than he called back Akimaru Jirō (1897–   ), an intendant lieutenant-colonel, from his post in the staff office of the Kwantung Army in Manchuria. Iwakuro's plan was to establish, as a secret adjunct to the Accounts Bureau of the War Ministry, a war economy research group headed by Akimaru. Its task was to produce quickly a thorough analysis of the war potentials of major countries, including the United States and the USSR, and of Japan's own plans for a war economy. Endō Takekatsu, chief of the Intendant Section, promised to collaborate, and the research group became operative in January 1940.[20]

Because of the secretive nature of its activities, the research group went into hiding in Tokyo, the location being changed several times. But its members, six university professors and a banker, remained unchanged once they had been appointed and begun their work.[21] Akimaru had previously studied under one of them, Professor Arisawa Hiromi of Tokyo Imperial University, who at one time had lectured in the army's special career training program. The inclusion of such a "leftist" scholar, whose knowledge of British and American economics was indispensable, is testimony to Akimaru's seriousness of purpose, for in 1941 Arisawa was awaiting trial for political crimes as a result of his role in the popular front movement.[22] Such intimidation by ultranationalist organizations was one reason the group had to remain inconspicuous. Partial records of their activities, which have survived both Akimaru's orders for destruction and the cataclysm that ended the war, give convincing evidence of their labors.[23]

An impressive list of sources was consulted. Prominent among them were German and Russian books and research papers concerning America's war potential. Possibly the group's conclusions were affected by the Russian ideological bias against capitalism and by the excessive self-esteem of the Nazis. More likely they would have been predisposed by their own nationalistic sentiments not to refute the Russian and German predictions in assessing the outcome of a war between Japan and the United States. Nonetheless, their research was ruled by sober realism. Among the books used was *Economic Problems of the Next War* by Paul Einzig, published in London in 1939. The author's name suggests German descent, but he was educated in

Paris, and after 1921 held important posts in London's leading financial papers. In 1929 he was naturalized a British citizen. The book gives a high estimate of American war productivity. Indeed, Einzig's estimates were nearly identical to those of Akimaru's group.[24]

As the research progressed, Iwakuro initiated an unofficial peace feeler toward the United States, which eventually led to the establishment of contacts with the American government through two American clerics, Bishop James E. Walsh and Father James M. Drought. In March 1941 Iwakuro himself arrived in Washington, where he and his colleagues, in collaboration with the two priests, formulated a basis for further conversations with the State Department. They communicated with both the American and the Japanese government. Unfortunately, Foreign Minister Matsuoka Yōsuke's obstinate inaction at the outset and later insistent objections to the whole scheme resulted in the failure of the plan.

Iwakuro brought with him to the United States Colonel Shinjō Kenkichi (1897–1941), who had been a staff member of the Financial Affairs Division of the Cabinet Planning Board.[25] His assignment was to investigate America's productive potential at first hand. On August 15 Iwakuro returned to Yokohama alone, taking with him the results of Shinjō's investigations. Shinjō estimated that Japan's steel production capacity was one-twentieth that of the United States, which also produced several hundred times as much petroleum as Japan, while America's aircraft production was five times greater, as was the size of its industrial labor force. Overall, he judged that Japan's mobilized war production potential was at most 10 percent that of the United States.[26] As far as Iwakuro was concerned, the only policy recommendation that could come from these figures was that negotiations aimed at reconciliation be continued, and from the day of his return to Japan Iwakuro worked zealously to convert the chief officials of the government and the military to this view. At the Army General Staff office he spoke before an audience that included the chief-of-staff and practically all his subordinates down to staff officer level. When a section chief reprimanded him that war with the United States was unavoidable, Iwakuro queried, "What is the prospect of winning the war?" "It is not a matter of winning or losing it any more," was the answer.[27] The officer's sentiment was similar to the view Navy Chief-of-Staff Nagano was about to express at the Imperial Conference of September 6, that a nation which does not rise against "injustice" is destined for extinction.

On August 23, according to Iwakuro, at the General Headquarters-Cabinet Liaison Conference, Army Minister Tōjō Hideki (1884–1948) indicated for the first time a favorable response to Iwakuro's arguments against war by ordering him to hand in a written report. Happy that at last his conclusions were about to affect national decision-making, Iwakuro visited Tōjō the next day, expecting to resume the conversation, only to be abruptly informed that a written report was no longer necessary and that he was to be transferred to a new post as commander of the fifth guards infantry regiment. Thus Iwakuro was removed from a position where he could directly influence national policy. After Pearl Harbor, as the war began to turn from bad to worse for Japan, Iwakuro was shipped overseas, apparently upon orders from Tōjō, to the Burmese front, where fierce fighting and likely death awaited.[28] Why did Tōjō change his mind about considering Iwakuro's arguments? The deterministic view that war was inevitable must once more have prevailed overnight, leading to the conclusion that if Japan had to fight the United States under any circumstances, a study of their war potentials, particularly one with a distinctly antiwar bias, would not be of much use.[29]

Toward the end of September, about a month after Iwakuro's failure to convince Tōjō, Akimaru presented his report to the top officials of the army in a closed session at the Army Ministry. Akimaru was the sole member of the research group present, for no civilian was allowed to attend. The report pointed out that the Japanese economy could rely only on the economic bloc embracing Japan, China, and Manchuria, which had already reached the limits of its productive capacity. Hostilities might be sustained for two years by drawing upon the stockpiles of war materials, but thereafter the Japanese economy would constantly decline while American productivity would continue to grow. The German economy had likewise reached its peak and could only be expected to deteriorate. Consequently, Japan was not prepared to fight a war.[30]

In concluding the meeting, Sugiyama Gen, chief of the General Staff, commented on the report. The research, he said, had been carried out well and its analyses appeared sound. However, its conclusions were at variance with the supreme will of the state. This, he went on, made it imperative that every copy of the report be immediately destroyed.[31] Here again was an image of the future which concluded that a war with the United States was unavoidable and which made a man such as Sugiyama reject all information that argued against going to war.

So far, two extreme images of the United States have been discussed. One, held by the navy, had strong overtones of chauvinistic spiritualism, locating American civilization at the opposite pole to Japan's own civilization. The other, that of the army, at least as expressed by Iwakuro and Akimaru, was more materialistic, taking full cognizance of Japan's economic deficiencies and believing it unwise to engage the United States in war. There was, however, a third image, between these two extremes, that was enormously influential in the years preceding the war. This was a Pan-Asianist image, derived from a theory of international justice and justifying Japan's position in China in the name of an Asian Monroe Doctrine. This was an important ingredient of the Japanese images of war with the United States.

Pan-Asianism in this sense perhaps originated in 1905, when the Japanese, elated at their victory over Russia, had to face the humiliation of racial discrimination in the United States.[32] The Japanese learned then that to be faithful to international law alone would not assure them justice. Power was more important, and a nation like the United States, which possessed power and affluence, was able to define international justice by forcing a weaker nation to accept its dictates in the name of international law. If Japan were to accept such a mixture of national interest and international justice as unavoidable in *realpolitik*, it must lay claim to a certain area of Asia as its own domain and apply the same kind of international justice toward the United States, if not to lesser nations within this area. This was the Asian Monroe Doctrine.

To be sure, others saw international law and justice as Americans viewed them. Maida Minoru, a popular American-trained journalist, asked in a book published in 1929, "Is it legitimate for Japan to rebel against the Open Door policy of the United States in the western Pacific simply because the latter has been enforcing a 'closed door policy' in Latin America?"[33] His reply was a prompt and unequivocal "No!" Japan, he argued, had to consider the matter of good faith among nations, for the principle of the Open Door in China had been the subject of international agreement when in 1889 the powers gave their consent to Secretary of State John Hay's proposal, and it had been confirmed and reinforced by such agreements as the Anglo-Japanese alliance of 1902 and the Nine-Power Treaty of 1922. In contrast, the Monroe Doctrine had been unilaterally announced by an American president, and the United States had never sought the consent of other powers to keep the door closed in Latin America. In Maida's opinion, if the principles of the Open Door and equal opportunity were faithfully observed, the cause of peaceful development in the Pacific would be well served.[34]

It is important to note here, however, that Maida's recommendation that Japan remain faithful to international agreements was predicated upon a hopeful assessment of the future of the world: a state of harmonious cooperation among nations, in which Japan would be allowed free access to raw materials and unrestricted export of finished products. He wrote:

Japan is a country whose territory is small and whose resources are scarce. It has to depend upon other countries for securing such materials. Furthermore, to sustain the livelihood of its excessive population, Japan finds it imperative to place a high priority upon exporting its products abroad. A country like Japan must welcome a liberal policy of international cooperation (like the Open Door) and rejoice over its growing acceptance among nations.[35]

It would follow that should these conditions for any reason be limited or cease to operate, Japan would regain the freedom of action to move whichever way it chose, including denouncing the system of international peace based upon a legalistic observance of the status quo.

An example of these developments can be clearly seen in the writings of Inahara Katsuji, a journalist who had studied political science and political economy at Stanford and Harvard immediately after the Russo-Japanese War. As a journalist he headed the foreign news division of the Osaka Asahi Press and was chief editor of an English daily and of the journal *Contemporary Japan*. He attended the Washington Conference as a member of the Japanese delegation. His books on foreign affairs numbered nearly a dozen, including *Gaikō dokuhon* (Reader in diplomacy), originally published in 1924, the year the anti-Japanese immigration act became law in the United States. In this book Inahara tried to be sympathetic toward the United States, reminding Japanese readers that their discrimination against the Chinese was very similar to American treatment of Japanese immigrants.[36]

After the Manchurian Incident, however, when the United States issued a barrage of criticism against Japan, Inahara drastically altered his stance. He ceased to be a moderate. Now, as one of Japan's foremost publicists, he repeatedly denounced the principles and practices of international justice as "hypocritical." For example, in an article printed in the December 15, 1931, issue of *Ekonomisuto* (The economist), he wrote that after having rejected the spirit and system of the League of Nations, the United States was sneaking into it as an observer. Furthermore, he charged, America's record of domineering behavior in Latin America was indisputably criminal. And yet, he went on, "This nation with a grave criminal record such as this has established itself in a position to watch over Japanese activities in Manchuria. How brazen and conceited can a nation get?"[37] A few months later for the first time he proposed in the same magazine that Japan should adopt an Asian Monroe Doctrine. Inahara's argument was practically identical with that of Maida Minoru, but he drew precisely the opposite conclusion: "After all, as long as the United States maintains the Monroe Doctrine—that is, a 'closed door policy' —and still insists on enforcing the Open Door policy, it is only natural and should not be objectionable at all that Japan, acting on the principle of equality, should establish an Asian Monroe Doctrine—that is, a 'closed door policy'—and further demand that the Open Door policy be applied to Central and South America."[38]

Such arguments for an Asian Monroe Doctrine, a kind of Pan-Asianism that was becoming prevalent in Japan at this time, implied a Japanese-led Asian solidarity that would condone inequality among nations within the region. This brand of Pan-Asianism was "externally provoked," for its model was found abroad. In contrast, there was another kind which may be characterized as "intrinsically based." Its fundamental beliefs were that the Japanese and Chinese had originated from the same stock and shared a common script for writing, and that Asia was a community of peoples sharing a common destiny. Such a notion of shared destiny was always present in the minds of Japanese and constituted a major ingredient of their self-image.[39] To choose just one example, Ishibashi Tanzan, the post-war prime minister (December 1956–February 1957), was a Pan-Asianist of this sort. He was president of a publishing house whose major publication was the weekly *Tōyō keizai shimpō* (Oriental economist), which was rivaled in economic journalism only by *Ekonomisuto*. Ishibashi wrote on Japanese foreign relations constantly in this journal. As the conflict in China stalemated and American economic sanctions were stepped up, Ishibashi came to view the war within the framework of Japan's efforts to establish a new order in East Asia. On New Year's Day 1939 he appealed in his journal that an independent managerial system for the Sino-Japanese community be established in order to bring about a new order in China. In the fall, when Ambassador Joseph C. Grew denounced Japanese policy in China, saying that the so-called "new order" was infringing upon American treaty rights in China, Ishibashi responded with an article entitled "Mr. Grew's Irresponsible Speech." He wrote that "Grew spoke honestly, but his words ignored one fundamental issue." He had failed to make clear that "the United States must try to understand what Japan wants and must give support to its efforts to find a way for national survival."[40] Ishibashi's hopes were unfulfilled.

About the time the Akimaru group was reaching its antiwar conclusions on the basis of more strictly economic considerations, Ishibashi, anticipating open hostilities with the United States, exhorted the Japanese to make economic preparations as far in advance as possible.[41] It was also around this time that Admiral Takahashi Sankichi declared in Ishibashi's economic weekly that Germany had a 99 percent chance of winning the Battle of Britain and urged Japanese expansion southward to score a victory over American policy in East Asia. "This action would precipitate a war with the United States at any moment," he wrote.[42] His conclusion was much the same as Ishibashi's call for economic preparedness. Upon learning of the conclusion of the Atlantic Charter in August 1941, Ishibashi wrote:

Those nations who have destroyed world peace are no other than Britain and the United States, who possess more than half the entire wealth of the world. In other words, the chaotic situation in the world today began to emerge as soon as they became disqualified to lead in bringing economic prosperity and peace to each and every nation of the world.[43]

A few weeks before Pearl Harbor he admitted that Japan's efforts to readjust its relations with the United States were sharply limited by its desire to maintain the Rome-Berlin-Tokyo Axis alliance, to obtain a satisfactory resolution of the China Incident, and to establish the so-called Greater East Asia Coprosperity Sphere. In other words, Japan had already prepared itself to wage war.[44] "Japanese expansion on the Asian continent and in the Pacific is bound always to collide in one way or another with the policy of the United States, which aims at maintaining the status quo."[45]

Ishibashi's basic line of argument might be termed the logic of the "have-not" nation. In November 1937, after Italy joined in the Anti-Comintern Pact previously signed by Japan and Germany, Ishibashi published an article entitled "A League of the 'Have-Not Nations' Will Contribute Greatly to the Cause of World Peace." To those who feared that tensions would arise leading to a war between the "have" and the "have-not" nations he replied that conflict was inevitable even without such a league. With the formation of the league, on the other hand, "we can expect some reforms to be effected by the 'have' nations."[46] The principal significance of the Axis alliance, as far as Ishibashi was concerned, was as a military and diplomatic tool to keep the United States from interfering in the endeavors of the Axis powers to realize a new global order.[47]

Apart from Ishibashi, certain prominent Japanese leaders also expounded the Japanese romanticism of the have-not nation. In fact, its first extended, public elaboration was put forward by Prince Konoe Fumimaro (1891–1945), in an essay entitled "Opposed to the Anglo-American Centered System of Peace" that he published in a nationalistic journal shortly before leaving Japan to attend the Paris Peace Conference.[48] Twenty years later, as prime minister, Konoe was to announce the establishment of the New Order in East Asia and the Greater East Asia Coprosperity Sphere.

As a university student Konoe had been concerned about Japan's social problems and had shown a rather serious interest in Marxist idealism.[49] His socialist leanings, however, had to be diverted in a less harmful direction because of his close familial relations with the Imperial House. Konoe's answer to his dilemma was to remain a socialist on the level of international politics, arguing Japan's right to make demands as a proletarian nation upon the capitalist nations of the West. Thus, he believed, could he circumvent that sacrosanctity which made socialism within Japan incompatible with its national polity. But in the process of manipulating his socialist ideals Konoe's nationalism had to be transformed into a kind of internationalism. Japanese nationalism was extended to the Asian continent through his concept of Japan's mission to liberate Asians from external forces coming from the West. It was a form of Pan-Asianism that was to grow among the Japanese by the mid-1930s.[50]

These views also meshed well with Konoe's images of the United States. In his 1918 essay Konoe had described the United States as selfishly pacifist. But when he viewed the devastation of the European countryside in the wake of the war, he became a convinced admirer of Woodrow Wilson and his proposal to establish a league of nations.[51] But despite Konoe's attraction to Wilson's ideals, neither Wilson nor the contemporary United States could provide an answer to Konoe's quest for a solution to the problem of establishing equality among the industrialized countries, including Germany and Japan. In 1935 Colonel Edward M. House published an article in the American journal *Liberty* entitled "Wanted—A New Deal among Nations." Arguing that a new deal was needed in international society as well, he proposed sympathetic solutions to Japan's economic problems.[52] Shortly afterward Konoe responded to a request from the editor of *Liberty* by contributing an article in which he expounded his time-worn theory of international justice.[53] Konoe had just returned from a trip to the United States, where he had been impressed that some Americans still held moderate and sensible views about the Japanese.[54] It may be that he was hopeful such moderate views might in due course become influential in the United States and that he now found reassurance in the concrete measures proposed by House.

Matsuoka Yōsuke (1880–1946), Konoe's foreign minister, provides another example. He lived on the west coast of the United States, mainly in Portland, Oregon, and Oakland, California, from 1893 to 1902, at the sensitive age of thirteen through twenty-two. This was a period when racial prejudice, already strong against Chinese coolie immigrants, was beginning to turn against the Japanese as well. Matsuoka's nationalistic sentiments had to undergo trial on many occasions, but he apparently concluded that to be treated as an equal, one must behave as an equal. If hit for no reason at all except that one happened to be smaller and yellow, he would say that one should not lose a moment in hitting back. Once a white aggressor was given the impression of capitulation, the yellow man would never be able to raise his head as an equal.[55]

In the international crisis that followed the Manchurian Incident, Matsuoka headed the Japanese delegation to the League of Nations. In the spring of 1933 he refused to accept the compromise solution proposed by the Lytton Commission and denounced the powers that were "crucifying" Japan, which had stood for the cause of international justice against the "have" nations. In a demagogic oration, he made a special appeal to the patriotic sentiments of the Japanese. His call for the triumph of justice over the injustices that existed in international affairs may merely have echoed the fantasies of Japanese militarism. Yet Matsuoka felt he had to hold to the lessons he had learned as a youth in the United States. When the League Assembly denounced Japan, 42–1, he stood up, holding his head high, and led the entire Japanese delegation out of the Assembly, never to return.

This determined gesture of defiance was maintained through the conclusion of the Axis alliance, which was designed to support Japan's efforts to establish a New Order in East Asia. If the United States could rely upon the Monroe Doctrine to support its preeminent position in the western hemisphere in order to sustain American economic stability and prosperity, why could not Japan do the same with an "Asian Monroe Doctrine"? This was going to be the first serious attempt by the Japanese to acquire for themselves a status of equality with the United States. Thus international justice would shine forth at least in the relations between Japan on the one side and the United States and other Western countries on the other. Since such an attempt meant the destruction of the world order the Western powers had developed and controlled, strong united resistance to Japanese action was anticipated. To cope with this Matsuoka believed to the last that Japan must stand undaunted, never showing the least sign of defeatism.

It is interesting to compare this posture of firm resolution, which he recommended that Japan assume in its foreign policy, with the images of Japan held by influential Americans such as Joseph Grew and Henry L. Stimson. As ambassador to Japan Grew had once recommended to his government that in dealing with the Japanese a resolute posture must be maintained.[56] Had both Matsuoka's and

Grew's recommendations been completely incorporated into the foreign policies of their respective governments, the results would have been mutual escalation of resoluteness, leading eventually to open military confrontation. Stimson, too, as secretary of war held a similar image, only slightly more pronounced in his deprecation of the Japanese as "Orientals." To his mind the Japanese were like "puppies" who would retreat to where they had started if a whip were swished firmly before their eyes.[57] If such images of Japan were prevalent among American decision-makers, the chances of open hostilities were infinitely increased, for most Japanese decision-makers tended to give greater priority to defending the nation's honor than to saving the lives of individual citizens.

Both Konoe's and Matsuoka's images of the United States were in some way or other related to Japan's final decision for war. A more extreme attitude arose out of the spiritualistic self-image held by many Japanese. A typical form of their argument in support of war might be called "surgical," for they equated Japan's predicament in 1941 to the case of a cancer patient whose life might be saved by a surgical operation. He might die anyway, but if out of fear he avoided the operation, he was sure to die. As Admiral Nagano said, the surgical operation for Japan was to strike out and see. To sit idle, doing nothing, was to capitulate to American pressure and accept their conditions for peace. This would mean a slow but sure death for Japan as a nation, for a nation that could not rise to defend its own land was already spiritually dead and destined for extinction.

Likewise, Okada Kikusaburō of the Army Ministry's War Preparations Section said, when the United States and Great Britain froze Japanese assets in July 1941, that Japan had been forced into starting a war. In his judgment, with petroleum imports completely cut, "within two years Japan will have exhausted all its power to defend itself . . . As a result, without doing a thing, Japan will be doomed to national exhaustion and collapse. Or Japan may find a course to national rejuvenation by striking out right away in a situation where the only other alternative seems slow death."[58] Accordingly, he ordered the staff members of his section to prepare immediately for war. About the same time Army Minister Tōjō Hideki told Prime Minister Konoe that it was sometimes necessary to "jump with one's eyes closed, from the veranda of the Kiyomizu temple" in Kyoto.

Thus did he indicate the pressing need for a prompt decision even if the leap might result in death at the bottom of the ravine hundreds of feet below.[59] Such a remark is characteristic of the "surgical" arguments Japanese were advancing to remedy what they considered a "fatal" disease. It was better to gamble with whatever resources they had left than to await the inevitable fate of "advancing impoverishment" and national collapse. Of course, some dissented that to strike out against the United States would more surely bring "absolute and complete impoverishment" to Japan. Yet such opinions found little support, for they sounded far too cowardly in comparison with the chauvinistic arguments that called for the defense of national honor and the national polity.

So long as chauvinistic spiritualism defined the fundamental mood of the Japanese, it was immensely difficult to make an objective assessment of war potential even in the sector of the national economy. Objectivity was distorted by ambiguity, and ambiguity was disguised in heroism. Altogether, the economic focus of what purported to be "economic" was lost. Suzuki Teiichi (1888–   ) of the Cabinet Planning Board epitomizes such ambiguity. As a minister of state he participated in cabinet meetings and even appeared before the emperor in Imperial Conferences. In the process of deciding upon supreme national policies, his expert opinion was frequently sought. But his views were blurred by his own nationalistic spiritualism. For example, at the fateful Imperial Conference of September 6, 1941, he prefaced his statement by saying that he was going to explain the "elasticity and resilience" of Japan's national strength. He then proceeded to give a high estimate of spiritual rather than material strength, declaring: "In regard to the spiritual strength of both the men in service and the people behind the battle line, who together constitute the essential sources of our empire's national power, it is my conviction that there is nothing to fear even if in the near future our empire finds itself in an extremely difficult situation."[60] The main body of Suzuki's explanation was a theory of "progressive impoverishment." By starting a war Japan could capture Southeast Asian countries where natural resources were abundant, and those resources could be turned into a major part of Japan's material strength by the beginning of the second year. This assessment of the value to Japan of the natural resources of occupied countries[61] was completely at variance with the conclusions of the Akimaru group, which had excluded as impractical the possibility of utilizing Southeast Asian resources.

That this type of thinking characterized the attitude of the Cabinet Planning Board is corroborated in an article contributed by its vice president, Miyamoto Takenosuke, to the September 1, 1941, issue of *Ekonomisuto*. Miyamoto, who held a doctorate in engineering, acknowledged that the hostile encirclement the countries standing for the status quo had set up around the Japanese islands posed a threat unprecedented in Japan's history. Nonetheless, he insisted, "no matter what pressure may be brought to bear upon Japan, if the status quo countries believe that the will of the Japanese people might be broken and they might surrender, those countries have a profoundly false understanding of the Japanese character. Not only are the Japanese people determined to repel any kind of pressure, but it must also be noted that the strength of their *elasticity and resilience* will increase in direct proportion to such pressure." (Italics added.) If the United States and Great Britain did not take this "traditional spirit" seriously, he concluded, their notions of the Japanese were "drastically mistaken."[62]

Japanese images of war with the United States were of two kinds. One was similar to that of Tokutomi Sohō, which held that open hostilities between Japan and the United States were only a matter of time. The other was one that would help the Japanese fight any foreign war, should it occur. It mattered little whether the enemy happened to be America or not. Beneath the superficial differences between the two, however, lay a common system of values, which supported the superstructure of prewar Japanese political culture and centered around the peculiarly Japanese concept of the national polity. When an international situation provoked the Japanese people's sense of crisis, this concept brought to a halt the functioning of what might be called "Western" rationalism, replacing it with nationalistic sentiments that resulted ultimately in blind ultranationalism. The top officials of the army who rejected the report of the Akimaru research group are eloquent cases in point.

Once the decision for war had been made, the Japanese could turn to another concept to support their war effort. This was the idea of conflict between the have and have-not nations of the world and the theory of justice that accompanied it. The Japanese demanded equal status with the advanced Western imperialist countries, but they ignored the unequal treatment they accorded their Asian neighbors. In the Japanese mind Asia constituted a sphere in which Japanese influence was to be supreme and whose liberation from Western imperialism was solely a matter for Japan to determine. There was little awareness of the ethnocentric, selfish motivation that lay behind such "liberation" or of the self-deception inherent in an Asian Monroe Doctrine that condoned and glorified Japanese expansionism in the name of "eight corners of the world under the one roof of Japan's imperial benevolence." Had Japanese behavior toward their Asian neighbors derived from a sense of sharing in the destiny of Asians as a whole and forming a community based on common cultural roots, the outcome might well have been a racial war with the Western world, where many were easily aroused over the idea of the "yellow peril." Nevertheless, the Japanese remained largely unconcerned about such implications of their own idealism.

From Ruth Benedict to Herman Kahn: The Postwar Japanese Image in the American Mind

It would seem natural that the enormous changes that have occurred in Japan between 1945 and 1973 should have led to parallel changes in the American image of Japan. The Japan that was seen as barbaric, feudal, bloodthirsty, and treacherous at the end of a terrible war should be seen very differently, one would think, at a time when peace has prevailed for many years, the Japanese economy has become the second most important in the free world, Japanese-American trade is one of the heaviest streams of trade in the world, and American visitors to Japan and Japanese visitors to the United States are numerous.

Obviously this change can be studied in many ways. One can review public opinion polls on Japan—and that is done below. One can review the attitudes expressed in the mass media—newspapers, magazines, movies, television. That I have not done, except for some notes on the relative volume of material on Japan available in some of these media. One can study what Americans learn about Japan in school and in college. This is only briefly alluded to below because this, too, involves a scale of research that was not possible. One can examine what American intellectuals think about Japan. This is easier, because, as is pointed out below, American intellectuals, despite the fact that a considerable number by now have been invited to lecture and travel in Japan, have not had much to say about Japan. Finally, one can do what I have done: examine what those Americans who are experts on Japan and who reach a substantial audience who want to find out about Japan, or who make themselves somewhat expert in order to write books on Japan, have had to say about Japan and the Japanese in the postwar period. The following essay takes this last line, while admitting that it is only one of many possible, that any conclusions that flow from it are tentative, and that undoubtedly many other approaches to studying the American image of Japan (some demonstrated in other essays in this book) are available.

But before considering what we learn from this approach, let us review some other approaches to studying the American image of Japan and what we discover from them.

A social scientist is immediately drawn to the public opinion poll, the survey, as a means of studying one nation's image of another, for here we find the validity given by random samples covering an entire population and the reliability given by repeated use of the same questions over time. But for our subject of the American image of Japan, public opinion polls are not too rewarding. The fact is, as has been pointed out so many times, the image of ordinary Americans of Japan is blurred. Harold Isaacs points out, in *Scratches on Our Minds* (1958), that in 1942 more than 40 percent of Americans could not locate China or India on a map. By the end of the war in 1945, the figures for the ability to locate China and India were still only 43 and 45 percent. Respondents were not asked to locate Japan, but in view of its much smaller size it is doubtful that they could have done as well as they did with China and India. In May 1945, a sample of respondents was asked if they knew where the following places were: Okinawa, Osaka, and Kyushu. Thirty-three percent knew where Okinawa was, 43 percent where Osaka was, 41 percent where Kyushu was. Among college-educated, the figures were 54, 72, 72. I am suspicious of these figures. I assume that the correct answer in all three cases was as simple as "Japan."[1]

The material available to Americans for the shaping of their image of Japan is fragmentary. The *Reader's Guide to Periodical Literature,* which indexes only major American magazines, shows that the number of pages of references to Japanese materials has stayed constant for over twenty years—generally about a tenth of 1 percent of all the references are to Japan (in 1971–72, for example, 3 columns out of 2,612). On the other hand, France and Germany do not get a particularly larger allotment.

The *Cumulative Book Index,* which includes all books in English, whether published in this country or abroad, showed between one- and two-tenths of 1 percent of its space taken by books on Japan. The *New York Times Index*—and here we move up, to discuss not the popular American mind, which is probably affected by magazines, and may be affected by books, but to discuss the American elite, whose main ideas about foreign countries are shaped by the *New York Times,* and by very few other sources—showed substantial coverage of Japan in the early years of the occupation: about one- half of 1 percent of its space in 1945 and 1946. From then through 1971, the Japanese items in the *New York Times Index* ranged between a low of one-tenth of 1 percent to about three-tenths of 1 percent, aside from exceptional years such as 1951, 1952, and 1960, when it went a bit higher. The average for Japan is not much less, however, than that given to France, about half of that given to Great Britain, about a quarter of that given to Germany.

Americans have been so little interested in what they think of Japan that despite the scale of the American public opinion surveying industry, there are very few surveys of American opinion on Japan. Hazel Gaudet Erskine, in *Public Opinion Quarterly* for Winter 1963,[2] reprints findings from "virtually all questions on familiarity with international issues that have been asked nationally since the publication of Hadley Cantril's *Public Opinion, 1935–1946.*" There are no questions on Japan. There are no questions on American attitudes on Japan in the *Public Opinion Quarterly*'s regular quarterly survey, "The Polls," since 1963. The only substantial series of questions on Japan ever to have been asked in American public opinion polling history and made publicly available, apparently, are those dealing with American attitudes toward Japan in connection with Japan's war with China, asked between 1937 and 1940. Consistently, 2 percent or less of Americans felt more sympathetic to Japan. The percentage of those sympathetic to China rose steadily from 43 at the beginning of this series, to 76 at the end. This scarcely means much today.

Private polls have been conducted for the Japanese Consulate General in New York by the Gallup Organization and some material from them for the period fom 1960, when they began, to 1970 is to be found in Kitamura Hiroshi's *Psychological Dimensions of U.S.-Japanese Relations* (1971).[3] The only question reported asks about Japan's dependability as an ally. In 1960, 55 percent of respondents thought Japan was "not dependable," 31 percent thought it was, and 14 percent had no opinion. This was, we see from later polls, an exceptional year in American attitudes toward Japan, clearly influenced by the mass demonstrations against the Japanese-American security treaty and the cancelling of President Eisenhower's planned visit. For 1961, only 38 percent thought Japan was "not dependable," 41 percent thought it was, and "no opinion" rose to 21 percent, reflecting the lesser interest in the question after the sensational events of 1960. There have been modest ups and downs since, but the general pattern has been between 39 and 45 percent seeing Japan as dependable, 31 and 38 percent seeing it as not dependable, and between a fifth and a quarter having no opinion.

One wonders, too, if the meaning of the question has not changed over the years. While in the earlier years of the 1960s the belief that Japan was not dependable as an ally may have indicated a negative point of view, in later years, as the impact of the Vietnamese war was more deeply felt, a substantial number of Americans might well have wished that some of our allies were not so dependable.

My reading of these responses is that whether or not Japan is a dependable ally was not a salient question for Americans before the broad awareness arose among Americans that Japan was a serious economic power. People divided on this question of dependability on the basis of well-known demographic features which offer no surprises. Thus in a breakdown of the 1970 question, we find the educated seeing Japan as more dependable than the less educated (66 percent for the college-educated, against 23 percent for grade school-educated), a similar pattern for occupation, the young most favorable (59 percent for the twenty-one to twenty-nine year age group as against 35 percent for fifty and over), and the West most favorable.[4]

A rather better source of information on general American opinion on Japan is the fascinating *Asahi*-sponsored poll by Louis Harris in early 1971. (The following comments are based on the *Asahi Evening News* report of March 17, 1971.)

Let us first consider what people *know* about Japan before considering what they *think* about it. Twenty-nine percent say they have read books on Japan, 35 percent have seen Japanese movies, 31 percent say they know a Japanese personally, and 14 percent have visited Japan. All this looks very substantial. But it is hard to believe the first figure of 29 percent. Professor Morton Kaplan of the University of Chicago "cannot accept it at its face value," and Professor Hans Baerwald of the University of California at Los Angeles "thinks the figure is about right if the books read include James Michener's best-seller, *Sayonara*" (*Asahi Evening News*, November 16, 1971). I agree with Professor Kaplan. The movie figure also seems suspiciously high to me. Japanese movies are shown only in art theaters, and then infrequently, or in movie theaters frequented by Japanese-Americans. The figure on Japanese known also appears excessive. Japanese on the mainland are only two-tenths of 1 percent of the population. Of those who have visited Japan, 80 percent did so in the course of military service in Japan and Korea. Thus only 2.8 percent of the American population has visited Japan independently of military service.

When we consider what Americans know of Japan, we are on more secure ground. Fourteen percent correctly identified Premier Satō; 5 percent correctly identified Mishima Yukio; 2 percent Mifune Toshirō; 2 percent Yoshida Shigeru; and another 2 percent Matsushita Kōnosuke. One percent identified Kurosawa Akira, and 1 percent Ozawa Seiji. No other Japanese is recognized by as much as 1 percent of the American population. These were the percentages of correct identifications when the name was presented by the interviewer. When asked to volunteer the names of famous Japanese, Hirohito was first with 33 percent, Tōjō second with 15 percent, Sessue Hayakawa, the Japanese-American actor, third with 9 percent.

Under these circumstances of almost total ignorance, it is questionable what weight we should assign general American images of Japan, but since this is the only survey available, we will summarize it. Given a selection of five statements about Japan, 85 percent of Americans agree, "The Japanese may not agree with us on everything, but we need their friendship in order to maintain peace and stability in the Pacific"; 66 percent agree, "The Japanese have become a really democratic nation since World War II. It is now a peace-loving country and stands on common ground with the United States"; 54 percent agree, "The Japanese fell under the control of the military before World War II. The same thing could happen in this country some day"; 25 percent agree, "Orientals, including the Japanese, are sly and devious—we should never trust them or rely on them as allies"; and 24 percent agree, "Japan, with its present rate of economic growth, will surpass the U.S. in average family income within the next 30 years, and will become a super power."

In view of the fact that 43 percent of the sample had heard of Mishima's suicide—the one event in recent Japanese history that was widely covered in the American press—it is interesting to note reactions to this event among those who had heard about it. Only 4 percent said it showed "Japan still remains a barbaric country"; 6 percent said Japan is "a very mysterious and inscrutable country"; 13 percent said Mishima's suicide was "a dangerous sign of revival of Japanese militarism"; 25 percent said "a sense of loyalty to the country still exists in Japan"; but the largest number, 43 percent, said "it was a unique incident which does not represent present-day trends in Japan as a whole." The latter also was the favored response of the better-educated and of those who had visited Japan (51 percent of both).

Among phrases that best describe Japanese people, "skilled craftsmen" came first (46 percent), then "energetic" (44 percent), "polite and reserved" (40 percent), "highly competitive" (33 percent), "intelligent" (24 percent), "serious and diligent" (19 percent), and then only in seventh place do we find the first negative characteristic, "sneaky" (19 percent).

Twenty percent of Americans still feel fear or hostility toward Japan as a result of World War II, 26 percent still feel very strongly about Pearl Harbor (18 percent "feel fairly strongly," 24 percent "not very strongly," 28 percent "almost forgotten"), and 64 percent feel dropping the atom bomb was both "necessary and proper." But only 51 percent of the youth from sixteen to twenty believe this, and only 53 percent of those from twenty-one to twenty-four.

What are we to make of such general views of Japan from people who inevitably know little about it? I would suggest that these views are for the most part not deeply based and are easily changeable under the concrete influence of Japanese-American political and economic relations. It is quite easy, to my mind, to shift American attitudes to foreign countries about which they know little—and this would include Japan—from friendliness to hostility, and vice versa, in very short order. In 1942, a poll showed that 56 percent of Americans thought Japanese cruel, 73 percent thought them treacherous, 63 percent sly. The parallel figures for Chinese were 3, 4, and 8. By the mid-fifties, I am sure, there were sharp changes in these figures.[5] Indeed, between 1951 and 1955 the number of Americans who had a favorable impression of the Chinese people dropped from 64 to 45 percent.[6] Undoubtedly there has been a very sharp favorable shift in attitudes toward China in the last three years.

The colleges and universities are one significant source of influences in shaping the image of Japan in the mind of America. Here 7 million Americans spend up to four years or more surveying various fields of knowledge, and 600,000 faculty members become specialized in instructing them. The college and university campus is the main setting, outside perhaps of the largest cities, for performances of visiting Japanese groups of actors and musicians, for showing of Japanese movies, for exhibits of Japanese art. And it is the only place, aside from the State Department and other government agencies, where sustained and consistent attention is given to Japan by a substantial body of experts. Certainly if the mind of America is to be affected on such a subject as Japan, the college and university campus must play a major role.

But these enormous numbers remain on the whole totally unaffected by any knowledge of Japan. It has been estimated that less than 1 percent of American college students receive "even the most superficial exposure to knowledge about Japan." But 80,000 are enrolled each year in courses on the history of East Asia, and if these courses use—as many do—the detailed two-volume textbook by E. O. Reischauer, John Fairbank, and Albert Craig, or its huge one-volume successor, then their exposure to knowledge of Japan is quite thorough. The entire field of Japanese experts involves a roster of about 500 scholars, both teachers and advanced graduate students, less than a tenth of 1 percent of the entire number of faculty. Class enrollments in Japanese in colleges and universities amounted to 4,322 in 1968 (against 34,000 in Russian, 200,000 in French), but the first six institutions listed—Hawaii, with by far the largest number (almost 1,000), Los Angeles City College, University of Washington at Seattle, California State in Los Angeles, San Francisco State, and San Jose State—suggest to me that at least half this figure consists of American students of Japanese descent who may be taking the course to learn about their heritage, or because it's easy, or for various other reasons that do not reflect an interest of non-Japanese Americans in Japanese.

Thus, some informed Americans on Japan come out of the colleges and universities—more than from any other place, one would think. Yet the numbers are tiny.[7]

Perhaps the ideal method for a study of shifting American images of Japan is that developed by Harold Isaacs in *Scratches on Our Minds* (1958) for his study of American images of China and India. It is indeed regrettable that Isaacs excluded Japan from that study. The essence of the method is to study in depth the attitudes and images of those relatively few individuals who count, either in shaping attitudes toward and images of a country such as Japan, or in shaping attitudes and images in general in this country, or who, even without the capacity to shape attitude and image directly, express significant attitudes because they hold important positions in economy and society and can act upon and change reality.

The first group includes that section of the world of scholarship who are specialists on Japan. It is to them that most people who want to know something about Japan go. It is in this sense that the American scholarly experts on Japan are important, and among them pre-eminently E. O. Reischauer. He is the author of one of the most accessible general surveys of Japanese history, *Japan: Past and Present* (Knopf, 1946), which, after going through revisions in 1952 and 1964, eventually emerged in a new form as *Japan: The Story of a Nation* in 1970; of *The United States and Japan* (Harvard University Press, 1950, which was revised in 1957 and 1965);* and of much of the material on Japan in the major text, *East Asia* (Volume I, *The*

*One index of influence is the sales figures for *The United States and Japan:* as of early 1973, 25,000 in hardcover, 78,000 in paperback. This compares very favorably with the sales of any but the most popular books on Japan.

Great Tradition, by Edwin O. Reischauer and John K. Fairbank, Houghton Mifflin, 1960, Volume II, *The Modern Transformation*, by Fairbank, Reischauer, and Albert M. Craig, 1965), single volume edition, *East Asia: Tradition and Transformation*, 1973. He is of course also the best-known American ambassador to Japan, a writer of articles on Japan in the *New York Times Magazine* and elsewhere, a frequent commentator and discussant on Japan on television, in the press, at international conferences. The role of such a man in shaping image cannot be underestimated. In an area where there is little knowledge and little opinion, he provides a good deal of both. Other American experts on Japan, through their books, articles, and discussion, are also key shapers of American images of Japan.

The second group that Isaacs surveyed are opinion-makers in general—those who, not specialists on some Asian country, nevertheless have access to minds and can shape opinions. This is an exceedingly important category. In this country we have few opinion-makers who consider themselves to some extent experts on Japan. Our major columnists write only occasionally about Japan, and none of them knows much about it. Yet what they think and know about Japan is exceedingly important. The Alsops, Buckleys, Restons, and all the rest reach those people who have opinions and whose opinions count.

The opinion-makers' opinions derive in large measure from those of the experts in the first group. It is not difficult to detect in the writing of columnists or of correspondents for *Newsweek* and *Time* and leading American newspapers the influence of such books as Ruth Benedict's *The Chrysanthemum and the Sword*, Herman Kahn's *The Emerging Japanese Superstate*, or Nakane Chie's *Japanese Society*. And while Benedict and Kahn were not Japanese experts, they drew much of their thinking from Japanese experts. In some cases the Japanese correspondents of American newspapers are Japanese experts themselves, fully conversant with the literature on Japan—for example, George Packard and Ivan Hall.

Finally, we have the world of major actors in politics and economic affairs. They are of course not generally experts on Japan though they have probably visited it; they are not opinion-makers in their principal roles, yet what they do affects American opinion on Japan. If they feel that Japan has been insufficiently open to American investment, or insufficiently supportive in our dilemma in Vietnam, or whatever, it will affect what they do—and what Americans think.

I have given a rather crude picture of opinion-making on subjects which are not salient to American thinking (as domestic issues are, and some foreign issues on occasion are), and have suggested that if for this essay I had interviewed such people in depth, we would know something of the changing postwar American image of Japan that could be attained in no other way. Unfortunately, owing to limitations in time and resources, I have not. Lacking that, I believe the most revealing index to significant American thinking on Japan are those major figures in categories one and two, the scholars and the opinion-makers who do so much to shape significant American opinion on Japan—the opinion, that is, of those who know something, those who care to some extent, and those who are in positions where their opinions can count. What I have done is to read and analyze, with an eye to underlying image, the work of some American scholars of Japan and those who have tried to make themselves expert on Japan, insofar as such books have reached substantial audiences.

In the first category, that of the scholars, the work of E. O. Reischauer is paramount. In the second category, that of semi-experts on Japan whose books are read and whose ideas filter down to others, I would list the work of Ruth Benedict, *The Chrysanthemum and the Sword* (Boston, Houghton Mifflin, 1946), for the early post-war period—still read and still probably the most widely known book on Japan among American intellectuals—Herman Kahn's *The Emerging Japanese Superstate* (Englewood Cliffs, N.J., Prentice Hall, 1970), and Zbigniew Brzezinski's *The Fragile Blossom* (New York, Harper and Row, 1972). None of the writers are specialists on Japan, all are scholars, all have in large measure surveyed "Japan from a distance" (Benedict, of course, was never there), but all have substantial audiences. These audiences—in the case of Kahn and Brzezinski—include far more than the readers of their books. They are prolific writers in other media; Brzezinski has summarized his main thesis in *The Fragile Blossom* in *Newsweek*. They are prolific lecturers and speakers before many significant audiences; Kahn in particular is famous for his briefings, and many of them these days, to American businessmen, professionals, and political figures, deal with his views on Japan. On a lesser plane of influence we can add the books of informed foreign correspondents, and I have used two in the analysis of images that follows: Robert Guillain's *The Japanese Challenge* (Paris, 1969; New York, 1970), and Richard Halloran's

Japan: Images and Realities (Alfred A. Knopf, 1969). Guillain is a French correspondent, but the book was published in this country, widely reviewed, and may be considered as part of the American opinion-making process. Halloran is the chief *New York Times* correspondent in Japan. It would be interesting to consider to what extent images of Japan in America and in European countries coincide. I would imagine there is much similarity.

Thus what I have done is to select a sample of books—more than a sample, since nothing really important dealing with contemporary Japan that is generally read by Americans who are not students has been omitted, except for specialized works such as James Abbeglen's *The Japanese Factory*—and considered the image of Japan projected there. The approach is admittedly partial and dangerous. If one deals with the works of experts and semi-experts, to what extent can one distinguish "image" from "reality"? But this is a problem in all research of images and there is no easy way of solving it. I have assumed that even experts may have "images" which may or may not be sufficiently supported by reality. To counter this *lèse-majesté* toward experts, I would add that even the images of ordinary people are based to some extent on realities. After all, if 19 percent of the American people think Japanese people are sneaky, it is undoubtedly owing to what is widely known as the "sneak attack" on Pearl Harbor.

Another possible approach to studying American images of Japan might have been to take the middle-level of American opinion-forming magazines—*Time, Newsweek,* and the like—and see what images they project. I have quoted from them on occasion in what follows. But their more general images so fully follow the central opinion-makers, Reischauer, Kahn, and Brzezinski, and are so parallel to those of informed correspondents such as Halloran and Guillain, that in effect one is generally dealing with derivative opinions when one examines the news magazines.

Aside from the basic Isaacs technique, which I consider the best approach to studying images, there is one other approach to studying American images that would be desirable. That is to examine a sample of business magazines, specialized and general, and of businessmen. The fact is the central means whereby America is brought into contact with Japan is through business. The images of the businessman are not based only on what he has read in the newspapers or on the current view in educated opinion-making circles; his views are based on direct contact with a reality. In addition, his views are important. They may not shape the opinions of the educated but they have enormous influence on political figures, for when business interests are at stake, businessmen can make them count. Thus what business-men believe helps shape what politicians do—and what the generality of Americans, following their leaders on issues on which they know and care little, will also believe. So we have the story of the textile quotas. Desirable as this approach would have been, I must leave it to the future.

Before turning to an examination of what I conceive to be these central image-shaping books, let me consider one other group of opinion-makers: the American intellectuals.

The American intellectuals—that group which, through the pages of *Partisan Review, Commentary,* the *New York Review of Books,* and similar journals, and through its influence on American publish-ing generally, magazine and book, has done so much to shape the attitudes of Americans who count—have no particular views on Japan at all. One will search the pages of the magazines I have men-tioned—and some others—in vain to find any discussion of Japan. Only one figure in this intelligentsia has written a book on Japan: David Riesman, who published, with his wife, *Conversations with Japan* (New York, Basic Books, 1967). A fascinating book, it is I believe the least read of his works, and the modesty of its impact is indicated by the fact that it is the only one of his books not to have been published in paperback. One can find an article on Japan by Daniel Bell published some time ago in *Antioch Review.* Sidney Hook wrote an article a number of years ago on a visit to Japan. Saul Bellow has visited Japan recently and may write something. Herbert Passin, the distinguished scholar of Japanese society, has written some articles in *Encounter.* There are a few other articles. All in all, this is a very small budget of opinion and information from the leading members of the American intellectual establishment on a great country, and I doubt whether one can say that this establishment has any distinctive and general views on Japan at all, aside from those that derive from the opinion-makers whose work I will attempt to characterize.

One way in which the rest of the world comes into the ken of the American intelligentsia is literature; another is politics. The politics of Japan has been too confusing and specialized to be of much interest to American intellectuals. After all, Japan presents neither a Mao nor a Castro, neither a Nasser nor a Nehru, not even a Salazar or a group of Greek colonels. Literature is another matter; it is at least *noted* by the intellectuals. But to someone like myself who has a deep appreciation of modern Japanese literature the treatment in the serious organs of American intellectual comment is shockingly uneven and inadequate. There are a number of examples.

In 1969 the English critic, D. J. Enright, who has spent time in Japan and written a book on Japan, reviewed in the *New York Review of Books* a Japanese novel, Mishima's *Thirst for Love*, and a book on Japan by the American anthropologist, David Plath, *Sensei and his People*. He wrote:

> Isn't the market for Japanese fiction just about swamped? [No more than two or three books of modern Japanese fiction in translation are published in a year in the United States.] Or maybe, since I have passed straight from reviewing Mishima's *Forbidden Colors* to reviewing Mishima's *Thirst for Love*, it is simply my personal market whose thirst has been quenched . . . temporarily, at least. Moving from the first novel's urban scene of "gay" bars to the Japanese version of *Cold Comfort Farm* in the second, one notes that something remains similar: the largely arbitrary nature of what is felt and thought and done and suffered, as if Mishima's motto was "Only disconnect."
>
> In an article in *Life* in 1966, John Nathan said that "reading a Mishima novel can be like going to an exhibit of the world's most lavish and ornate picture frames. . . ."
>
> Is this general absence of motivation as we understand it a Japanese thing? Is Mishima merely being representatively enigmatic and inscrutable? . . .
>
> In *Sensei and his People*, which is not a novel . . . , most of the time you do understand why people do what they do . . .
>
> It is certainly an interesting record, but not exactly soul-absorbing, and that the book should have been hailed with such advance enthusiasm [by E. O. Reischauer and Kenneth Rexroth] I would interpret as a sign of the thinness in humanity of the modern Japanese novel as available in English. (*New York Review of Books*, September 25, 1969.)

Perhaps the most widely reviewed of Japanese novels in translation in this country until Mishima's recent novels was Tanizaki's *The*

Makioka Sisters. The record of the reviews has been surveyed by Charles E. Hamilton:

The American reviews . . . have been marked by an air of discomfiture, some dismissing it with factitious phrase, others more rudely. *Time* found it dull in the main, but worthwhile as "an exemplification of the Oriental wisdom of bending with adversity." Donald Barr, in the *New York Times,* spoke inaptly of Jane Austen and credited it with "veracity," and in the *New Yorker,* Anthony West guyed the book at scurrilous length as a mere exercise of medical naturalism.[8]

Perhaps nothing is more representative of the place of Japan in the mind of the American intellectual than that the *New Yorker* review of Japan's most important modern novel should ridicule it as an example of the "medical novel." Two years earlier, the *New Yorker* was kinder to Tanizaki's *Some Prefer Nettles,* but was incredibly patronizing: "And if he is by western standards only a minor master, he has an unusual ability to create beautiful images and to give pleasure." (June 18, 1955.)

Nor did the awarding of the Nobel prize to Kawabata lead to any deeper understanding of Japanese fiction. *The Sound of the Mountain* was reviewed anonymously in *Book World*—not an important publication, but perhaps representative of how the uninformed reviewer in the daily press might respond—under the title "Pidgin Hemingway" (May 21, 1970): "Halfway through I began to toy with the idea that the Japanese are just so different that we are unable to appreciate or judge their literature. It seems to me a mark of something that a celebrated Japanese author should be so ill-used by his American publisher, who commissioned and approved this translation." The translation was by Edward Seidensticker, a leading scholar in the field of Japanese studies, praised by Howard Hibbett in the *Saturday Review* (June 6, 1970), by Ivan Morris in the *New York Times Book Review,* by E. Dale Saunders in the *Washington Post.* But note that all these admiring appreciations of Seidensticker's translation were by Japanese specialists.

The dilemma involved in the treatment of Japan in the serious American intellectual press devoted to literary matters is that the Japanese specialist, whatever his talents (Donald Keene, Edward Seidensticker, Ivan Morris, Howard Hibbett, and others are certainly talented), is precisely a *specialist*—as perhaps is inevitable if anyone is to master Japanese—and thus does not play a major role in shaping the ideas generally of educated Americans about Japan. Only major intellectual figures could have done so—if they had become interested in, as Edmund Wilson became interested in, and made important, areas of literature that were not part of the canon that American intellectuals took seriously. But Edmund Wilson did not become interested in Japan, nor has anyone else of his stature.

The ideas of Americans on matters with which they have no personal experience or which do not move their sense of personal interest may also be shaped by lesser figures, the writers of best-sellers and movies who nevertheless project an image of a country that may take hold. One thinks of the role of Pearl Buck's *The Good Earth*, book and movie, in shaping the image Americans held of China, of *Mother India* in the twenties in shaping the ideas Americans held of India. There are no such books about Japan. One thinks in vain of a best-seller that might have shaped the American mind and its thinking about Japan. *Sayonara*, by James Michener, comes closest—but it is really about Americans in Japan. Oliver Statler's *Japanese Inn* comes far behind. An authentic and charming book, it tells us nothing about contemporary Japan. There is the *Tea House of the August Moon*, play and movie—but that is about American soldiers in Okinawa. There is nothing, fiction or nonfiction, of the kind that becomes a best-seller, that could have shaped the American popular mind on contemporary Japan. In its absence, the images that would have been discovered in a Harold Isaacs-style search of the American mind would have been fugitive indeed. The content might have been that of a cruel and incomprehensible Japan in World War II, overlaid by an almost equally incomprehensible Japan as expressed in the amazing products of Japanese technology that now appear everywhere in the American market. Underneath them both, one assumes, there is still the basic image of exotic Japan—Fuji, cherry blossoms, geisha, temples. How all this is put together in the American mind, God only knows. Perhaps, just as in the case of Japan itself, these multiple images are not integrated very well together at all. To *The Chrysanthemum and the Sword* has now been added the television set.

What is striking when one reviews the central opinion- and image-

makers of Japan in this country—though admittedly all such conclusions must be, if easy to document, impossible to prove—is how
much has remained constant between 1946 and 1972, even while such
a fantastic change has taken place in the nature of Japan itself, in
Japanese society, in the Japanese individual, in Japan's role in the
world, and in its relations with the United States. For example, is it
not striking that Brzezinski should title his 1972 book *The Fragile
Blossom*, so evocative of *The Chrysanthemum and the Sword?* Of
course this enormous change has had some effect. As we have seen
from the *Asahi* poll, the feeling about Pearl Harbor has faded, and
almost fully positive images about the Japanese now occupy first
place in the American mind. This change has of course affected what
the central shapers of opinion on Japan have to say. It is intriguing to
contrast Professor Reischauer's first version of his elementary book
on Japan in 1946 with the latest in 1970. Perhaps the first change to
note is simply how much larger the newer version is: 345 pages with
a bibliography, against 192 pages, without. Inevitably, one sees the
fading of wartime animus and wartime views and the rise of a more
positive view. Thus, in the earlier version, Professor Reischauer
wrote:

Isolation has also made the Japanese a highly self-conscious people, un-
accustomed to dealing with foreigners individually or as a nation. The
Japanese are always conscious that they are Japanese and that all other
peoples are foreigners. Isolation has made them painfully aware of their
differences from other peoples and has filled them with an entirely irrational
sense of superiority, which they are anxious to prove to themselves and
others. Isolation has made it difficult for them to understand the attitudes
and actions of other peoples. In short, the factor of geographic isolation
. . . has helped fashion national traits which eventually, and almost inevitably, led Japan to political isolation and to crushing defeat in war.[9]

The contrast with 1970 is striking:

Geographic isolation and cultural and linguistic distinctiveness have made
the Japanese highly self-conscious and acutely aware of their differences
from others. In a way, this has been a great asset to them in the modern
age of nation-states, for they faced no problem of national identity . . . On
the other hand, extreme self-consciousness bred of isolation has been a
handicap in other ways. It has made the Japanese somewhat tense in their
contacts with others. They have shown relatively little sensitivity to the

feelings or reactions of other peoples. At times they have seemed obsessed with a sense either of superiority or of inferiority toward the outside world. Japan's isolation may help to explain some of the extremes in her international relations and also, perhaps, the uneasiness Japanese feel today about their place in the world.[10]

One would expect the general softening of language. Isolation now has positive as well as negative effects. But what is worth noting is how much remains the same: for example, the Japanese difficulty in relating to the rest of the world.

There are contrasts in the view of the United States in the two editions of the book. Five years of Vietnamese war, many years of revisionist history, had somewhat changed the American attitude to America—and one cannot underestimate Americans' attitude toward their own country as an influence on their attitude toward other countries. As the United States declines in prestige and virtue in the eyes of its own citizens, other countries must to some extent rise in their estimation. Thus, contrast the two treatments by Professor Reischauer in 1946 and 1970 of the negotiations preceding Pearl Harbor:

> The moderates, appalled by the danger of war against a coalition of foreign powers but aware that the army would never be willing to withdraw empty-handed from China, desperately sought some compromise which would satisfy both the United States and the militarists at home. The United States, however, refused to compromise with aggression. (1946)[11]

> The United States . . . was unrealistically insistent that no settlement could be discussed until Japan had relinquished the fruits of her aggression since 1931. Japan would have to yield first and discover what the terms were later. (1970)[12]

In the later version, as we see, the United States has become "unrealistic." To that extent, one appreciates better the Japanese dilemma.

Then, of course, there is the atom bomb. While Americans in general, along with President Truman, have no regrets, this is not true of intellectuals. In the earlier version, Reischauer wrote with no comment that "moderate bureaucrats . . . were spurred into immediate action by the dropping of two atomic bombs, which all but wiped out the cities of Hiroshima and Nagasaki, and by the Russian declaration of war."[13] In 1970 he writes: "The end was in sight, but the

Americans, without stopping to think fully about what they were doing, proceeded . . . to drop on the cities of Hiroshima and Nagasaki the two atom bombs they had at long last completed, wiping out in two big puffs close to 200,000 lives and ushering in the horrors of the nuclear age."[14]

We have also become more aware of the effect of American racial attitudes and policies on our relations with other countries, and this too affects our estimates of other countries (but also makes some writers sensitive to Japanese ethnocentrism, as a peculiarly exaggerated version of a general human attribute). Thus there is no reference in the earlier version of Reischauer's *Japan* to American racial attitudes toward the Japanese. These become important in the latest version:

> The ultranationalistic movement . . . was fundamentally anti-Western, and this coloration was strengthened by the realization that, despite Japan's status as a world power, Westerners were still not willing on racial grounds to accept Japanese as full equals. At the Versailles peace conference in 1919 Japan had argued for the inclusion of a clause on "racial equality," but this had been blocked by the United States and Britain . . . In the United States, Orientals had much earlier been declared ineligible for naturalization on racial grounds, and California and other western states put their children into segregated schools and denied them the right to own land. To ease the strains of this situation, Japan and the United States worked out in 1908 a "Gentlemen's Agreement," which brought a virtual end to Japanese immigration. Despite this, Congress in 1924 passed an Exclusion Act . . . This was deeply resented by Japanese of all types as a gratuitous insult. Though really a part of American rather than Japanese history, it is worth noting that anti-Oriental racism in the United States was to reach its peak in the early days of World War II, when the whole Japanese population of the West Coast, loyal, native-born *nisei* citizens and their inoffensive, elderly, immigrant parents alike, were driven out of their farms and homes and herded into concentration camps.[15]

Having had a good deal of time to reflect on our sins, the sins of others have declined in gravity. Similarly, having become aware how hard it is to change another nation—look, after all, at our attempts to make South Vietnam and other countries into democracies—we are appreciative of how Japan helped us in our efforts to make Japan a democracy. We see the democratization of Japan as less of an American success and more of a Japanese success. Thus the arrogance that characterized early American attitudes has been much moderated. We will not find arrogance from Professor Reischauer even in 1946, but as an example of what I mean about early American attitudes, consider this quotation from an editorial in the *New York Herald Tribune,* occasioned by the fact that an American sergeant provided blood to save Tōjō's life when his attempt at suicide was unsuccessful:

> In volunteering the blood, the sergeant was a bold man . . . he was . . . making himself a symbol. The destructive and self-destructive impulses of ancient Japan can only be halted and turned to better expression in the modern world by a massive transfusion from the main intellectual and social blood stream of modern culture . . . We find that in the act of destroying the savage and barbaric in Japan we must pour out [a] great transfusion of Western thought and institutions if our enemy is to be left neither a primitive danger nor a corrupting corpse in our own society. (*New York Herald Tribune,* September 13, 1945, p. 22).[16]

Professor Reischauer's treatment was inevitably affected by the twenty-five-year history of postwar Japanese democracy. In 1946 he wrote: "Seven centuries of domination by the feudal military class has left patterns of thought and behavior which have not been easy to discard in recent times and which will not be easily discarded even today."[17]

Yet even in 1946 he considered it likely that a new democratic system was being firmly established:

> They are pragmatists, and in the past have shown themselves capable of abandoning old customs and habits of thought when convinced there was something better. The leaders of the early Meiji period, when they realized that their feudal political and military system was inferior to the nation states and citizen armies of the West, made a startling about-face and did away with feudalism. It now appears the Japanese are making another abrupt about-face.[18]

The 1970 treatment reflects the new skepticism about American capacities to change the internal constitution of other countries:

> The Americans gave themselves full credit for the remarkable transformation of Japan during the occupation, but little of this would have been possible without the firm foundations of democracy that the Japanese already possessed: universal literacy, high levels of governmental efficiency,

strong habits of hard work and cooperation, and more than a half century of experience with democratic electoral and parliamentary institutions. The supposed lack of democratic foundations made the American reform program radical; their actual presence made it successful.[19]

Thus there have been inevitable changes in American images of Japan, but what is striking is how much has remained the same in the midst of change. Even the preceding quotations, selected to represent change, suggest how much has remained the same. The following points seem to characterize the present attitude of the best-educated Americans toward Japan: that they are *characterized by radical paradoxes*; that connected with this sense of radical paradox is a sense of *alienness*—and whether we see Japanese as alien because they are paradoxical, or paradoxical because they are alien, I am not sure; that one aspect of their alienness is their *insensitivity* to others, their peculiar relations to other people; that because of this paradoxicality they are basically *unpredictable*—they may change from one thing to another overnight; that because they are unpredictable one must approach their present prosperity, growth, and stability with a sense of extreme caution—in effect they are fundamentally *unstable;* that since they are unstable, we must in particular be distrustful of the *Japanese commitment to democracy*. Admittedly there are attitudes and images that run strongly counter to all these. These images are held not only by Americans who are fundamentally hostile to Japan and the Japanese—that would be natural—but by most American Japanese experts too, and therefore, those who help shape educated Americans' attitudes on Japan.

The classic statement of Japanese paradoxicality is to be found in Ruth Benedict's *The Chrysanthemum and the Sword*. She summarizes some of the paradoxes on the first two pages of her book: Japanese are "unprecedentedly polite," but also "insolent and overbearing"; "incomparably rigid in their behavior," but also "they adapt themselves to extreme innovations"; "submissive," but also "not easily amenable to control from above"; "genuinely brave," but also "timid." They "act out of concern for others' opinions," but also possess "a truly terrifying conscience." They show a "robot-like discipline," but "soldiers [act on their own] . . . even to the point of insubordination." They show a "passion [for] Western learning" but "fervid conservatism." In short: the chrysanthemum, but also the sword.[20]

And in Benedict we find, if not the classic statement of Japanese alienness, an exceedingly powerful one, in the words that open her book: "The Japanese were the most alien enemy the United States had ever fought in an all-out struggle . . . we were fighting a nation fully armed and trained which did not belong to the Western cultural tradition. Conventions of war which Western nations had come to accept as facts of human nature obviously did not exist for the Japanese."[21]

Professor Reischauer agreed, in 1946, that the Japanese were a bundle of paradoxes: "Nowhere in the world is proper decorum more rigorously observed by all classes . . . when they meet a situation to which their accustomed patterns of courteous conduct no longer apply, they are likely to react more violently than other people. This may be one explanation for the amazing contrast between the courtesy and docility of the modern Japanese at home and his cruelty and excesses as a conqueror abroad."[22]

Japanese paradoxicality and alienness remain the dominant image of the Western observer, whether friendly or less friendly. Inevitably the opening theme of almost any book on Japan is that of the basic contrast—itself imbued with paradox to the Western observer—of Japanese traditionalism and modernity.

The sense of alienness can be expressed in many ways, but certainly one way in which one sees it operating among informed observers today is in the tendency to see Japanese as quite different from the people of other developed countries. Consider the following:

It is a truism that Japanese are not sensitive to others or to the reactions they arouse and are incredibly clannish. (William P. Bundy, *Newsweek,* May 1, 1972, p. 46.)

. . . the Japanese project an air of insecurity in their relationship to the outside environment and strong inferiority-superiority complexes (the former usually toward the more powerful Western states, the latter toward the less developed Asian countries). (Brzezinski, 1972.)[23]

The Japanese paradox is seen in many forms—as Asian people with a Western economy, the contrast between tradition and modernity in social life, the paradox within the Japanese economy itself with its modern and traditional sectors, the paradox presented by a people emphasizing hierarchy and nevertheless possessing a democracy, and so on.

Thus, consider the opening passage from Brzezinski: "The initial impression one obtains from a stay in Japan is that of a highly stable and apparently cohesive society. The social fabric seems to be tightly knit . . . It appears to be responsive to the Japanese desire for a clearly demarcated social hierarchy while providing a ladder for the many who are capable and ambitious enough to climb upward. As a result, most Japanese know their precise place in society."[24] But this passage is written as a foil to the author's argument that the initial impression of stability conceals a rather fragile "metastability."[25]

Or consider an early passage from Guillain: "Japan is a whole tissue of contradictions. As soon as some statement, firmly based upon observed evidence, is put forward, a conflicting and equally well-based statement can be advanced either to nullify or refute it."[26]

The theme of paradoxicality merges into the theme of a fundamental instability. The instability is seen both in personality and in social structure and would seem to be inevitable in a character and society characterized by paradox, where one is never on stable ground. Thus, even a contemporary sympathetic observer such as Herman Kahn, summing up the modern Japanese, strikes, to Western eyes at least, an image of fundamental instability:

Individual male Japanese often describe themselves with such terms as egoistic, emotional, introspective, illogical, hypochondriac, stoical, persevering, disciplined, conformist, diligent, respectful, loyal, honest, polite, and unbelievably rigid about the requirements of various kinds of duty, but as less interested in the letter of a written agreement than in its emotional connotation and context, very anxious to avoid stark confrontations and uncertainty in almost all situations (social, business, governmental), tending to dislike and look down upon Koreans, and finally as having a realistic ability to learn, indeed almost always to be interested in self- or national-improvement.[27]

This summary, in the most positive and enthusiastic book about Japan to be produced by an American scholar and intellectual, fully conforms to the popular *and* scholarly image of the Japanese who entered into a career of military expansion and began the Great East Asian War.

If these are the images of the observer most confident of Japanese stability, it is hardly likely that images of others more uncertain will project a greater air of confidence. The main thesis of Brzezinski's *The Fragile Blossom,* written it would appear almost to counter Herman Kahn's optimism, is that Japanese stability is suspect—characterized by a "metastability."

Benedict had already established, through her descriptions of the paradoxes of the Japanese character and its ability to make rapid shifts, the groundwork for seeing Japan as unpredictable and unstable, though with her own subtlety she did detect an underlying pattern that gave a basis for prediction:

> The right-about-face of the Japanese in defeat is hard for Americans to take at face value . . . Very few of the Westerners who knew Japan predicted that the same change of front characteristic of the prisoners of war might be found in Japan, too, after the defeat. Most of them believed . . . that defeat would be in her eyes an insult to be avenged by continued desperate violence . . . Such students of Japan had not understood giri. They had singled out, from among all the alternative procedures that give one an honorable name, the one conspicuous traditional technique of vengeance and aggression. They did not allow for the Japanese habit of taking another tack . . .
>
> [The Japanese] need terribly to be respected in the world. They saw that military might had earned respect for great nations and they embarked on a course to equal them . . . When they failed . . . , it meant to them that aggression was not the road to honor after all . . . The goal is still their good name.
>
> Japan has behaved in a similar fashion on other occasions in her history and it has always been confusing to Westerners.[28]

We still see the expectation of rapid change among modern observers, but one sees it in the form of the uneasy expectation of a change that might quite overturn everything we may count on and take for granted.

Brzezinski quotes Katō Shūichi to the effect that there have been three periods of modern Japanese history when "the country was very receptive to Western ideas. Each . . . followed immediately upon a great change in society . . . Each continued roughly for ten or fifteen years. Each was succeeded by a period of nationalism."[29] Brzezinski continues:

> What is striking about these shifts is the suddenness with which they come . . . As a result of this predilection for abrupt change after considerable gestation, Japanese society can be said to be characterized by a kind of metastability, that is to say, a stability that appears to be extremely solid until all of a sudden a highly destabilizing chain reaction is set in motion by an unexpected input . . . once instability is set in motion, insecurity tends to intensify the instability.[30]

The possibility of rapid and unexpected change is troublesome to Americans because Japan is an ally, an important trading partner, and part of the democratic world—and if it should cease to be an ally, if its economy goes into a tailspin, and if it turns against democracy, this must inevitably have grave repercussions for the United States. Despite the fact that the Japanese might legitimately on the basis of recent experience have greater distrust of American stability in some of these respects than Americans might have of Japanese, the sense that Japan might very rapidly become something very different—and much more uncomfortable to live with—is a potent part of the image of educated Americans of Japan.

Benedict and Reischauer had, of course, early cautioned about the difficulties involved in establishing a stable democracy in Japan. We have already quoted Reischauer's caution. Consider Benedict's: "The true difference between the Japanese form of government and such cases in Western Europe lies not in form but in functioning. The Japanese rely on old habits of deference set up in their past experience and formalized in their ethical system and in their etiquette."[31]

> What the United States cannot do—what no outside nation could do— is to create by fiat a free, democratic Japan. It has never worked in any dominated country . . . The Japanese cannot be legislated into accepting the authority of elected persons and ignoring "proper station" as it is set up in their hierarchal system . . . The Japanese themselves, however, are quite articulate about changes . . . which they regard as necessary. Their public men have said since VJ-Day that Japan must encourage its men and women to live their own lives and to trust their own consciences . . .

> The Japanese have taken the first great step toward social change by identifying aggressive warfare as an "error" . . . They hope to buy their passage back to a respected place among peaceful nations . . . Japan's

motivations are situational. She will seek her place within a world at peace if circumstances permit.[32]

Strangely enough these modest and reasonable cautions, in the light of Japan's history in the thirties, have become even sharper among present-day observers, who continue, after two and a half decades of democracy, to have doubts about Japan's ability to maintain democratic government.

The great unknown in all of this is the extent of popular commitment to democracy itself. Democracy was imposed on Japan from outside, though it does appear to have been genuinely accepted. That acceptance, however, was reinforced by two conditions, one external, one internal . . . the enormous prestige of the United States strengthened the appeal of Western democracy . . . The internal condition was that of economic recovery . . . How deep the Japanese commitment to democracy will prove itself, especially should economic difficulties become acute, no one can say with certainty.[33]

Admittedly all nations are unstable and no one can judge with certainty any nation's commitment to democracy. Yet I believe it is our sense of Japanese paradoxicality, alienness, and instability that leads to a sense of greater unpredictability than with other countries.

Thus, Herbert Passin describes conditions of social strain in Japan. Brzezinski quotes this passage approvingly, and uses it to support his own expectation of instability:

The dislocation and mobility of vast rural populations, the difficult adaptations to urban life, the loss of supporting community and family institutions, the periodic inflation, the unevenness of advance in various sectors, the sharp short-term ups and downs, the inability of housing and amenities to keep up with urban growth, the crowding of schools, transportation and other facilities—all of these will combine to keep aspiration and opportunity continuously out of balance. All of the people will be frustrated some of the time, and some of the people will be frustrated all of the time.[34]

Brzezinski continues:

This frustration might express itself in two alternative ways. One would involve a widespread rejection of the existing system, the adoption of the view that the evil by-products of rapid growth are the inevitable consequences of capitalism and of the existing Japanese Establishment . . . This essentially left ideological position . . . would feed on the rising nationalism of the younger people, stamping the existing system with the label "made in U.S.A." . . .

Paradoxically . . . Yukio Mishima could well become the symbol and inspiration for this outlook . . .

The other alternative would involve a more conservative response. The existing Establishment would adapt and co-opt the rising social concern as its own, and would make the growing ambivalence—not to speak of hostility —about the GNP part of its own program to recapture "the Japaneseness" of Japan, while still providing the masses with continued prosperity . . . one may also expect from this side more emphasis on Japan's cultural unique-ness and national distinctiveness—the old Yamato spirit—as part of a broader program to make Japan into a uniquely Japanese domestic success story.[35]

And even sympathetic observers see aspects of the Japanese char-acter that raise doubts about the stability of the commitment to democracy:

The younger generation, while ostensibly revolting against group unity and stressing individualist values, more often than not also craves some form of group life. As Robert Jay Lifton notes: ". . . But underneath this ideal of selfhood, however strongly maintained, one can frequently detect an even more profound craving for renewed group life, for solidarity, for the chance to "melt" completely into a small group, a professional organization, or a mass movement. . . ."

And Robert Huntington comments that "The Japanese personality has weak, indistinct, permeable boundaries between the self and other; is de-pendent as opposed to independent, group-cooperative rather than self-reliant; conforming rather than innovative, and accepting of personal rather than rational-legal authority."[36]

I have presented a hypothesis, I am well aware, rather than proved it. Underlying sophisticated American attitudes toward Japan, I argue, is the sense of alienness, paradoxicality, instability, and unpre-dictability, and these attitudes have remained as a basic component of the American image of Japan since World War II (whether this was any part of the American image of Japan before World War II, I do not know—I suspect one would have found alienness and para-doxicality, but probably without the additional corollary of instabil-ity and unpredictability).

One must always be uneasy in writing about something as tenuous as images from evidence as scanty as that which I have used in this essay, and of course one must make the saving concession that what I have described is a hypothesis. But the scope of the hypothesis will become clearer if I specify how I have used and understand the concept of "image." The word "image" incorporates a surprising ambiguity. In relation to "attitude" or "opinion" (a distinction between these two is made in social psychology, in that the former is taken as more general than the latter), "image" suggests at one and the same time something more solid and long-lasting than mere attitude and opinion—and something more fleeting and slight. Thus we are all acquainted with the idea of "image" as a fleeting impression (such as in Debussy's *Images*, or what we would expect from a book titled "Images of Japan"). But at the same time the reason we are concerned with images is that we also think of them as just the opposite of fleeting impressions, as the firm substratum of attitude and opinion, based on emotionally meaningful experience and communication, such that it would not be easy to change an image. Image in this sense has something of the character of the concept of "prejudice" as used in social psychology. In the case of "prejudice," too, one must consider whether it is lightly held and easily discarded or whether it is anchored in emotional needs and early and significant experience. Even if one refuses to give prejudice so awesome an origin, one may still see it as a basic attitude, one which organizes impressions and experiences so that the prejudice itself does not change.[37]

My concept of "image" in this paper has been that of an orientation that is more basic than attitude and opinion, more long-lasting, conceivably rooted in some way, just as prejudice may be, in personality needs, but in any case serving to organize impressions and experiences so that the underlying image retains its character and is not easily changed. Thus "image" to my mind bears some of the same characteristics as "prejudice" except that it is not necessarily pejorative. There is a relation to the notion of "image" as fleeting impression, because it may well be true that it is the fleeting and half-understood impressions and experiences of childhood which serve to create and give content to the longer lasting, more basic image. Harold Isaacs, in both *Scratches on Our Minds* and *The New World of Negro Americans* (New York, John Day, 1963), describes how some of these casual impressions of childhood serve to fix an image and yet, even if the basic image is fixed by events that are them-selves apparently of little importance, the images may well be tied to important emotional needs. Whatever the relationship between image as simply organizing experience and image as organizing ex-perience on the basis of emotional needs, in this essay I limit myself to the former. I simply assume that an underlying orientation may develop toward a subject, and that this orientation serves to organize further and subsequent experience and knowledge. It is this kind of image that I have attempted to define.

Having defined the concept of image as I have used it (and this usage has emerged inductively from a review of the literature seeking for what seemed to be fairly basic organizing orientations), three other questions arise. First: Is it possible to have more than one basic or underlying image toward a subject? Have I described "the" image of Japan or "an" image of Japan? Second: What is the relationship between this image and reality? "Reality" raises even more problems than "image" but presumably one may develop an understanding of Japan that, it would be agreed by those qualified to judge, is in con-formity with existing and important aspects of Japanese society, politics, economics, culture. In other words, there are "true" and "false" images. Where does the image I have described fall? Third: What is the importance of images in any case? In other words, do images shape international relationships, international policies?

The first question is perhaps the easiest. I am perfectly willing to concede this is "an" image of Japan. Thus it is possible for other images to be held by the same people who hold this one, or for other images to be held by persons who do not hold this one. It is possible that some American policymakers see Japan as stable, predictable, dependable, comprehensible. (See the essay in this volume by Priscilla Clapp and Morton Halperin.) I would only argue that what I have described is an important and pervasive image, found among Japa-nese experts and those who, trying to become knowledgeable about Japan, base themselves on Japanese experts.

The images of stability, predictability, and comprehensibility, how-ever, I tend to think, are images that are not really held but rather images that are promoted by those who hope to improve Japanese-American relations. But it is not necessary to go that far: one can concede there are other images in circulation.[88]

The second question: Is this image the "true" Japan? One consideration weighs heavily upon me in suggesting that this is as true an image of Japan as we can formulate: it is that the American image of Japan I have described is based in large measure on *Japanese* images of Japan. Thus two leading Japanese scholars and intellectuals (Maruyama Masao and Katō Shūichi) see Japan as unstable and unpredictable, and are doubtful about the prospects of Japanese democracy. I am not suggesting a full equivalence between the image of Japan I have attributed to American writers and that held by these distinguished intellectuals. Nor is it only intellectuals who hold such views in Japan. Alienness, paradoxicality, instability, and unpredictability seem to characterize Japanese views of themselves and their society. After all, Benedict, Kahn, Brzezinski, and other writers on Japanese society must draw upon Japanese sources, individuals, and scholars. While something in American society and character may contribute to American images of Japan, I have the impression it is overwhelmingly something in Japanese intellectual life or perhaps indeed something basic in Japanese society and personality as communicated by Japanese scholars and intellectuals that has made the largest contribution. The American image of Japan thus may reflect the Japanese image of themselves. I hesitate to go beyond that to say that this image reflects a basic reality of Japan.

We may see the conflict in the American mind between the view of Japan as exotic and unpredictable and the view which tries to discount the unfamiliar elements in the reactions to the *seppuku* of Mishima as given in the *Asahi* poll. As we noted, a large minority of Americans were willing to see it as an exceptional event "which does not represent present-day trends in Japan as a whole." Let us recall, however, that the Japanese themselves were divided as to how to interpret this incident. And when one considers that two of the best covered news events with some reference to Japan in 1972 were the Lod airport massacre and the killings of members of the Red Army in the snows of Karuizawa, it seems not unlikely that the image I have described is further anchored in the American mind—and these events too raise the question of the relationship of this image to Japanese reality.

Finally, on the relationship between image and policy, I would like to suggest first of all that the image I have described, and other international images, generally have a positive and a negative form. While the image does not change (or changes slowly), the valence may change. Second, while the image may have an effect on policy, policy also has an effect on image, and we have striking cases of the image changing from positive to negative or negative to positive while much of its underlying content remains the same.

Specifically, consider the history of the American image of India. Poverty has always been part of that image. Spirituality in the service of political ends, as in the case of Gandhi, has been part of that image. When we are on good terms with India, we think of making a contribution to solving India's poverty, and we are impressed by such statesmen as Gandhi and Nehru. When we are on bad terms, we see poverty as India's fault and get impatient with it, and we see the strong and distinctive line of Indian leaders as sanctified hypocrites. The change from one form to another is in large measure the result of policy changes. Most Americans were sympathetic to Bangladesh and to India as its supporter. Initially the pro-Pakistani policy of the United States received little support or comprehension in public opinion. But Americans—educated Americans, the kind that go to Council on Foreign Relations events—cooled rapidly in their attitude toward India in late 1971 and 1972 as a result of the deterioration of American-Indian relations, even though these same educated Americans might have initially opposed American actions. In time, the reasons for the deterioration in relations is forgotten, and what is left is the reality of bad relations which affect the valence of the long-held images of India.

The story of American images and policies toward China is somewhat similar. We have seen three distinct and sharp phases in our relations with China since the 1940s: China, the heroic ally of World War II; China, the implacable Red enemy of the 1950s and 1960s; China, the remarkable success story of the 1970s. American attitudes have shifted from for, to against, to for again. Throughout, I suspect the main content of the image of China has remained constant—hard-working, intelligent, pragmatic. Our attitudes have shifted on the basis of whether or not we have seen these qualities of the Chinese image exerted to oppose the United States. Just as we may admire at one point the Indian emphasis on religion, and denounce it as superstition the next, so we may admire Chinese intelligence and hard work at one point, and fear it as serving devilish ends at another. What is not possible is to see Indians as totally indifferent to their religious precepts, or to see Chinese as lazy and stupid.

We have never failed to see the Japanese as "skilled craftsmen," "energetic," "polite and reserved," "highly competitive," "intelligent," and "serious and diligent," but the valence of these terms has changed as we have seen Japan first as enemy, then as client and ally, and now as competitor. Changing realities and changing policies have given a different weight and meaning to these terms.

Does the image of Japan I have described—as paradoxical, alien, unstable, and so forth—also have a positive and a negative form? In this case, there seems little doubt the content of the image predisposes us to be uncertain and suspicious of Japan. Thus even if an image may coexist at different times with friendship and with enmity, some images by their nature predispose more to one or to the other. As Harold Isaacs demonstrated, Americans—because of their image of China—seem predisposed to be friendly and positive toward that country; because of their image of India, they are predisposed to be less positive and less friendly. This does not mean that policy considerations may not lead us to be closer to India than to China, as we were in the 1950s and 1960s, but the weight of the images held seem to make most Americans happy with the opposite arrangement.

I suspect that the weight of American images of Japan also puts a strain on our relations with Japan.[39] But since interest binds us so closely together, there is all the more reason to examine critically the images we hold, to become fully aware of them, and not to allow them—insofar as they are not a clear reflection of a firm reality—to influence policies. Policies based on interest should guide images, and images based on who knows what should not guide policies. So we should study images, but in order to be better able to act on the basis of rational judgment.

8 MICHIO NAGAI
and
TAKEO NISHIJIMA

Postwar Japanese Education and the United States

Since the Meiji Restoration of 1868 there have been three stages in which American influence on the Japanese educational system has been of paramount importance: the period of the Education Ordinance of 1879, the period of the Taishō New Education Movement (1912–26), and the period of the American Occupation (1945–50). All three were times of intense change in Japan, both domestically and internationally. The process of educational reform during the early Meiji era was one of trial and error, and in the years between the establishment of a national educational system in 1872 and the promulgation of the Imperial Rescript on Education in 1890, reform and tradition vied for preeminence. With the Rescript on Education, the educational system crystallized and, until after World War II, was characterized by a highly centralized administration with the emperor at its apex, by the unification of education and politics based upon a Confucian ideology, and by the bifurcation of elite and mass education. These "three pillars of prewar Japanese education" were rejected by Occupation authorities in the immediate postwar years, the period which is the subject of this essay.

In terms of Japanese-American relations as they bore on Japanese educational history, the postwar years may be divided into three

periods: the Honeymoon (1945–48), the Cold War (1949–50), and
the Conservative (1951–60). The first period was a time of unparalleled amity between the United States and Japan. In domestic
politics it was likewise a period of harmony, for sharp differences had
not yet arisen between conservative and progressive forces in Japanese society. The Japanese people felt liberated by the Occupation
forces and by the progressive democratization policies that issued in
rapid succession from Occupation headquarters (SCAP), including
the institution of the unitary "six-three" educational system (six
years of elementary school followed by three years of junior high
school). Japanese ruling circles, however, made strenuous efforts to
incorporate into these policies, in one form or another, the principles
of *kokutai* or "national polity," the prewar system of Confucian
nationalism under the rule of the emperor. Thus, two contrasting
forces were operating. On the one hand, Japanese liberals worked
harmoniously with the progressive elements in SCAP, while Japanese
teachers eagerly adopted American teaching methods that stressed the
autonomy and freedom of the child and served as an antidote to the
strict centralized control of the past. On the other hand, the structure and personnel of the Ministry of Education survived, and tradi-
tionalist politicians resisted the abolition of the Rescript on Education
despite the passage of the Fundamental Law of Education under
which "democratization" of education was officially recognized.

During the second or Cold War period, postwar democratization
continued but was increasingly affected by the shift in U.S. policy
toward Japan. The United States now wished to transform Japan
into a "bastion of anticommunism," and the government, exploiting
this switch, began to reverse the radical policies of democratization
promoted by the Occupation. Among the progressive elements in
Japan a new image of the United States as virulently anticommunist
appeared.

The Conservative period began in 1951 when Japan, having
achieved independence with the conclusion of the San Francisco Peace
Treaty, turned its attention to economic development presumably for
the benefit of the people. As an ideological prerequisite, the ruling
classes undertook to instill patriotism from above and, in keeping with
the theme "harmonize education with national power and customs,"
attempted a return to prewar educational forms. The government and

the Ministry of Education, in their efforts to eliminate the liberal American style educational system of the Honeymoon period, revived moral education, made local boards of education appointive (in 1955), carried out evaluations of teacher performance (from 1956 to 1958), and consolidated a system of guidance from above. A hierarchical structure was created, leading from the government party, to the Education Ministry, to the appointed prefectural board of education, to the principal, to the head of the faculty, to the teacher, to the child.

In opposition to such trends, progressive forces, spearheaded by the Japan Teachers Union (JTU), attempted to protect the fruits of postwar democratization and launched a political struggle under the slogan "education for peace." With American techniques as the point of contention, conservative and progressive forces thus collided in the arena of education. The JTU, in alliance with the left wing, took the stance of preserving "American ways" of education while at the same time opposing "American imperialism" politically. In contrast, the government, closely tied to the United States through the U.S.-Japan Security Treaty, adopted an "anti-American" stance in support of a prewar style educational system.

All through these three periods, the one constant image of America held by all categories of people in Japan was that of a superpower capable of controlling global power relations. For Japan, especially, the United States was the victorious, occupying nation; and even after the signing of the San Francisco Peace Treaty, the United States remained the most important power, capable of swinging Japan's destiny.

Beyond this generalized perception, however, America represented different images to different groups of people. Japanese leaders during the Honeymoon period regarded the United States not only as a great superpower but also as a country embodying such principles of democracy as freedom, equality, and fraternity. Conservative leaders during the Cold War period, however, began to see in the United States not so much a tradition of liberal democracy as that of a prosperous free enterprise system. Thus, they were willing to build a closer cooperative relationship with the United States for the sake of free enterprise prosperity; and they thought the two countries would share a common concern over the spread of communism. In sharp contrast to conservative leaders during the Cold War and Conservative periods, progressive educators and JTU leaders began to see the United States as a dangerous capitalist nation likely to increase international tension in the Far East. This image eventually spread to larger numbers of intellectuals and educators, especially after the outbreak of the Korean War. In spite of a highly critical view of these people toward America's global strategy, however, many of them retained an image of the United States as a country of liberal democracy insofar as its domestic and social policies were concerned.

It might be useful to look briefly at several individuals prominent in education in the postwar years with a view to determining their images of the United States. During the Honeymoon period the images held by the elite were determined to a large extent by the four general directives issued by SCAP and the 1946 report of the American Education Mission rejecting the three pillars of prewar education in Japan. Even before SCAP began to order reforms, however, the ruling classes were critical of the wartime militaristic educational system and showed an understanding of liberal American principles of education; at the same time, they desired to protect traditional cultural values that accorded the emperor an ascendant position.

One representative of this outlook was Maeda Tamon, minister of education from August 1945 to January 1946. At the end of the war Maeda had been an official in the Home Ministry. A Protestant, he had served in 1938 as head of the Japan Cultural Center in New York and was well acquainted with the United States. He became minister of education in the first postwar cabinet on the recommendation of Ogata Taketora, a junior acquaintance and fellow employee at the *Asahi shimbun*. Maeda embodied the dualistic view described above: he was at once an antimilitarist exponent of international peace and a nationalistic supporter of the imperial system. His ideal was a peaceful, constitutional state in which the people would participate in politics while the *kokutai* was maintained under the sovereignty of the emperor. To him the source of evil was militarism, which grew out of extreme chauvinism and a highly regimented system of education. Such militarism, he felt, had denigrated the peace-loving "Yamato spirit" and the Imperial House and had caused the war with the United States. The Imperial Rescript on Education had been not a tool for regimentation and militarism but rather a statement of general human morality that provided standards for being "a good parent, a good child, a good married couple." Building from the rescript, the people should perfect their own individuality, the better to serve the imperially-ruled society of Japan. On one occasion, when asked whom he would choose if the United States were to send an educator to confer with the Japanese, Maeda responded, "Dewey or a follower to be named by Dewey."[1] Until John Dewey did arrive, it was the hope of people like Maeda, who had experienced the liberal education of the late Meiji period, to loosen the regimentation of education that since the early 1930s had provided the basis for militarism, and to allow teachers to create teaching conditions through their own efforts.

The union of *kokutai* nationalism with support for an American style liberal educational system is epitomized by Maeda. Thus, while he insisted that "the first thing one must consider is the defense of the *kokutai*," he also urged the introduction into Japanese education of individualism, internationally valid knowledge, and scientific methods of thought. When asked by a SCAP official about his ideas on educational reform in Japan, he answered that he would like to see a civics curriculum established. Maeda proposed to adapt to a Japanese form of democracy the things he had learned during his years in the United States. He sought to impart through the educational system a process of political participation by which the people in a given locality could, through their own efforts, develop a cooperative way of life.

The first step by the Japanese toward an autonomous reform of education, with Minister Maeda as ideological protagonist, was taken with the issuance in September 1945 of the "Educational Policy for the Construction of a New Japan," the first systematic postwar policy formulated by the Ministry of Education. Asserting that defense of the *kokutai* and construction of a peaceful nation were the primary goals of education, the ministry demanded the eradication from textbooks of material that inculcated militarism. As a result, teaching materials widely used in Japan—such as "Sailor's Mother," "Landing in the Face of the Enemy," and "The End of the Unsinkable Ship" —were censored. When the policy statement was issued, the head of SCAP's Civil Information and Education Section (CIE), Harold Gould Henderson (who had been a lecturer at Columbia when Maeda was in New York) reportedly called Maeda and applauded the new policy. Clearly the picture of American education that Maeda had acquired during his long residence in the United States before the war had become his ideal for the development of Japan's postwar educational system, an ideal that closely paralleled the views of the American Education Mission.

Maeda's liberalism had been inspired by his teacher Nitobe Inazō, principal of the First Higher School where Maeda was a student in the last years of the Meiji era, and was reinforced by the free and open search for knowledge permitted to the elite under the dual-track system devised by Education Minister Mori Arinori during the early Meiji era. This was a "hothouse liberalism," nurtured along the First Higher School-Imperial University route from which the intelligentsia emerged. After the war Maeda adhered to Nitobe's teachings hoping, as he wrote in *Sansō seishi* (Meditations at a cottage), that he might be "a bridge between Japan and America." It was his firm conviction that the civilizations of the East and West would one day merge, despite the antitheses that existed between Japanese and American culture (for instance, Americans were extroverted, Japanese introspective; Americans valued freedom, Japanese unity). Before such a fusion could come about, however, Maeda believed it essential that Japan be reborn as a "cultured"—that is, a peaceful—country.[2]

It was intellectuals such as Maeda, products of the prewar elite system of education, who cooperated with the progressive elements in SCAP and were the major actors during the Honeymoon period. Nearly all the leaders in the postwar educational reforms were graduates of the First Higher School, including Maeda (who graduated in German law in 1905), Education Minister Abe Nōsei (in literature, 1906), Tokyo University President Nambara Shigeru (in English law, 1910), and Education Minister Tanaka Kōtarō (in German law, 1911). The intent of these "*kokutai* liberals" was to disseminate among the people the liberalism they had learned at the First Higher School. Their goal was a cultured, peaceful country; their strategy was reform from above through the authority of the progressive faction in SCAP. Equation of the national polity with the emperor was essential to their sense of integrity; their villains were the military.

174

Maeda's successor as education minister, Abe Nōsei, was a man with a wondrous sense of balance that permeated his famous greeting to the first American Education Mission. His aim was to balance and combine Japanese and American thought in several respects. First, he called for a balance between the Throne and democracy (he advocated democracy under a "people's emperor," with the Rescript on Education serving as the model for the morality of the public). Second, he wanted a balance between nationalism and internationalism, rejecting the extreme chauvinism characteristic of Japan's traditional educational system and looking to the rest of the world for stimulation and enlightenment that would promote a "universal and humanistic international education." At the same time he criticized the imposition of imported American ideals. Finally, he desired a balance between science and mythology, for while he hoped that Western science would become the cornerstone of the future Japan, he also had a high regard for the mythical and historical foundations of the Japanese state.

The basis for Abe's concept of the concinnity of seeming opposites was his faith, befitting a Kantian scholar, in "universal human truth." While seeing the source of Japan's misfortunes in America's superficial qualities as the "country of jazz, movies, and dollars," he advocated democracy as the keynote of education, not because the victorious United States was able to impose it, but because it was based on fundamental human nature. On the other hand, Abe feared that democracy might be imposed from above and be accepted in a conformist, bandwagon fashion, as militarism had once been. In this, he in fact prophesied the subsequent trauma of Japan's cultural revolution.

Tokyo University President Nambara Shigeru, another leader of educational reform during the Honeymoon period, was also a proponent of postwar spiritual and cultural revolution, although, like most of those who participated in the postwar educational reforms, he expounded "cultural revolution from the podium." He gained prominence in February 1946 when he was elected chairman of a committee of twenty-nine Japanese educators set up by SCAP to work with the American Education Mission. The composition of this committee set the pattern for the drafting of the postwar educational reforms, which were drawn up largely by educators and scholars unconnected with the Ministry of Education. Although the Educational Reform Committee was created by a directive from SCAP and cooperated with the American Education Mission, it proposed educational reforms from a perspective that was to some extent independent of the Americans. As Nambara wrote:

Although some of us felt at the time that Japan was not ready for a six-three system, I thought that, as a result of Japan's defeat, we should adopt it. It was said that we were merely copying the American system, but it was also true that Japan's previous system of schools and education had originally been imported from western Europe. So after the war it was natural to look at American institutions and adopt their good features.[3]

According to Nambara, the idea of the six-three system was not totally new to Japan but had been discussed in elite circles since the Taishō era.

Men such as Nambara, who responded positively to American liberalism, were members of the "progressive" intellectual elite who had made it to the top of the prewar educational ladder. They were the finest products of Meiji education, sophisticated men who supported the elitist culture (often referred to as "Iwanami culture" because it was diffused through books issued by the most respected publishing house in Japan) that had flowered during the period of Taishō democracy. That culture had fortified the training of the elite in modern western European philosophy and was now being channeled into trying to realize, through the power of the American Occupation, the democracy that could not be achieved before the war because of the obstruction of the military.

In addition to the views of such progressive policymakers, what was the response of the ordinary teacher to the reforms made during the Honeymoon period? One teacher has written:

Immediately after the defeat, the official national textbooks were censored on orders from SCAP. And the half-million or so teachers scattered throughout Japan, who had their pupils inking out material that until the day before they had been teaching as correct—what were they feeling? what were they thinking? Unfortunately, one cannot find anyone who recorded his feelings and thoughts on censoring the textbooks.[4]

His words imply that many teachers were unable to comprehend fully the significance of this event, to say nothing of the wider meaning of the Occupation. Their acquiescence was a product of their training in prewar normal schools, where standardized teaching materials were memorized exactly as presented in endless drills that left no room for the development of a critical approach to learning. As a result, many teachers who had cried out against "American devils" and sent their pupils off to the battlefield suddenly began to mouth slogans about democracy and a peaceful nation. As one teacher described the situation:

Most teachers, in all schools, could not rejoice over defeat but neither could they mourn. Such sentiments were never expressed in the teacher's lounge, for everyone was expressionless, in a state of bewilderment. When told what was the proper attitude to take toward the Occupation army, they communicated it to their pupils.

Amid such apathy, some teachers found conversion easy and changed about with alacrity. The teacher quoted above went on to say:

As if we had forgotten the things we had told the children during the war, we now preached democracy and peace. There were also those who were quick to go around explaining democratic education to the teachers. Such people had practically all been educational leaders during the war, but now, quick as a flash, they were beating their chests for democratic education . . .
    "They used to call the principal 'my lord'
    And the teachers 'vassals.'
    These stupid fools—
    Now they denounce the imperial system."[5]

Mizuno Shigekazu has recounted the same phenomenon at another school. At the end of the war he was being trained as a kamikaze pilot, but defeat came before his mission. When he returned home and went back to his school, he found that an English teacher whom he had greatly respected had made a complete turnabout. During the war the teacher had preached the evils of the United States and Britain; now he praised them for their democracy. Mizuno felt an intense hatred upon seeing this once-respected teacher in high spirits, riding in a U.S. army jeep and translating for the Americans.

By rights this teacher should have reflected severely upon his own responsibility for the war; only then should he have looked to the future to decide what he would teach accordingly. But far from doing this, he was convinced that by submitting to the Occupation he was freed of responsibility and had become a new teacher.[6]

Careful consideration of the issue of immediate responsibility for the war could have provided a personal basis for the examination of educational problems and generated pressures for reform among Japanese teachers. But this did not happen. Some teachers were, however, greatly influenced by the report of the American Education Mission and tried to use it as a point of departure. The mission totally condemned prewar Japanese education and contrasted it with the American system at two levels: centralized administration of education as against decentralization of authority and popularly elected boards of education, and separation of elite and mass education as against a unitary system.

What most impressed certain teachers was the idea of separating education from politics. Kanazawa Kaichi, the retired principal of an elementary school in Tokyo, has described his reaction to the report in 1946, especially to the assertion that "the maximum potential of education can be fully realized only in an atmosphere of freedom. The creation of such a climate is the job of administrators; they must not create a hostile atmosphere." During the war Kanazawa had propounded the "American devils" concept and sent his pupils to the front. As a result, he thought, twelve of his forty students had died. The American Education Mission report served as a personal turning point, enabling him to overcome his feelings of responsibility and commit himself to a new educational system that was a negation of the prewar pattern.

One pedagogue who saw the implications for democracy in the American Education Mission report and had great hopes for an educational system along American lines was the late Munakata Seiya, a professor at Tokyo University and an ideological leader of the Japan Teachers Union. As he read the mission's report, Munakata recalled, he was unable to hold back his tears. Before the war he had opposed prevailing practices in education and had called for a more humanistic orientation. During the war, however, he had been forced to acquiesce and, as president of a women's junior college, had worshiped at the school's Shinto shrine and extolled the emperor. With the report of the American Education Mission, he felt liberated from the deep spiritual pain of this experience.

Munakata interpreted the report as built upon three tenets of education: a social studies curriculum, the six-three system, and a board of educational system. He believed that the values embodied in the Fundamental Law of Education, combining American style democracy and respect for the individual with an emphasis on peace, had been derived from the report. In his thinking we can observe a logical progression that developed during the Conservative period and has continued into the present in the ideology of the Japanese left wing, wherein concurrence with the Education Mission report led to support of the peace constitution and to defense of the Fundamental Law of Education.

The "new education" teachers snatched eagerly at American theories of education. But while asserting that they should develop school curricula themselves, they had little idea of what to do. These leaders of Japanese educational reform in the first three years after the war can be divided into three groups: the social studies group took as a model a manual prepared by the Ministry of Education in 1947 under the guidance of the CIE. This manual, *Modern Curriculum*, incorporated many of the curriculum revisions instituted in several American states (including California and Virginia) and aimed to put into practice John Dewey's progressive educational theories. Its central course of study was the "social studies curriculum," which first appeared in Japan at this time. In form a combination of the prewar history, geography, and ethics curriculum, in actuality it was a Japanese version of the Virginian Plan, based on Dewey's idea of "learning by doing." For example, in the social studies classes at Tokyo's Sakurada Elementary School, where the first social studies curriculum was initiated in 1946, students studied the postal system by delivering the mail themselves.

The core curriculum group was dubious about the efficacy of creating separate curricula for social studies, science, and so forth and advanced the idea of an empirical education that would parallel the circumstances of daily life. They envisioned a course of study having at its core themes from life itself. Representing this movement was the Core Curriculum Federation, established in 1948, which at its height was known as the "unofficial Ministry of Education"; its publication achieved a circulation of 40,000.

The local education group wanted to develop a curriculum based upon empirical studies of the local society constituting the environment of each school. The city of Kawaguchi in Saitama prefecture

whose foundation was filial piety. Education began with love for
one's relatives; lacking this, it was nonsense to speak of love for one's
fellow man. Hence the degradation of dignity in postwar Japanese
education. Considerations such as these led, during the Conservative
period, to the teaching in the classroom of respect for the emperor
and to the revival of ceremonies marking national holidays. However,
this revivified patriotism based on Confucian morality was unable to
repress postwar Japan's utilitarian morality which emphasized economic progress and personal success. The values of a competitive
society that esteemed academic credentials were taking root, and the
competitive entrance examinations, now strengthened by the six-
three system, were growing increasingly rigorous.

In response to these trends, the Japanese educational left wing,
centering about the Japan Teachers Union, became increasingly
politicized. During the Honeymoon period the JTU, striving to bring
about educational reforms from below, had avoided theoretical
studies of education, the view then being that teachers were workers
and the study of education a luxury. At that time the union emphasized wage demands and, as an extension, flung itself into the political
struggle. While Saitō Kihaku was chief of the JTU's Cultural Bureau
in Gumma prefecture, activities concerning educational practices
were avoided by the union as being "not the sort of thing for a union
to do." Union militants tended rather to have a political orientation,
fighting fiercely for the rights of teachers as workers and demanding
a system of minimum wages. Inevitably, conflict arose between the
union and SCAP, which held that education as a whole must be considered, and resulted in SCAP intervention in the board of education
elections of 1948 and ultimately in its attempt to purge the teaching
ranks of "reds." Consequently, there have always existed within
the JTU images of America both as an "army of liberation" and
as "anticommunist." Teachers first became active in pacifist and antiwar movements in the early 1950s, when "Don't send our pupils to
war again" became a JTU slogan. The movement was a response to
the international political environment, characterized by the Korean
War and the San Francisco Treaty, and focused on opposition to
American bases in Japan. In subsequent Diet elections the JTU supported the Socialist party in its battle with the ruling conservative

parties. Instead of moderate educational practitioners, activists advocating political positions reigned supreme in the JTU.

This political orientation was also visible in the JTU's Education Study Conferences established in 1951. For example, under the slogan "Protect the children in communities around the bases," the conferences attacked the allegedly evil influence of locally stationed American forces on public morals. At the same time that the JTU was stridently proclaiming its opposition to American imperialism, however, it staunchly defended the views of the American Education Mission in matters concerning the administration of education. Thus, its platform advocated elective boards of education and the right of teachers to formulate curricula independently of the government. The relationship between politics and education and between the teacher and the worker has been a continuing issue within the JTU. It was during this period that some teachers were threatened with being labeled "red" and dismissed or demoted. An elementary school teacher who was an elementary and junior high school student during the Occupation has recalled that a junior high mathematics teacher was suddenly fired for being "red," and how stunned he was watching the teacher go.[7]

In the political sphere the Conservative period was punctuated by violent confrontations between conservative ministers of education and the JTU. But in the classroom the conflict was not so clear-cut. The broad base of the educational system was composed in large measure of so-called "nothing else teachers," individuals who had drifted into teaching simply to make a living, because "there is nothing else I can do." There were also many who vigorously pushed for studies of the educational system. A number of diverse experiments were tried by various groups, among whom four stand out: the realists, the historical educationists, the systematic educationists, and the defenders of the social studies curriculum.

The realists in general welcomed American educational theories that respected the individuality of the child and gave the teacher considerable leeway in developing teaching materials; but at the same time they criticized those theories as being in many ways inapplicable to the daily lives of Japanese children. For example, they claimed that social studies classes tended to become merely games that imitated the process of delivering mail or operating a bank. Many sociologists likewise criticized the new educational system for failing to take cognizance of the wretched realities of Japanese society—its economic poverty, spiritual and moral chaos, and the ever-present danger of global war.[8]

Such considerations gave rise to the "compositions on life movement." Originating for the most part among teachers in the poorer rural areas, where Japanese traditions remained strong, this was an indigenous school of thought that resembled American empirical theories of education. Several of its practitioners wrote books describing their experiments: Muchaku Seikyō's *Yamabiko gakkō* (Country school, 1951), Konishi Kenjirō's *Gakkyū kakumei* (Revolution in the classroom, 1955), and Tōi Yoshio's *Mura wo sodateru gakuryoku* (Educating the country village, 1957). Admittedly, without the importation of American style education, such "realistic" experimentation might never have taken place. The fact that Muchaku's methods were adapted to the new postwar junior high schools and were derived from courses in the social studies curriculum is evidence of this. Moreover, at the time elected boards of education, which gave teachers wide latitude in their approach to teaching, were still operating. In its emphasis on empiricism and democracy the movement reflected educational theories imported from the United States. For example, in *Yamabiko gakkō* Muchaku recounts how the children started by examining their own allowances and progressed to studying the school and village budgets. Konishi describes efforts to eliminate schoolyard bullies through discussions among the pupils and the creation of more democratic human relationships and to develop egalitarian, nonhierarchical teacher-student associations.

The realists' rejection of blind acceptance of the new American style education was less a sign of accommodation with existing social norms than the expression of a desire for indigenous reforms and an effort to stimulate a reexamination of rural Japanese society and culture. Muchaku did not adopt the methods of the standard civics curriculum, which stressed adjustment within an already-democratized society; rather, he taught the children how to cope with the world through their own efforts—for instance, how to mechanize agriculture so that future farmers could become more prosperous.

These teachers also taught their pupils to examine their own lives, hence the term "compositions on life."

The second group of innovators were the "historical educationists." The major spokesmen of this school were educators and scholars of Marxist persuasion, whose educational theories were drawn from Soviet pedagogy and proposed the elimination of social studies, the establishment of independent history and geography curricula, and the systematic teaching of history. In their system an anti-American nationalism would naturally become dominant. The Conference of Teachers of History, a private educational organization, was established as early as 1949, with the objective of maintaining a link between the historical educationists and elementary and junior high school teachers. Later, in response to the efforts toward "patriotic upbringing," revival of the mythical National Creation Day, and the reintroduction of Japanese mythology in the schools, this organization worked vigorously to promote "scientific historical education." One teacher has written why he was converted from the social studies curriculum to the viewpoint of the historical educationists:

I did not mean to denigrate Dewey's educational theories, but I thought it improper that Japan, which had resisted the United States all the way up until defeat and occupation, should start viewing everything from the perspective that "If it's not American it can't be any good" . . . The social studies curriculum should at that time have emphasized how occupied Japan could become independent and what kind of Japan we should be thinking of, and I simply could not get used to an American style social studies curriculum with nothing of Japan in it.[9]

As a result, from about the time of the San Francisco Treaty this teacher began once again to teach Japanese history, a subject theretofore underemphasized.

Another teacher described his feelings as follows:

I felt anxious about the type of child we would be educating if we practiced a social studies curriculum derived from and heavily colored by regional studies in the United States. We were in a period of general self-examination regarding the errors of the war; even so, in a way I was worried that a people without a nationality might be created.[10]

This teacher, stimulated by a flood in the city of Kumamoto, began to study the history of floods since the Tokugawa era and the losses peasants had suffered because of them and to teach this history to his pupils.

The third group, the "systematic educationists," developed out of criticisms of the new American curricular emphasis on the student's personal experiences and adaptation to society. Its proponents initiated the "modernization" program that aimed at introducing into the elementary and junior high school curricula the latest techniques of modern natural and social sciences. Their activities led to a serious debate on education among teachers, usually carried on apolitically, although about 1954 the Educational Study Assembly of the JTU argued that pragmatic, problem-solving theories of education were the product of American colonialist educational policy. The critics of the new curriculum acknowledged that it decreased the emphasis on scholastic achievement and that the problem-solving method introduced by SCAP was a good antidote to prewar methods by which knowledge was pumped into the student. On the other hand, because the new approach tended to overemphasize spontaneity on the part of the child, the content of education tended to become fragmented, and as a result, coherent, formalized knowledge was neglected. Such fields as natural science, history, and foreign languages, in which systematized knowledge was particularly necessary, suffered in consequence. It was in reaction to this trend that the Conference of Teachers of Mathematics was organized in 1951 and developed a systematic approach to teaching mathematics. The foremost advocate of this method, Tōyama Kei, criticized education based on life experience as an American import that short-sightedly pursued immediate utilitarian goals. Urging that it be replaced by a curriculum based on the scientific approach, he and other systematic educationists established their own organization and strongly opposed efforts by the Ministry of Education to determine the content of education, demanding that teachers be allowed to determine what and how they would teach.

These three groups all criticized in varying degrees the Occupation-imposed educational reforms. However, there were those who defended the problem-solving approach to teaching and life-experience theories of education. Among them were the members of the Society to Achieve the Original Purposes of the Social Studies Curriculum, led by Ueda Kaoru, Shigematsu Takayasu, and others, which called for "solution of real problems by the child" and stated in its program, "We reject the position that the simple injection of knowledge is adequate, and we disagree both with the intellectualized education of the so-called systematic educationists and with moral education based on specific formal virtues."

To conclude, the influence of the United States on postwar Japanese education is impossible to calculate precisely. The power of the United States did bring about a revitalization of Japanese education, but once the Occupation ended, a reversion to prewar practices soon became apparent. Eventually, all that remained of American educational influences were features, such as the educational theories of Dewey, that had been introduced before the war and had already become rooted in Japanese education, as well as certain elements suited to the indigenous situation (the six-three system, for example, was quite compatible with the utilitarian Japanese infatuation with academic degrees). The democratic approach to education instituted by progressives in SCAP has not been sufficiently strengthened in subsequent Japanese policy, with its emphasis on economic growth. Japan in the 1970s is still wrestling with questions of overall educational reform. The prewar system, characterized by administrative leadership in education, the teaching of patriotism, and the differentiation of elite and mass education, are likely to be closely scrutinized by the coming generations to determine their merits and demerits in relation to the system, methods, and contents of education introduced after the war.

America as Seen by Japanese Travelers

Nations and peoples form images of one another in a variety of ways. Where many countries occupy the same continent, images derive mostly from constant and direct contact, and we might expect the resulting images to correspond to reality. At the other extreme, in a remote tribal society in which information about the outside world is relatively limited, images would be more ambiguous and even mythical.

In Japan image formation has followed an interesting and somewhat unusual pattern of development. Because of its geographic location and relative inactivity in international affairs, its people have had little direct contact with foreign countries; yet their extremely high literacy rate and the vast quantity of information available to them have made them one of the best-informed nations in the world. Despite a lack of direct contact with other cultures, the Japanese have been reading about them for many decades. This is especially true with regard to the Western countries, about which a vast literature, including numerous travelogues, has accumulated during the past one hundred years. The importance of this travel literature as a source of information about and images of the West is the theme of this essay.

In 1866 Fukuzawa Yukichi, the liberal thinker and educator,

published his well-known *Seiyō jijō* (Conditions in the West), describing the history, geography, and social and political institutions of the West on the basis of a trip to western Europe and the United States. It was then two years before the Meiji Restoration, and Fukuzawa was one of the few young Japanese who had traveled overseas. The book had an incredible circulation for that day—several hundred thousand copies. Fukuzawa then wrote another work, *Bummeiron no gairyaku* (Outlines of civilization), an introductory yet profound study of world conditions and international relations. It might be called the first best-selling nonfiction work in modern Japan; total sales reached one million within ten years of its first printing. To sell a million copies of a book is rare in Japan even today, when the publishing business is prosperous and people are more affluent and literate than a century ago.

Why were these books such a success? Who read them? In the first place, the Tokugawa seclusion policy, in force since the beginning of the seventeenth century, meant that very few Japanese had had any contact with foreigners, and Fukuzawa's books were eye-openers for the Japanese; everything he said was new. Furthermore, it was not only interesting but vitally necessary for the public to know about foreign countries, as Japan was about to open its gates to the world. It should also be noted that education under the Tokugawa regime was widespread, the literacy rate was high, and thus there was already in Japan a reading public on a mass scale.

Finally, Fukuzawa's popularity should be put into historical perspective. He was not the first Japanese whose travel accounts were widely read, but part of a tradition going back to the Buddhist monks who studied in China as early as the seventh century. Kūkai, the monk who founded the Shingon sect of Buddhism, for example, upon returning to Japan after years of study in China, wrote a theological treatise entitled *Sangyō shiki* (The three doctrines), in which he discussed the three important religious-philosophical systems in China: Confucianism, Buddhism, and Taoism. It was not printed, of course, but *Sangyō shiki* was one of the philosophical classics of medieval Japan. Intellectuals of the day, especially those in holy orders, had to read it as a guide to thought. Western history, too, abounds in similar examples. Marco Polo's report from the East aroused the adventurous and impelled the navigators of fifteenth century Europe to set sail for Asia. In the modern period, as Thomas Znaniecki's study of Polish peasants has demonstrated, many Europeans decided to emigrate to the United States after reading reports from that country. Indeed, writing about other cultures has formed one of the most popular genres in the literary traditions of both East and West. What was unique about such reports from abroad in Japanese cultural history is that, in comparison with Eurasian nations, far less information on other societies was available in a purposefully isolated island country like Japan. Only very recently has visiting another country been anything other than an exceptional adventure for Japanese. In such a society a handful of individuals like Kūkai or Fukuzawa were the windows through which its people viewed the world. In a period of vast sociopolitical change such as the Meiji Restoration, it was natural for the Japanese reading public to turn to Fukuzawa's books to obtain current information from abroad.

A second cultural tradition contributed to the popularity of the travel record in Japan: *miyage-banashi* or the "souvenir-storytelling" tradition in Japanese rural life. During the fifteenth century pilgrimage groups known as *kō* came into existence in many Japanese villages. Each year a representative of a particular *kō* was sent by the village on a pilgrimage to a particular shrine, often that at Ise. If the village was located in a remote area, the trip would take several months and would be costly for the farmers. The *kō* functioned as a financing organization; its members contributed an annual fee, and the money was given to the *kō* representative for his travel. In addition, there were contributions called *sembetsu* or "bon voyage money." The receipt of *sembetsu* obligated the representative to bring something back from his trip for the giver. This would usually be some small thing bought at the shrine with the money. Such gifts were known as *miyage*,[1] which literally means "shrine box" but is synonymous with "souvenir." With the distribution of *miyage* to all who had given him *sembetsu*, the pilgrim's mission would be completed. In addition to the tangible *miyage*, the traveler was also expected to make an oral report on his trip to all *kō* members. Since he had represented the whole village in visiting the shrine, his experience had to be shared by those who believed in the same shrine. The oral presentation was called *miyage-banashi*, the most popular form of the travelogue tradition in Japan.

Indeed, this *sembetsu-miyage* pattern of obligation still exists among contemporary Japanese, albeit in modified form. Of course, rural Japan is declining and *kō* organizations have disappeared as a result of modernization and urbanization. But replacing the village unit there are business corporations, and instead of pilgrimages, business trips abroad. When an urban executive goes abroad on business, his associates will very likely contribute some *sembetsu* apart from the travel allowance provided by the company, and he must not hesitate to accept the money. Foreigners are often amused to see Japanese tourists shopping at duty-free shops throughout the world, buying large numbers of small items. This strange activity is simply *miyage* shopping. It would be both rude and ridiculous for someone not to bring *miyage* to those who had given him *sembetsu*. But the tradition of *miyage-banashi* is also alive. An executive returning from an overseas business trip may be solicited by the editor of the company newsletter to write about what he has seen during the trip, or he may be asked by his associates to talk to them about it for, say, two hours. Those who travel to new places are still obliged to report their experiences to friends and relatives back home. It is a Japanese social institution.

In this context, there is good reason to suspect that Fukuzawa's books were written and accepted as a new manifestation of an old tradition. They were *miyage-banashi* on a national scale. On Fukuzawa's part, he saw it as his duty to report to his countrymen all he had seen and heard. As a result of his success, Fukuzawa earned a considerable amount of money, but his goal was not primarily profit. He felt an obligation to tell his countrymen what went on in the world; his experience had to be shared. Indeed, the public expected Fukuzawa's *miyage-banashi*. Furthermore, Fukuzawa had received *sembetsu*, in the sense that he had been one of the privileged few chosen to go abroad at the expense of the nation. Many who followed him to distant lands also adopted his style by writing of their experiences in the form of essays, diaries, or poetry, and many of their writings were published either commercially or privately. The number of such publications, as well as their readership, has been exceedingly large.

Another tradition in Japanese travel literature must be mentioned. The travelogue in Japan had had a fully developed aesthetic style before the modern era. Travelogues were not only candid nonfiction reports; they also could be a form of poetry. A number of literary figures gained fame through travel reports in the medieval period—for example, Saigyō, who wrote of his extensive poetic tour of Japan, and Bashō, a haiku poet who narrated his experience in the remote Tōhoku countryside in his masterpiece *Oku no hosomichi* (Narrow road to the deep north). In Japan an individual's life cycle has often been perceived as a process of travel in a space-time continuum. It is not surprising, then, that Fukuzawa's books should have enjoyed enormous popularity. They fitted into an existing tradition of travel literature in Japan. Nevertheless, something new was added: a practical value as guides to Western civilization. They served as textbooks in practical education. If a book introduced certain new developments in the West—for instance, in the field of technology—it meant that Japan also had to make an effort to cope with these developments. Unlike continental Europe, where intellectuals have been able to travel to other nations since the fifteenth century, modern Japanese intellectuals have had to learn about other countries, especially Western countries, primarily through books.[2]

Of course, there were efforts on the part of the government to send scholars and students to study in Europe and the United States, but the number was relatively small because of distance and cost. Therefore, the majority of the intellectual population in Japan had to be content to learn about foreign countries through books, including travel reports. Indeed, prior to World War II persons newly returned from the West usually received extremely good offers from major universities and government agencies and were regarded as the best sources of information about the outside world. In addition, until very recently anyone who visited a foreign country was expected to write an article or a book and was usually approached by a publisher or two upon his return.[3]

The United States provided the initial impetus that compelled Japan to discontinue its policy of isolation. In response to Commodore Matthew Calbraith Perry's visit in 1853–54, the Tokugawa government sent Ambassador Shimmi Masaoki to the United States in 1860. On board the accompanying naval ship *Kanrin-maru*, the first to cross the Pacific, was Fukuzawa Yukichi. The embassy was composed largely of samurai, and its members proved to be the first writers of travelogues about the United States. A seven-volume collection of their diaries was recently compiled,[4] containing numerous descriptions of American culture. They are interesting not only as historical documents but also as an important source of early Japanese perceptions of the United States.

The aspect of American life that seems to have struck the Japanese visitors most strongly was the informality, kindness, and hospitality of the American people. Morita Kiyoyuki, an aide to the ambassador, wrote: "It is customary among Americans that even in front of high officials they stretch their legs on the table, rest their chins in their hands, never bow, and seem to have no etiquette. But whenever they see someone in trouble, they are extremely kind. Therefore it is wrong to generalize that Americans are impolite." Another aide, Kimura Yoshitake, commented:

I consider the people of this country thoughtful and polite. They celebrated the establishment of a new relationship with us, and even the lower classes expressed their delight in our visit. Government officials especially were very kind to us and never behaved in an insulting or despising manner. Naturally, this is basically because of the prestige of our nation, but at the same time it is a sign that the American people are well educated.

Cultural differences between the two countries were found to be extreme. The visitors were excited by the Panama railroad, curious to see five-story buildings in Washington, and amazed to find a faucet through which they could get hot water at any time. And there were many episodes of culture shock. The ambassador's aides were dismayed when they were invited to dance parties. As Morita's diary describes these parties:

We were taken to the dance hall. Men and women were together and packed in tightly. Somehow a man approached a woman and after greeting, he took the left hand of the lady with his right hand, placing his left hand on her back. The woman put her left hand on the man's shoulder. Many couples danced to music until they were practically out of breath. We, as spectators, really felt dizzy watching their movements. The noisiness of the scene was beyond description. There was nothing really wrong with it, yet I could not bear to watch it. A little while later the official in charge came to Mr. Ambassador and said he had taken us there because this was part of American life, but that if Mr. Ambassador were not particularly interested in it he might leave at any time. Mr. Ambassador replied that he would like to leave immediately.

The social status of women was another focus of interest. "Women have prestige over men. For instance, when the number of chairs is insufficient, women sit on the chairs and men stand," commented Nonomura Tadazane. Ekitō Naotoshi wrote: "Women wear bracelets of silver and gold and dresses embroidered with gold. They seem to be decorative and luxurious. They are sociable, and even young women are not shy at seeing Japanese for the first time. They greeted us and shook hands. They seem to have much firmer character than Japanese women."

Food habits were a source of many awkward moments for the Japanese. Ambassador Shimmi wrote in his diary that he found it extremely frustrating to try to become accustomed to the food served in the United States. Apparently he ate little at formal dinners, preferring to wait until he had returned to his private room at a Washington hotel, where he would cook his favorite *miso* soup with ingredients he had brought from Japan. His *miso*, however, was soon exhausted, and toward the end of his stay the only foodstuff left was some dried radish that one of his aides had brought. Sitting alone in his room, the ambassador chewed the Japanese radish and wrote, "The only dream I have now is to go back to my country after my mission is complete and eat good steamed rice with *tsukemono* [Japanese pickles]." Nonomura Tadazane described the menu of a shipboard dinner:

Mr. Ambassador and other high officials had their supper in their private cabin; we ate in the dining hall, where more than a hundred people sat together around a long table. First, they served something like *suimono* [Japanese clear soup] in a big bowl; the second dish was salmon but with a strange sticky liquid over it. Many kinds of food were served, but for me they were inedible. The only thing I could eat was bread. I put some sugar on the bread so that I might not starve.

Another topic that interested the Japanese visitors of 1860 was the racial situation in the United States. Basically, their attitude toward the black population in America was unfavorable, and they thought that segregation was a natural arrangement. Morita Kiyoyuki related a touching experience:

Since we have arrived here, many of us have given small things such as fans, toys, woodblock prints, and so forth to those Americans who have taken care of us—waiters, maids, and other service people. The hotel employees, without exception, have received something from someone in our group. It was found, however, that we gave the gifts almost exclusively to white people. One black woman said in tears that the black people were very sad at not receiving any gifts because of their color. I was so struck that out of sympathy I gave her a fan. She was very grateful for it.

In contrast with the Japanese samurai who traveled to the United States in 1860, Japanese travelers today are in a totally different setting. Whereas only about fifty Japanese crossed the Pacific on that first voyage, today masses of tourists take 747s to the United States every day. Furthermore, through schools and the mass media the Japanese people are well informed (some say overinformed) about America. Fukuzawa's epochmaking *Seiyō jijō* would mean little to the Japanese public in the middle of the twentieth century. According to a survey conducted in Hawaii in 1970, more than 90 percent of a Japanese tour group had seen American movies and television programs about Hawaii before they went, and some of them said they had come to the islands "to ascertain whether all the things said about Hawaii were true." Japanese tourists now come from very diversified groups in Japanese society, ranging from farmers to secretaries, salesmen, nurses, and housewives. The day when only privileged elites such as diplomats and eminent scholars had the opportunity of foreign travel has passed. The increase in the number of tourists since the 1950s has been dramatic. The number of Japanese who traveled abroad in 1952 was a mere 13,000; even in 1960 the number was just 57,000. Thus the 640,000 Japanese tourists in 1970 represent a fifty-fold increase over the 1952 figure. The age of mass tourism is here to stay. In terms of cultural contact, this is very significant. Direct contact between different cultures on a mass scale is something new. The exotic and faraway sound of the words "to go abroad" has disappeared in present-day Japan.

There are no precise figures on the number of Japanese tourists who have visited the United States in recent years. According to a survey by the Foreign Ministry in 1970, 82,000 people visited America in 1968, 129,000 in 1969, and 203,000 in 1970. The total number of passports issued during those three years was 320,000, 470,000, and 640,000 respectively. Of those who traveled abroad, 26 percent went to the United States in 1968, 27 percent in 1969, and 31 percent in 1970. From these figures it is obvious that the number of Japanese visiting the United States in recent years has been significant and increasing year by year. Exact figures for 1971 are not yet available, but it is estimated that 250,000 of 800,000 Japanese overseas travelers visited America. Even if it is true that many go only as far as Hawaii, staying there for only two weeks or so at most, such a large number of travelers to the United States is unprecedented in Japanese history.

Japanese mass tourism has continued the travelogue tradition and has produced a vast quantity of travel literature. There always seems to be a market for travelogues, even those with an amateurish style. According to the *Japanese Publishers Yearbook*, 2,300 travelogues were published in Japan between 1950 and 1970. Most dealt with trips to Europe; only 250 concerned the United States. Thus, even though nearly a third of the passports issued in Japan have been for travel to the United States, the proportion of travelogues about that country has been relatively low. This gap may be reflected in the somewhat simplistic images that emerge from these accounts.

Generally speaking, most of the travelogues on the United States in the past twenty years have been favorable to the country and its people. Contentwise, approximately 70 percent are written in a more or less positive tone. America is usually depicted as a great new country. The adjectives most frequently used to describe Americans are "frank," "honest," "generous," and "kind." For example:

At any rate, Americans are kind to foreigners. For instance, when I was almost lost in a big building, someone who happened to pass by took me to the office I was looking for . . .

I was standing on the street waiting to catch a taxi. An American approached me and asked if I was in trouble. They are very anxious to help people, and everyone seems ready to extend assistance to a foreigner . . .

Americans display their emotions openly and express their opinions very clearly whether they know what they are talking about or not. I like them for this . . .

When they are too kind, we find it embarrassing. However, we have to understand their goodwill, admire their frankness, and respect the courage with which they carry out a proposed idea or plan.

Negative reactions to the United States occur in several different contexts, but American food is often singled out for unfavorable comment.

I can't stand American food, it is so bad and tasteless . . .

The meals I had at my dormitory were very bad, and American restaurant food is flat and tasteless . . .

If the beef we had when visiting the meat packers was bad, what is it like throughout the rest of the country? How can Americans be satisfied with such bad beef?

Most Japanese find American food distasteful because of its standardization. As one traveler put it, "When seen in supermarkets and cafeterias, American food seems to be cooked mechanically, never made by human hands. It often doesn't taste good."

Numerous similar examples might be cited, but one very important fact that emerges is how little the descriptions differ from those written by the Japanese ambassador and his aides a hundred years ago. American generosity and kindness is one of the most consistent elements in Japanese perceptions of the United States and has survived periods of anti-American sentiment in Japan. The complaints of the samurai about American food and the criticisms of contemporary tourists contain more similarities than differences—the only difference is probably that a tourist today will eat American hamburgers anyhow, while the samurai did not. In short, Japanese stereotypes of the United States today are echoes of images created one hundred years ago. In that sense, Japanese images of America in the past century have been static.

At the same time, a new type of person travels to the United States. Oda Makoto is a typical example. Awarded a Fulbright grant to study at Harvard University in 1958, he later wrote that his attitude toward the trip had been extremely casual: "It happened that I wanted to see America. That's all." There was no serious decision on his part about going abroad. He took a plane and traveled as if he were taking a local train. He also decided that he wanted to experience and participate in American life rather than to "see" the country. He observed more similarities than differences between himself and his American friends at the university. For instance, he was pleased to know that his classmates were discussing Sartre and Camus. The essay he wrote upon his return, entitled *Nandemo mite yarō* (I want to see everything), instantly became a best-seller. More than a half-million copies were sold during the decade 1960–70, and the book is still on the market with steady sales figures. Its readers are mostly young students, and Oda has been one of the idols of the younger generation.

In this very provocative book he says: "What I felt in the United States was not the weight of Western civilization. Rather it was the extreme form of civilization on its dead-end street." For him, America's problems are not only for Americans to solve but should be a matter of concern to all who share in the civilization of the twentieth century—including, of course, the Japanese people. In this sense Oda is different from Japanese travelers who emphasize the "materialistic," "egoistic," or "cold-hearted" aspects of the United States. Such travelers have written:

American products cover the world and they enjoy profitable markets. Also, Americans complacently believe that they were victorious in World War II wholly by themselves . . . People from Europe and other countries still come to the United States to live, so most Americans are rootless. In addition, they are extremely materialistic and self-centeredly individualistic. They do not think of the future; only present affairs are important to them . . .

While traveling through America I felt as if I were in a lukewarm bath. I finally went mad because of the dull monotonousness.

Oda, in contrast, does not criticize the United States in such conventional terms. He argues that criticism alone is not productive. For Oda and his generation America is not *their* problem but *our* (that is, Japan's) problem. As he notes, "To think about America is synonymous with thinking about Japan." The younger generation of Japanese he represents are more interested in hippies, drugs, pop art, and other aspects of contemporary young Americans who are now searching for an "exit"; young Japanese are also looking for an "exit" from the dead-end street.

This point needs elaboration. First of all, Oda is not anti-American. Quite the contrary, he is sympathetic toward Americans. But what is characteristic of his generation is that they do not feel overwhelmed by the United States and are free of superiority or inferiority complexes regarding that country. For them, America is not a faraway place. Rather, it is something that has been carved into the mind of every Japanese youth. As Tōno Hōmei, the art critic, wrote in his book *Kyozō baiyōkoku shi* (Record of an illusion-producing country):

I wanted to see America not as an object to look at but as something silently penetrating the lives of us Japanese. Our generation has grown up under the pressure of the constant cultural presence of America. I cannot formulate any theory about the United States without considering the "internalized America" that exists in the minds of Japanese.

While in the United States such travelers no longer think of Japan in terms of *wabi, sabi,* or *zen.* Past generations of Japanese used to discuss these traditional aesthetic concepts when they were asked to talk about Japan, and they were capable of appreciating their value. But to the young, traditional Japanese culture seems remote. In fact they, like Americans, tend to look at traditional Japan as part of the "mysterious Orient"; their psychological distance from American culture appears far less than from old Japanese values. There is a feeling that many of the problems confronting the contemporary United States are ones Japan too faces or will face eventually. Japan is only a few steps behind America on the path down the dead-end street. When Japanese criticize American "materialism" or "standardization," they are projecting their own anxieties concerning Japan.

Oda sensed "the smell of America" as a mixture of many contradictory elements, but he has noted that the "smell" also pervades Japan. What seems to be essentially "American" is often universal, so that it may be "Japanese" at the same time. Thus, for Oda and his generation the United States is no longer a strange, exotic foreign country. It is an experience to be internalized by Japanese as well as Americans. This in part accounts for their sensitivity to changes within American society. These changes are meaningful to young Japanese as they ponder the present and future of their own society.

Oda revisited the United States in 1964 and was particularly impressed by the changes that had taken place among the youth. He wrote:

Talking to young Americans, I could not help but think that the United States was becoming more leftist. At least I did not see many pseudo-realists such as dominated the youth scene a few years ago. Instead of computer-happy philosophy, young Americans today are trying to think matters through, tracing them back to fundamentals. For instance, rather than repeating the word "freedom" as a monk might repeat a sutra, they try to

understand what "freedom" means to Vietnamese (in addition to Americans)
. . .

> After enjoying my talks with these Americans, I came back to Japan to find pseudo-realists dominating the country. I felt as if I had returned to the America of a decade ago.

His point is clear. He has a firm belief that the United States will change for the better in spite of its difficulties. Likewise, Kuni Masami, who lives in the United States, wrote in his 1969 book *Amerika wa nagareru* (America in transition):

> "Profit-seeking, uneducated" Americans are now being replaced with a new breed, namely, young, "thinking, truth-seeking" Americans. One of my young American friends was extremely angry about the American taxation system and quoted the theories of Karl Marx. When I said that certain parts of Marx were outdated, he then referred to Mao and other contemporary revolutionaries.

The difference between these writers and those of preceding generations lies in the content of evaluative terms. The older stereotype was that Americans are good because they are frank, generous, and kind; Oda and the writers of his generation would say that Americans are good because they are eager to achieve a new era. Japanese travelers for many generations have seen the United States in a positive evaluative framework, but for different reasons. These reasons are so different that the images of America held by Japanese today may be said to be undergoing a drastic transition. The old images of "kindness," "generosity," and "materialism" are now being challenged by new images and new perspectives. Of course, the older images still inform the majority of Japanese travelers, and guidebooks published by the tourist industry still emphasize and reinforce the stereotypes. But it would be unrealistic to disregard the new images of the United States that have emerged in Japan.

Finally, changes within Japan have affected tourist images. A recent survey disclosed that, while the number of Japanese visiting the United States has increased, more and more tourists are becoming interested in visiting other parts of the world. Travelogues about Europe, China, the Soviet Union, Africa, and South America have increased at the expense of ones about the United States. Though travel costs to Europe are considerably higher, with the growing affluence of Japanese society, many tourists seem to be looking for the cultural traditions of Europe rather than the "material" wonders of America; or they may be interested in observing the more "natural" ways of living in Asia and Africa as an escape from the polluted air of Tokyo. Until a decade ago the typical Japanese traveler went to the United States and was impressed by American democracy and industrial achievements; and their *miyage* would be certain industrial products Japan did not possess. But today, no longer so amazed by American goods, tourists are returning to Japan with antiques and handicrafts from Europe in place of industrial products from America. Under such circumstances, Japanese perceptions of the United States are becoming more mutable and diverse than in the past. In an era of worldwide changes in images of America, the perceptions of Japanese travelers are no exception.

PRISCILLA A. CLAPP
and
MORTON H. HALPERIN

U.S. Elite Images of Japan: The Postwar Period

The attitudes of the elite policymaking community in the United States on any subject are derived from a complex set of influences. To examine the development and interplay of American images of Japan as they have been reflected in U.S. policy toward Japan, one must consider first of all the attitudes of the American public and the range and variety of images of Japan. Second, one can examine the set of shared images about the world, and Japan in particular, that are common to the large majority of policymakers and related to broader American foreign policy goals. These shared images tend to be reflected in major foreign policy statements and provide continuity in U.S.-Japanese relations from year to year and administration to administration. Finally, a number of divergent and somewhat conflicting views of the nature of Japanese-American relations can be identified. Often these divergent images are related to some very direct domestic pressures on the policymaking community; other times they appear to be determined by the organizational interests of a specific group in the government or by that group's approach to foreign policy in general. The extent to which these divergent views become translated either in decisions or in the style of U.S. relations with Japan depends largely on the relative influence a particular group has over the policymaking process.

American Public Attitudes toward Japan

A discussion of American public opinion toward Japan must be prefaced with this observation: in contrast to the Japanese public, which is relatively very interested in the United States, the American public focuses very incoherently on Japan and tends to shift with particular events, as they are reported in the American press. This means that, although the average levels have remained fairly constant, public opinion does fluctuate from time to time. In 1960, for example, public opinion polls in the United States reflected a sharp increase in public misgivings about Japanese dependability (in the wake of the Security Treaty revision and the cancellation of the Eisenhower trip to Tokyo). The next year this feeling was back down to previous levels.

Public Opinion Polls

Over the last decade both the Gallup and Harris polls have done, for Japanese clients, a series of studies of U.S. public opinion on Japan. We shall draw from three of these polls for the following discussion of American public opinion. While these polls provide some useful insights into the context from which policymakers must extrapolate in shaping American foreign policy, it should be remembered that polls are somewhat manipulative and can produce seemingly different results according to the questions asked.

In the absence of any crises in the U.S.-Japanese relationship, public feelings about Japan seem to remain fairly constant, with confidence in the relationship holding an edge over lack of confidence. In March 1970, for example, 44 percent of those polled considered the Japanese dependable allies, mainly because they have proved their friendship, contributed to good trade relations, and shown appreciation for U.S. assistance. The majority of this 44 percent was college-trained, male, and of the postwar generation (in their twenties). Some 36 percent of those polled, however, felt that Japan was not a dependable ally, because the Japanese are untrustworthy and capable of betrayals such as Pearl Harbor. The Americans who felt this way about Japan tended to be less educated (grade school level) and over fifty. The other 20 percent had no opinion of Japan.[1]

A year later, in March 1971, a similar poll found that "Americans view the Japanese people in basically positive terms," citing favorable personal attributes and technological and economic achievements, but that there was evidence of a significant residue of mistrust. One in four respondents felt that "Orientals, including the Japanese, are sly and devious—we should never trust them or rely on them as allies." Despite the inconsistency in attitudes toward Japanese society in general, as reflected in this poll, some 59 percent (and 72 percent of those who had been to Japan) felt that Westerners could develop an appreciation for Japanese culture.[2]

A third poll, conducted for the *Yomiuri shimbun* in the fall of 1971, found indications (probably because of the nature of the questions asked) that a majority of the American public lacked confidence in the U.S.-Japanese relationship.[3] It implied that an "overwhelming majority" of Americans were convinced that the U.S. government should be considering its own interests first, rather than equal partnership with Japan.

The *Yomiuri* poll found that five out of eight respondents feared a Japanese defense build-up. The *Asahi* poll was even more specific: 69 percent agreed that the Japanese military role should be limited to self-defense, and 72 percent were convinced that Japan should not have nuclear weapons.

With regard to trade, both polls reflected that a majority sees more trouble ahead. Of those polled for *Asahi,* 50 percent agreed that "the Japanese economic advance is so great it now poses a serious economic threat to Western countries, including the U.S." In the *Yomiuri* poll 70 percent felt that U.S. industry was threatened by Japanese imports. When asked to attribute reasons for the Japanese economic success, those polled for *Asahi* considered cheap labor to be the prime factor (83 percent), with other reasons being the diligence of Japanese workers (49 percent), a free ride from U.S. military protection (50 percent), cooperation between government and industry in exporting (44 percent), and technological expertise (38 percent).

The *Asahi* poll and the consulate poll both inquired about the sources of information of their respondents. In the consulate poll 54 percent relied on television, 50 percent on newspapers, and 22 percent on radio. Some 21 percent had personal experience and only 5 percent had learned about Japan in school courses. Of those polled for *Asahi,* 29 percent had read books about Japan, 35 percent had seen Japanese movies, 31 percent had Japanese friends, and 8 percent had visited Japan. It is obvious that the public media played the major role in developing the American public's images of Japan.

The Press

More often than not, mistrust is bred by a lack of understanding. That Japan does not loom very large in the interests of the general public is evident in the sketchiness of U.S. press coverage of Japan. Furthermore, American correspondents in Japan rarely speak fluent Japanese and often miss important issues until they are brought to their attention. The chances of misinterpretation are much greater than they would be in any European country.

Press coverage tends to focus on more exotic events, such as student riots, Mishima's suicide, the sergeant lost on Guam since World War II, the extreme aberrations of political revolutionaries, interspersed with images of Japan, Inc. The *New York Times,* for example, can be characterized as one of the most sophisticated American newspapers in reporting foreign affairs, but a survey of its index for 1970 reveals that articles on Japan for that year occupy nine columns of indexing, while those on West Germany take twenty-five columns. Of the nine columns on Japan, one is devoted to "U.S. bases and forces" in Japan and two relate to "defense and armaments." A breakdown of the reporting on "defense and armaments" is interesting; it emphasizes Japan's defense build-up, Mishima's suicide, and riots concerned with the expiration of the Security Treaty. In the section on Japan's "foreign relations," half the articles deal with Sino-Japanese relations and eighteen articles with U.S.-Japanese relations, most of which are concerned with the growing dispute over textiles. The majority of articles in the section on "politics and government" report on the activities of opposition parties, such as the socialists, the communists, the Sōka Gakkai, and Kōmeitō. It is probable that the reports on Japan in local newspapers are even more selective and sensational.

Relative Lack of Interest

It is rare that U.S. relations with Japan become an important domestic issue to Americans, and when they do, press coverage of events —no matter how balanced—encounters a public that is not prepared to understand the process by which these events have come about.

The circumstances surrounding the Security Treaty revision of 1960 are a most obvious example. Americans were baffled by the public clamor in Japan over a treaty that to Americans was a continuing commitment by the United States to look after the best interests of Japan. The easiest and most comprehensible explanation in the public mind was that there was a serious communist threat in Japan. Typical of this attitude was James Reston's comment that Japan "is one of the three major objectives of Communist policy . . . many of the intellectuals in Japan, many of the Socialists, and many of the trade union leaders have either cooperated with the Communists or acquiesced in their activities."[4] The reaction in Japan to the Security Treaty revision was considered a slap in the face to American munificence.

Facile explanations, however, seem to be a common means of grappling with difficult foreign policy problems on a broad public scale. It would be hard to prove that this characteristic was the fault of either press coverage or the public mentality. It is more likely a combination of both, in that the press reflects public attitudes as much as it influences them.

The very neat image of Japan, Inc. that has been so attractive to the American press—and public—as an orderly explanation for Japan's seemingly phenomenal economic exploits is the epitome of this public approach to foreign relations. It is easy to imagine a very cleverly designed and manipulated socialistic entity working to invade world markets with artificially low-priced, well-built products. The sinister implications of this image in the American mind are not difficult to find. In the first place, the Japanese, by purposely flooding the American market, are taking advantage of the benevolence and economic assistance they have been given by the United States since World War II. Furthermore, could such a highly integrated and finely tuned economic system really be based on democratic government?

The leading U.S. economist Paul Samuelson has found that "We veer from contempt of Japanese as capable only of making shoddy Christmas-tree ornaments, to thinking of them as supermen whose costs and precision Americans and Europeans could never compete with. Ugly racism has to be fought, in the economic as well as political and social spheres."[5] Thus carried to its extreme, the Japan, Inc.

idea suggests a racial bias on the part of the American public, inasmuch as it provides the only acceptable explanation for how an Asian country could have reached a technological level high enough to compete with the United States. Admittedly, this is an interpretation of the Japan, Inc. image that concentrates on its most highly suspect implications, but nevertheless they are there. The results of the public opinion polls, discussed above, support this interpretation.

One of the keys to the American public's image of Japan is its general lack of interest in Asia, with the exception perhaps of China. To the extent that the American public interests itself in foreign policy, the focus is clearly on Europe. There is a historical messianic interest in China, stemming perhaps from the early missionary work. However, the Vietnams, the Koreas, and occasional tiffs with Japan are really only diversions for the public. Consider the amount of time that it took the public to focus coherently on the war in Vietnam. These diversions penetrate the public consciousness only to the extent that they affect daily life.

Public interest in U.S. Asia policy must be viewed, therefore, in terms of its direct relationship to domestic interests; this really means that the majority of our dealings with Asia remain almost exclusively in the domain of the policymaking experts. In the case of Japan, however, one must also consider the extent to which business interests have become involved with Japan and, consequently, the occasional influence that they might have on policymaking.

Shared Images of the Policymakers

The views of participants in the foreign policy process of the American government are constrained by shared images of what the national security interests of the United States are. These images are basic beliefs, common to the majority of the participants in any given decision, about the functioning of the international system and the U.S. role in it. They combine perceptions of reality with preferences and objectives.

Although they are now undergoing change, it was these broad common conceptions that shaped elite attitudes toward Japan in the United States during most of the postwar period.[6]

1. The preeminent feature of international politics is the conflict between communism and the Free World.

2. Every nation that falls to communism increases the power of the communist bloc in its struggle with the Free World.

3. Military strength is the primary route to national security.

4. Nuclear war would be a great disaster and must be avoided.

5. The United States must maintain military superiority over the Soviet Union, including the capability to destroy the Soviet Union after a Soviet first strike.

6. The intentions of communist countries in Asia are essentially expansionist.

7. The surest simple guide to U.S. interests in foreign policy is opposition to communism.

8. The United States has the power, ability, responsibility, and right to defend the Free World and maintain international order. If the United States does not defend the principles of world order, no other state has the power to do so.

9. Peace is indivisible. Therefore, collective defense is necessary. The new international order is based primarily on U.S. assumption of responsibility, especially demonstrating the willingness of the United States to resist aggression. Thus any expansion of communist influence must be resisted.

10. The Third World really matters. (a.) It is the battleground between communism and the Free World. (b.) Western capital will generate economic development and political stability with a minimum of violence. (c.) Instability is the great threat to progress in the Third World.

11. U.S. prosperity depends on the economic health of other developed nations, a favorable U.S. balance of payments, and the preservation of the American gold supply.

Not all policymakers have shared all of these images at the same time, but the majority have shared most of them. For all policymakers this is at least a fair representation of the lens through which they have viewed foreign affairs until very recently.

Thus, faced with what they saw to be monolithic aggressive communist expansion, as manifested in the Korean War, policymakers in Washington became convinced that "the idea of a Japan left without strong outside support, questionable enough anyway in the light of events in Korea, appeared, quite naturally, as the wildest frivolity."[7] They saw Japan and Europe as two vital centers of industry in the world, which must be kept out of the control of the communist powers.

To most policymakers in Washington, Japan still provides a strong base for U.S. military power in Asia and thus serves as a deterrent to Soviet or Chinese expansion. In the early postwar period American policymakers also perceived an internal communist threat in Japan. There is now, however, a tendency to take Japanese political stability for granted.

In Asia "the ultimate ideal is a community of the free states of Asia cooperating for their common interests in the political, economic, and security fields, with which we are associated only to the degree that these states desire our cooperation."[8] Washington tends to feel that Japan, with its increased capacity and willingness to contribute economic assistance to the Asian countries, can serve to lighten the American burden in this area and promote greater stability in the developing countries.

Probably the great majority of U.S. policymakers focus on Japan only through this lens of shared images about national security interests. Japan occupies the attention of a very small section of the American elite. Most U.S. leaders have never been there, know very little about it, and are rarely called upon to think about it. Therefore, when policymakers, outside of the small group that is cognizant of Japan, are forced to focus on Japan, their basic terms of reference are necessarily their images of U.S. national interests. Those who are knowledgeable about Japan and sensitive to Japanese problems must also begin from the point of view of U.S. national interests. Even if they did not share a majority of these images, they would have to conform their suggestions to them most of the time in order to have them accepted by the rest of the policymaking elite.

It is easy to see how conflicts between U.S. and Japanese interests could arise. But it is also clear that, in terms of these shared images, Japan is a very important ally of the United States, and in the end it is essential in the minds of U.S. decision-makers to maintain that alliance for the good of national security.

Conflicting Images

With these broader, widely shared images of Japan in mind, we can turn to a consideration of the more specific and divergent images that can be found in different sections of the policymaking elite.[9] There seem to have been three basic approaches to Japan among U.S. policymakers in the postwar, or more accurately the post-Korea, period. Each of these views have, in consecutive order, tended to dominate U.S. policy in the postwar period, accounting in part for the inconsistencies and tensions in U.S. policy toward Japan. However, all three views can be found to some degree at all points in the postwar relationship.

The first of these views we shall call "inevitable harmony." Roughly, that is the notion that the interests of the United States and Japan are identical and that Japan can be counted upon to act as an agent of the United States in Asia. The second view reflects the idea of "creating a partnership" through diligent efforts on both sides to overcome the differences inherent in the two cultures, as well as divergent national interests. Finally, the third view, which includes a multitude of pessimistic feelings about the future of the relationship, is one of an "inevitable conflict of interests" between the United States and Japan. This last view is a less coherent philosophy about the relationship and serves more as a catch-all category for a variety of tactical and ad hoc approaches to the relationship. To characterize the postwar period in terms of these three views, it could be said that American policy toward Japan has been motivated primarily by a combination of the first two images, with elements of distrust (the third image) lurking in the background and occasionally coming to the fore when domestic politics have entered into the relationship.

To an extent these three divergent views are characteristic of different interests within the policymaking elite. The dominance of any one of these views at a particular point in time can be related to the influence that a specific part of the bureaucracy has over the policymaking process. Therefore, in describing these three views, an attempt will be made, as far as possible, to relate them to sections of the bureaucracy and to describe their role in policymaking at various points in the postwar relationship.

Inevitable Harmony

The idea of inevitable harmony seems to have characterized the period in U.S.-Japanese relations extending from the Occupation to the early 1960s, when Edwin O. Reischauer was ambassador to Japan. During this period American policy toward Japan was dominated by a sense that Japan's future was inseparably linked to that of the United States. The United States had been instrumental in fashioning the postwar political and economic structure of Japan, and Japan had accepted dependence on the United States in exchange for both economic and security assistance. It was inevitable that the national interests of both countries would be parallel, especially since the United States had done so much for Japan and Japan had so much to be grateful for.

As John Emmerson describes it, in the aftermath of the war "Americans suddenly saw the Japanese as friendly, attractive, and hospitable people. Japan's image was transformed into a romantic combination of flowers, temples, kimono-clad beauties, Zen Buddhism, and a graceful way of life."[10] For the U.S. serviceman Japan was a nice place to be stationed. During the Occupation the U.S. military had established a comfortable social position for itself in Japan. And the military had considerable say in the conduct of U.S.-Japanese relations, partly because the Occupation was followed immediately by the Korean war, when Japan suddenly became a major U.S. base in Asia.

Thus, before the Japanese loomed on the economic horizon of the United States, U.S. interests were framed largely in terms of Japan's strategic importance, its role in the extension of U.S. military power in Asia. The only real threat to this harmonious relationship was communism in Japan. Economic resurgence and nationalism, according to this view, would contribute to, rather than threaten, the relationship. An economically viable Japan would be able to ease the U.S. military burden; a nationalistic Japan would be anticommunist.

The idea of inevitable harmony is in many ways a grand scheme for the protection of U.S. security interests in Asia. It envisions an economically strong, rearmed Japan promoting the interests of the United States in Asia and relieving the United States of a substantial portion of its burden.

Those who have advocated Japanese rearmament have generally based their case on arguments suggesting inevitable harmony. A rearmed Japan would inevitably pursue a course consistent with that of the United States. To civilian policymakers this would permit the

United States to decrease its defense expenditures. To military leaders it would complement and strengthen U.S. efforts.

Although, as we have pointed out, this view tended to be more prevalent in the immediate post-Korea period of U.S.-Japanese relations, traces of it can still be found today in the attitudes of a few U.S. policymakers. Perhaps the best personification of this view of Japan today can be found in the statement of former Secretary of Defense Melvin Laird. His development of the argument is worth quoting in full:

As we have all come to recognize in recent years, Japan's growing power on the Asian scene will make her one of the keys to peace and stability in Asia in the years ahead. [At San Clemente Mr. Nixon and Mr. Satō spent a large part of their time together reviewing] our mutual interest in the broad security problems of the Asian region. As they announced at the end of this meeting, and as I said after my trip to Japan last summer, the approaches of our two countries to these problems are complementary.
As a result of my trip to Japan last Summer, I gained a better appreciation of Japan's need for military equipment modernization if her forces are to become effective against sophisticated threats. Accordingly, we are encouraging Japan to modernize the equipment of her forces, and have placed our technical services at the disposal of the Japanese to help assess their needs and determine what equipment we might be able to provide within Japanese budget constraints.[11]

Another part of the inevitable harmony point of view is that Japan should take a much stronger political role in Asian regional organizations. This assumes a very great area of mutual interest not only between the United States and Japan but also between Japan and other Asian countries. It also disregards any residual feelings of hostility that other Asian countries might harbor for the prewar experience with Japanese political activities in the region.

Indeed, the inevitable harmony image has tended to characterize a section of the policymaking elite that is not too knowledgeable about Japan but that must bear the responsibility for maintaining a stance in Asia that will not disrupt the balance of power. It also seems to have been based on the assumption that the United States exercises essential control over Japan, to the point that Japanese national interests contrary to those of the United States will be subdued and kept under control through U.S. persuasion.

Creating a Partnership

Perhaps more than any other single event, the public dissent in Japan over the revision of the Security Treaty caused American decision-makers to begin reassessing the relationship. In the process of reevaluation, the voices of those advocating the development of a partnership began to dominate. Just after the events of 1960 Edwin O. Reischauer wrote an article in *Foreign Affairs* about the "broken dialogue" between the United States and Japan, pleading the case for the United States to begin looking at Japan more carefully and to consider that Japan was going to have its own set of national interests. Shortly after this article was published, he was appointed U.S. ambassador to Japan by President Kennedy. His appointment was seen as a recognition by the president of the growing importance of Japan and the need to establish a dialogue with the Japanese that would compensate for the many differences between the two cultures. In 1964, affirming the wisdom of Reischauer's appointment, George Kennan wrote, "The tasks of intellectual mediation between these two countries, where the technical difficulties of communication are truly formidable, is one for specialists. It is not accomplished, as many Americans like to believe, merely by thrusting ordinary people together and 'letting them get to know each other.' "[12]

Thus, during the period of the 1960s the attitude of U.S. policy-makers toward Japan came to be characterized more by the partnership image than by either of the other two images. However, it is also evident that this was a period in the U.S.-Japanese relationship when policy was left pretty much in the hands of the experts. Neither the memoirs of the Kennedy years nor Johnson's *Vantage Point* give more than passing reference to Japan; Japan was not on the front burner in the White House. U.S. policy toward Japan during this period was influenced very much by the middle-level bureaucrats in both the State Department and the Defense Department, most particularly those who had a continuing interest in U.S.-Japanese relations.

With attention riveted on Vietnam at the highest levels and an absence of any crises in U.S.-Japanese relations, the most significant policy issue to evolve during this period was Okinawa reversion. Perhaps the very fact that it arose before it was a crisis issue indicates that this was a period of growing awareness of a need to equalize the relationship between the United States and Japan and to create a partnership. Okinawa was an issue that had impressed Ambassador Reischauer when he first arrived in Japan in 1961. By 1966, when he left, a small group of policymakers in Washington had begun a concerted effort to make arrangements for Okinawa reversion before the fixed term of the Security Treaty expired in 1970. Thus the groundwork for reversion had been laid well in advance of the 1969 decision to negotiate a treaty, and the importance of U.S.-Japanese partnership had been impressed on those high-level policymakers who would have been in opposition to reversion if it had come to the surface suddenly as a crisis issue.

It can probably be said with confidence that this partnership image, the voice of reason and understanding, has really been the most important in shaping postwar relations between the United States and Japan, in spite of manifestations of the other two images in U.S. policy from time to time. The partnership image is certainly the attitude reflected through the years in annual presidential messages on relations with Japan. Even in recent presidential statements, for example, U.S. government policy is described as the promotion of a cooperative political interdependence, based on increasing economic interdependence within the context of the worldwide competitive system.

At this point it would be useful to describe more clearly the attitude we are calling the partnership image. Basically, it is predicated on the assumption that there are strong mutual interests between the two countries and that usually the leaders of the two countries share a common outlook. But it also recognizes the difficulties of overcoming cultural and other differences between the two countries to create a workable relationship. At the same time, tactical differences and domestic pressures are strong enough to sour the relationship, if measures are not taken to ease their effect. In other words, in the long term, the relationship is bound to be strong and friendly, if the inevitable short-term difficulties are handled with care.

John Emmerson has provided a good characterization of the long-term view.

In contrast to the American pain over China and our baffling crusade in Southeast Asia, the American postwar experience with Japan has been generally a happy one. The Occupation was a constructive effort and subsequent relations have developed a partnership which both nations have recognized as essential to security and stability in Pacific Asia. Turning from our frustrations in other parts of Asia, we see Japan as the hope for the future. This stable, economically powerful democracy is destined to become the leader of Asia, we say; and as we reduce our troops in Asia we contemplate the kind of stabilizing force the Japanese can be.[13]

The partnership image envisions an economically and politically strong Japan, participating independently in world affairs. While recognizing the importance of the security relationship, advocates of partnership are especially concerned about any manifestations in U.S. policy toward Japan that would indicate a U.S. desire to see Japan rearm or that would encourage any militaristic feeling in Japan. "I have always been against Japan's taking any larger military role than her present limited commitment to defense," says Reischauer. "I worry that in the coming period of crisis between the United States and Japan, a fundamental change in our relationship might lead Japan back to militarism."[14] There is also a fear of the tendency of the military to encourage and accept Japanese rearmament as inevitable. For Japan to be led down the road toward nuclear weapons would be folly. As Senator Fulbright rationalizes: "Japan is an American ally. With the enormous militarization of the United States, why would anyone need more arms?"[15]

These were basically the sentiments guiding those policymakers in the United States government who determined that Okinawa reversion would neither demand a substantial increase in Japanese forces for Asian security nor force nuclear weapons on the Japanese by insisting that the United States be allowed to keep them on Okinawa. In the Americans' search to find something to extract from the Japanese in return for reversion, both of these possibilities were considered and ruled out by the arguments of partnership advocates.

In its most refined form the partnership image advises that both American and Japanese leaders be more aware of the influence of domestic politics on the relationship and begin to compensate in their dealings with each other, with the hope that they might avoid placing themselves in intractable positions by responding too blindly to these domestic pressures. A sense of history and continuity is advocated for all official actions that are taken relevant to Japan. However, it is recognized, with frustration, that the public media on both sides tend to skew the significance of points of contrary interest in the relationship.

Advocates of the partnership image, while remaining confident in the basic stability of the relationship, find much to criticize in its conduct. In part, they blame the bureaucracy for not having the necessary sensitivity and flexibility to adapt to new situations. For example, Robert Barnett finds that, in an age when the United States is having to admit the limitations of its power in the world, "Much of the American bureaucracy—and the 'establishment' which buttresses it morally and intellectually—continues to operate on old assumptions of United States power and purpose."[16] Others have singled out individual elements of the bureaucracy: "our President, Mr. Henry Kissinger, and certain other people seem to have a much stronger sense that we are living in a balance of power world than I think to be the case."[17] But all of them recognize deficiencies on the part of the Japanese in their analysis of U.S. intentions.

Most who share this image of Japan agree that many of the shortcomings in the U.S. relationship with Japan are a matter of style rather than substance. "Perhaps even more important is the style in which they [U.S. government actions] are formulated and carried out. A style which suggests that we are insensitive to Japanese problems or oblivious to their feelings . . . can only convey to the Japanese the message that we are not prepared to treat them as equals."[18] And criticism of the 1972 presidential trip to Peking was likewise a matter of style: "All other things being equal, prior consultation with Tokyo was clearly called for before the President made his now famous announcement of July 15 [1971]. Not only would this have met the traditional diplomatic good manners, but it would have avoided awkwardness for a Japanese Government that was otherwise caught off-guard."[19]

Most of the advocates of a partnership are concerned with equalizing the relationship. They feel that the United States should not always expect to have its own interests prevail when they are contrary to those of the Japanese but should work out solutions that give equal weight to Japan's interests. However, there can be found those who envision a partnership in which Japan is the dominant partner. For example, Edwin Reischauer thinks "Japan truly will be the senior partner in our relationship in the future."[20] All of them would agree that signs of independence in the Japanese should be encouraged so that they would initiate a stronger foreign policy of their own, with less deference to the United States.

Inevitable Conflicts of Interests

There is probably no point in the postwar U.S.-Japanese relationship where it would not be possible to find some trace of lingering animosity and distrust toward Japan among American policymakers. In 1949, during the period when most were feeling very magnanimous toward Japan, Secretary of the Army Kenneth Royall caused a small storm when he was reported to have said that "We don't owe the Japanese anything, not even a moral obligation. We had the right—and the duty—to disarm them after the war, even though someone else may later cut their throats."[21] And a decade later Hanson Baldwin was editorializing that "the military chauvinism— never far beneath the surface in the Japanese—is still there, encouraged perhaps by a subconscious desire to get back at the conquerors."[22]

Many felt that the image, or the style, projected by the Nixon White House in its dealings with Japan betrayed a sense of inevitable conflict, if not economic then political. Observers were further disturbed by the fact that this approach represented the views of a minority, and the majority's plea for temperance went unheeded. The fear was that Japan could become so alienated by such rough treatment that it would take off down a road toward goals quite incompatible with U.S. interests. As William Bundy wrote in 1971:

What Americans must face up to is that their government's behavior toward Japan in the last year has created resentment and suspicion that will linger for a long while . . . A Japan alienated from the United States is not likely to rush into the arms of Peking.

Paradoxically, but about as surely as one can predict anything, the effect of such alienation would be to make Sino-Japanese rivalry naked and sharp. Then, unhappily, the U.S. would be back in the situation Professor Iriye has described, forced to choose sides between China and Japan—and headed for inevitable conflict.[23]

The Nixon White House seemed to believe that the Japanese must be shocked into action. U.S. actions appeared calculated to break Japan's psychological dependence on the United States and to make

Japan realize that, now that it had reached great power status, it could no longer expect favored treatment from the United States. The total effect of this style of relations was to imply that the alliance between the United States and Japan was not permanent and that Japan should stand on its own feet in a free-wheeling world dominated by several interacting powers.

During the Nixon years, many observers felt that the White House was dominated by a sense of power politics, in which the main actors on the international scene could only be the nuclear powers. Thus, despite lip service to the objective of a five-power world, Japan did not really fit in, being only an economic power. Both this policy objective and certain statements by Pentagon officials during the Nixon administration at times created the image that Japan was expected to become a nuclear power—that the acquisition of nuclear weapons by Japan was inevitable.

Despite a very vocal opposition, there were a number of constituencies from which the Nixon administration drew support and encouragement in its rough handling of Japan. First, a group of American leaders from all sections of the government felt burdened by the relationship with Japan. They sensed that Japan had been expecting too many concessions from the United States and that Japan relied too heavily on U.S. support in its dealings with other countries. What this group subscribed to was really a version of the "free ride" argument, because behind their frustration was a belief that Japan was taking the United States for a ride politically by refusing to take its own political initiatives internationally.

The second and most readily identifiable constituency for the inevitable conflict image emerges from time to time among U.S. business leaders and their government representatives. American business in general has been frustrated by the unique ability of the Japanese to manage the few advantages they have in the world market. American companies felt that trade relations were unfair because of severe restrictions in Japan on U.S. investment and imports. As mentioned earlier, some business leaders have developed the idea that Japan has been working overtime, at the expense of its population, to penetrate the American market. There have been further indications of the idea, among both industry and government leaders, that there is some mysterious relationship between Japanese industry and government that makes it possible to mobilize resources for a very precise economic assault on the world. Some sections of the Commerce and the Treasury departments, for example, are convinced that the Ministry of International Trade and Industry should be examined and emulated in order to discover the key to this phenomenon, when in fact MITI's influence on the development of Japanese exports was marginal at best, and at times a hindrance. (The Finance Ministry probably gave Japanese industry the more significant boost by subsidizing exports. MITI's influence was more indirect, through its control over patterns of import. Its control over the import of foreign technology, for example, gave advantages to Japanese heavy industry but restricted the input of foreign technology in the broad range of industries not designated for promotion.)

Obviously, all American business circles are not this simplistic in their image of Japan. But even the large, multinational corporations harbor a suspicion that the structure of the Japanese economy gives it special advantages. Furthermore, under the pressures of relatively serious economic decline, some American businesses have argued that the Japanese ought to show sympathy and return favors they received in the past.

There are roughly two subgroups among those subscribing to the "inevitable conflict" image of Japan. The first group believes that there is really nothing we can do to prevent or even forestall conflict with Japan—that Japan will only act in its own self-interest. Whatever measures we might devise to satisfy Japan would necessarily be contrary to our national interest. The other group, while agreeing that the long term will bring conflict, feels that short-term measures can at least forestall friction. Taking the partnership image in reverse, they see short-term partnership and long-term conflict. They would say that only the political arrangements the United States has made for Japan since World War II have kept Japan in line. The idea is that all the ingredients for a pre-World War II Japan are there; we must do what we can to forestall their development.

These feelings which began to surface in the United States in the late 1960s have been fed gradually by a series of futurist predictions about Japan and the Japanese economy. Herman Kahn presented images of a Japan that "almost inevitably will achieve giant economic, technological, and financial stature, that very likely . . . will become financially and politically powerful in international affairs, and that eventually . . . is likely to strive to become a military superpower as well."[24] While those making such predictions usually find no basic conflict for the United States in a strong and internationally responsible Japan, to those who cannot reconcile U.S. national interest with a strong Japan such predictions are frightening.

Some feel strongly that there is a racial tinge to the inevitable conflict image. "There is a real question whether Europeans and Americans are ready to accept the Japanese as full equals and meet them at least in part on their terms, rather than simply expecting them always to conform to a Western-dominated world community." And "One cannot blame the Japanese for wondering whether it [the Nixon Doctrine] means, that, for geographic or cultural, or possibly racial reasons, they fall into a different category from Europeans in American minds and should therefore not count on a shared defense relationship with us."[25] At least the image does imply a certain sense of condescension toward Japan by American leaders. But most critics of the inevitable conflict image agree that, whether the problem is one of racial discrimination or not, the style that has developed since 1971 in U.S.-Japanese relations does little to dispel such feelings.

Interplay Among the Images

If the partnership image—image 2—can be characterized as the attitude of interest groups with a deeply-rooted understanding of Japan, then both the inevitable harmony and inevitable conflict images—images 1 and 3—represent the attitudes of groups that have a more ephemeral and less educated interest in Japan. Those sharing image 2, while sharing the same basic national interests as those in the other two groups, are at the same time very sensitive to the interests that the Japanese must satisfy in their own country. They usually seek to modify U.S. policy toward Japan in a way that will meet the requirements of both sides. The attitudes of those who hold images 1 and 3, on the other hand, respond more readily to domestic or organizational interests in the United States.

It is relatively easy for a policymaker to make the transition from image 1 to image 3, depending on his perception of his own interests at the moment. For example, as long as U.S. business is benefiting from the Japanese market, the most convenient view of Japan would be inevitable harmony. As soon as Japanese industry begins to gain advantages over U.S. industry, the two countries are seen to be on a collision course. Similarly, it was not very difficult for military policymakers to make the transition from image 3 (wartime Japan) to image 1 (Occupation and Korean War). It befitted their own perception of national interests, as seen through the lens of military organizational interests, to accept that Japan was a loyal ally who would promote and support large U.S. bases in Asia.

The history of U.S.-Japanese postwar relations is very much a history of the interplay of images 1 and 3 against image 2. Until 1948 the military (image 1) was against an early peace treaty and did everything it could to keep the powers of SCAP intact and to keep the State Department (image 2) out of its business. A year after Kennan's trip to Japan in 1947 the National Security Council decided that SCAP would have to begin taking measures to prepare the Japanese for the termination of the Occupation by shifting responsibility as rapidly as possible to the Japanese. Gradually the arguments of those wanting an independent Japanese partner began to take hold, and Truman appointed Dulles to draw up an acceptable treaty.

Okinawa reversion, as we described earlier, was another example of the partnership advocates gradually winning out over a combination of those holding images 1 and 3. Pitted against early reversion were both those who thought the Japanese would acquiesce indefinitely in the U.S. occupation of Okinawa because their best interests were identical to those of the United States and those who felt inherent distrust for Japan. In the textile dispute, however, adherents of image 2 were never able to gain enough strength to overcome the arguments and interests of the image 3 group.

Thus, while we would agree to a point with those who say that "the American view of Japan seems to fluctuate between almost unconditional affection and unconditional antipathy,"[26] we would also contend that there is a strong middle group composed of officials and academics well versed in Japanese affairs who, in general, act as a regulating influence on U.S. policy toward Japan. The fluctuation between unconditional affection and unconditional antipathy, as it becomes reflected in policy decisions, usually occurs in periods when relations with Japan become a domestic issue in the United States and coalitions are formed within the policymaking elite to respond to severe domestic pressure. To a large extent, the outcome of decisions during periods of strain can be determined by the president's perception of the interests he must satisfy either to maintain his influence in the bureaucracy or to stay in office.

The Visual Panacea: Japanese-Americans in the City of Smog

This essay attempts to explore certain facets and types of images that were held by a cross-generational panel of Japanese-American leaders and communicators in the Los Angeles, California area as they appeared during intensive interviewing and reinterviewing in 1971 and 1972. Interpretations of the "true" intentions and actions of Japanese-Americans have spanned an unusually wide and imaginative gamut: from the observations made by Japanese liberal critic Ōya Sōichi of "Japanese immigrants with nineteenth century mentality living like museum pieces from feudal Japan,"[1] to the cries of American supporters of Japanese exclusion and the World War II evacuation of "Japanese, born to obey, obsessed with a determination to colonize California,"[2] to the more recent claim that Japanese-Americans are a model minority, that "the Japanese-Americans are better than any other group in our society . . . even in a country whose patron saint is the Horatio Alger hero, there is no parallel to this success story."[3] Dennis Ogawa, in his pamphlet *From Japs to Japanese: The Evolution of Japanese-American Stereotypes*,[4] has provided us with a critique of the history and possible functions of these perspectives in American society. My purpose here has been to attempt to filter through the cloudy mixture of competing views by asking Japanese-Americans themselves what images they have, how and why they might have changed, what possible sources exist, and what functions they might serve for them.

The Interview

Since this study is largely exploratory and primarily in search of fresh information and data from which some clues might be gained in answering my substantive question, I have chosen to rely on the interview approach. Sixteen open-ended questions were put to each panel member to insure some degree of uniformity in the inquiry, and responses to more specific questions dealing with clarification and enumeration of responses were also pursued. These sixteen questions, of which only the first eight and the sixteenth will be analyzed here, were devised to give the participants free rein with a minimum of interview direction. They were as follows:[5]

1. When you think of Japan, what comes to mind?

2. What are these impressions of Japan based on?

3. How long have you felt like this? or how long have you held these impressions?

4. How would your views and impressions of Japan differ from or be similar to those of your brothers and sisters; your husband or wife?

5. Your close friends?

6. Your parents?

7. Your grandparents?

8. And Americans in general? Would their views be similar or different from yours? In what ways?

9. What does it mean to be a Japanese in American society?

10. Why do you believe this is so?

11. How long have you felt like this? Or how long have you held these impressions?

12. Do you think your parents would share this view?

13. Your grandparents?

14. And Americans in general?

15. And how about your children? What does it mean or will it mean for them to be Japanese in American society?

16. Is there anything else that has crossed your mind concerning Japanese or American society?

The purpose of these questions was twofold: first, to glimpse the differences and similarities between the images the respondent might attribute to himself or herself vis-à-vis others as a result of possibly different or similar experiences, expectations, or information; and second, to understand the possible basis for and length of adherence to these images. In many instances the specific questions that were asked along with the broader ones served to bring out, often for the first time, thoughts rarely uttered or understood, experiences that had been forgotten, and observations of specific events that had been loosely connected to some grander theme. This form of probing provided invaluable clues to many hidden aspects of how our panelists view developments in Japan and its relations with the United States.

Interviews were conducted at either the home or office of the panel member and varied in length from two to five hours. Eighteen interviews were completed before President Nixon's announcement on August 15, 1971, of Phase I of his economic policy, while the remaining ten interviews and eight reinterviews were taken in late December 1971 and early January 1972. These interviews were hand-recorded with pencil and paper, and I have sought to reproduce them in considerable detail and length to give the reader a glimpse of the richness and complexity of the responses. All interviewees were promised complete anonymity.

The Panel: A Profile

Twenty-eight Japanese-Americans in the Los Angeles area, who hold positions of leadership in various key organizations in the Japanese community, graciously consented to assist me in this inquiry. I was acquainted with about a third of the members on the panel, and I had heard or read about most of the others. It should be stated that the panel does not represent a random or stratified sample in any methodological sense, and generalizations based on the data to all Japanese-Americans in Los Angeles or any other area in the United

States would be premature and unwarranted. My purpose has not been to obtain a cross-sectional representation of all Japanese-Americans but instead to seek out representative types of various generational and ideological leaders and communication actors in the Japanese-American community, who are often called upon to shape and voice the sentiments of the minority.[6]

The seven female and twenty-one male panel members were drawn from five different generational units in the Japanese-American community: three were Issei (first-generation Japanese who migrated to the United States prior to the 1924 Oriental Exclusion Act), ten Nisei (second-generation), two Kibei (second-generation Japanese-Americans who returned to Japan for their education), one "new-Issei" (a first-generation immigrant of the post-1945 period), and twelve Sansei (third-generation). With the possible exception of a few cases, the participants from all generations were products of lower-middle class, nonprofessional or agricultural families. All panel members had some college education and represented a variety of occupational pursuits: five were still students at local colleges, four occupied full-time positions in Japanese-American organizations, three were editors of Japanese ethnic newspapers, two were ministers (one Buddhist, the other Presbyterian), four were educators, two were dentists, and the others included a clothier, a textile importer, a social worker, a rice grower/restaurant proprietor, a realtor, a secretary, a pharmacist, and a retired insurance man. No panel member was related by family to any other member on the panel.

These twenty-eight individuals were members, and oftentimes leaders, of approximately seventy-five Japanese-American organizations and interest groups in the Los Angeles area. These organizations ranged from cultural ones such as the Southern California Kendo Federation (Japanese fencing) to religious groups such as the Young Buddhist Association of the Buddhist Churches of America; and from civic groups like the Japanese Chamber of Commerce and the Japanese-American Jaycees to activist organizations such as Asian-Americans for Peace. The panelists also represented organizations such as the Issei and Kibei Kenjinkai (prefectural organizations whose membership is drawn from immigrants of a particular *ken* or prefecture in Japan), the Nisei-founded Japanese-American Citizens League, the Sansei-oriented college fraternities and sororities, and groups of the Asian-American movement. Some also belonged to organizations with exclusively Japanese-American membership but affiliated with larger national and international associations such as the Japanese-American Republican Club, Southern California Japanese-American Dental Association, Veterans of Foreign Wars (Nisei Memorial Post #1961), Japanese-American Optimist Club, and the Japan-America Society. For the most part, there was very little overlap across generations for these organizational memberships with the possible exception of the Japanese-American Citizens League, which had members in all the generations. The panel also included several top elected and appointed officials of communities in and around Los Angeles, as well as a former mayor of one of the relocation camps established during World War II. Owing perhaps to their active involvement in community affairs, most panel members indicated that they came to "Little Tokyo" or to one of the other Japanese-American commercial and cultural centers in Los Angeles at least two or three times a week. Similarly, twenty-four panel members said that the majority of their friends were Japanese-Americans, while the remaining four stated that most of their friends were either Caucasian or Black Americans.

All Issei, Kibei, and "new-Issei" panel members have by definition lived in Japan at one time or another during their lives. Only the three Issei and one Kibei member have returned to Japan since deciding to reside permanently in the United States. In contrast, nine of the ten Nisei and four of the twelve Sansei have been to Japan, for a variety of reasons to be discussed later. In terms of religious preference, the panel members were divided into three groups with no glaring differences among generations: eleven were Christians, seven were Buddhists, and ten said they adhered to no specific religion. On the other hand, the majority of parents for all generations tended to be Buddhists. In terms of Japanese language proficiency and language spoken at home, all Issei, Kibei, and "new-Issei" panelists said they were able to read, speak, write, and understand Japanese; and two Issei and the sole "new-Issei" said they spoke only Japanese at home, while one Issei and both Kibei indicated that they spoke both Japanese and English at home. The majority of Nisei and Sansei participants indicated that they were able to speak and understand Japanese, but slightly less than a majority said they were proficient enough to read and write the language. Finally, the majority of Nisei said they spoke both Japanese and English at home, while the majority of Sansei said that they spoke only English.

The Interviewer

In the course of this inquiry, I have been influenced by and have drawn from two somewhat competing ways of looking at Japanese in America: that of a political scientist and that of a Sansei. These two outlooks are not easily reconcilable, or at times distinguishable, and yet there is always the temptation to emphasize one at the expense of the other. Paradoxical as this might seem, the possible implications are clear and can be stated quite succinctly.

As a Sansei who was born and raised in Los Angeles, I have been influenced by the Japanese-American community there and, to a certain extent, by the panel of leaders and communicators that was selected from it for this study. I would not deny the fact that I have probably been prompted to ask certain questions about Japanese-Americans, Japan, and the United States that only an insider might want to ask, could possibly ask, and perhaps should ask. I think because I am who I am, I might have received honest and candid responses from those whom I interviewed. My questions and some of my a priori assumptions about my own minority group are unavoidably linked to the fact that I share some common experiences with those whom I have tried to study. In this regard, it might be appropriate to note that I attended Japanese language and cultural school for approximately ten years during my boyhood and adolescent years. I am a Buddhist. My parents were evacuated during the war years. I visited Hiroshima, where my parents were raised and educated, when I was quite young and the city was still in ruins. Whether my personal characteristics and experiences in the Japanese-American community bring virtue or imponderable defects to this study is something the reader will have to decide. If normative or subjective judgments appear in this work, then they must be taken, at least to a certain extent, as consequences of being an insider, a fact that I cannot and would not want to deny.

At the same time, I might be seen by some as an outsider. Even though I did maintain contact with the Japanese-American community in Los Angeles, most of my activities prior to my college years were spent in East Los Angeles, the largest Mexican community outside of Mexico. Consequently, my closest friends are not Japanese-Americans but Chicanos. Furthermore, I spent my undergraduate years at Yale University, and now my graduate training at Harvard University, two environments quite different from the Japanese-American and Chicano communities. I am, in some respects, an outsider to two communities that have shaped many of my views on life in this society.

The other perspective that I have brought to this study is that of a political scientist. Political science, as a field of serious inquiry, has been able to provide little in terms of *direct* analysis of Japanese in America.[7] But what it tangentially suggests and what it can contribute to the voluminous body of works undertaken in the other disciplines in the social sciences and humanities seems quite promising and deserves greater future effort.

The Issei, Old and New

The Issei, both old and new, are the only panelists who can claim that Japan is the "land of my birth." For all other generations, Japan must be something else. In a general sense, the Issei represent the original or founding members of a "fragment" of Japan, which is "detached from the whole" of Japan and "hurled outward onto new soil."[8] Each fragment, to a certain extent, is imprinted with the distinctiveness of the departed Japan: in language, cultural mores, political values, and the reasons migrants might have or provide for leaving. The fragment, though, changes not only because it is merely a part lacking the whole which it has left, but also because the part is challenged by another whole. Each fragment that is spun from Japan is thus different from other fragments since it is a different part from an equally different whole. It also undergoes a different process of change since it is met by an equally different whole of America and, if it is not the first fragment, must also contend with equally different and changing past fragments.

Year one is important for the fragment, but so also is year two, five, or one hundred. How the original members of fragments view the whole of Japan that they left and perhaps have seen from afar is the theme of this section on old and new Issei. The other sections provide us with clues on how and what the original members transmit to succeeding generations within the fragment, as well as what views these succeeding generations have, given the changing nature of both the fragments and the whole.

The old and new Issei panelists represent different fragments of the evolving whole of Japan, the former migrating to America in the early part of the century and the latter after World War II. The three old Issei are all kenjinkai presidents, while the new Issei is a social worker in the Japanese-American community. All Issei leaders seem to share certain types of images: those which recall what Japan was like at the time of their departure; others which bear on having knowledge of what Americans and America might possibly offer for them that Japanese and Japan could not; some relating to where the Japan they left and have seen from afar stood in relation to other countries in the world; others on how Japan's progress is specifically related to their own experience in America; and finally those which deal with the distinctiveness of the Japanese people.

The images our old Issei panelists have of the Japan they left are intimately connected with both their actual or perceived position in a *ken* (or prefecture) and their specific reasons for coming to America. One Issei, who came to America in 1905, viewed the Japan he left in this manner:

I was born in Japan and left when I was twelve years old. My parents came to Hawaii when I was twelve because by the old custom of Japan, my father was put into an embarrassing position, and he signed a note and they took away everything. We came to Hawaii to get out of financial difficulties. I remember when I was five years old and my father was a share-cropper and didn't have any money or rice. One day he was taking rice to the landlord and as he was doing so I got a hold of his leg and told him he couldn't take the rice to someone else. I cried and cried. That's why we came to Hawaii.

On the other hand, the other two old Issei leaders, both of whom came to America in 1915, were at the opposite end of the social ladder and remembered a quite different Japan. Their Japan was one that was "beginning to change." They came to America not to escape financial difficulties but rather to see the reality of "Abe Lincoln and democracy." As one said:

The Japanese were in the old country mold, the feudal system. The eldest son succeeded the father and got the family property. Before I left the thoughts of the Japanese people were beginning to change. In 1912 and 1913 they introduced Ibsen's plays in Tokyo, and along with those came the introduction of other plays and literature from Europe. Then the principle of democracy was introduced and it awakened the rights of women and the people. But until this war (World War II) and until this emperor declared that he was a human being they thought he was a supreme being. And when I left Japan they still thought that way.

I always associated with Americans when I was in Japan and read so much about Abe Lincoln and democracy. I worshipped the American people and that is why I left all the family property to come here. I had servants and everything. I was from a very old family which was top grade in Kumamoto. We had a village background of eighteen hundred years.

Or, as our third Issei said:

When I was in high school, I fell in love with America. My father worked for a big silk factory, Matsui silk factory, and there was a manager there who always rode a horse. That was seventy years ago. He graduated from Keiō University and went to Germany and learned how to do things European style. I was so surprised when I first saw him. One day he told me, "Boy, if you go to Europe or America, you will live a good life." When I was a kid, I loved the American people . . . I remember when I went to commercial college. We had only American teachers. I looked at them and they were all well-dressed. We were hobos. That is why I wanted to come here. Entirely different way of living. My parents were against my going to America. They kept all my money. They said, "Why do you want to go?" If I stayed in the same town maybe I would have been the mayor like my father (who was mayor for eighteen years). But I didn't want that. Times are different. I wanted to come. Money is nothing. I am happy here.

Whereas our old Issei panelists have somewhat different views of the Japan they left, their images today of the Japan they have seen since being in America are much more similarly focused and include common elements and concerns. The overriding and the broadest image our old Issei leaders have of Japan evolves around a somewhat linear conception of Japan's progress from the time of its first contact with America and the Western powers to its present position in the world. This is essentially a favorable view in which Japan is seen as having acquired necessary political and social concepts as well as technological knowhow from the West, having learned an important lesson from its World War II expansionist venture, and having operated through some form of internal consensus or harmony that made all of this possible. Included within this broad image is the view that Western countries did not give Japan adequate credit or the opportunity to become one of the big, progressive powers (*senshin koku*). They feel that if Japan continues to progress as it has throughout its period of growth, it has the "possibility of growing much more than now." They also see a danger that Japan will depart from its twentieth century progress or national orientation if either the younger generation or the communists in Japan are not immediately steered in a more acceptable direction.

This somewhat linear conception of Japan's progress takes on two quite different meanings for the old Issei. On the one hand there is the idea that "what Japan has done in the course of its development I have also done in my own life"; on the other hand, "what Japan should really have done and what it is wisely doing now I have always done in my own life." Both contain an underlying student-teacher theme in which Japan, more so than the other progressive nations, had to learn and be taught; and the United States, the other progressive countries, and China had to instruct. Both views also see the Japanese as not "having a creative mind; they always copy but improve what they imitate and make it better." The two approaches differ, however, with respect to where the Issei places himself within this underlying relationship. In the first, the Issei is also a student, while in the second the Issei is also doing the teaching. The Issei who came to America to seek economic salvation provided the first meaning. As he said:

This is the first time that I have opened up about Japan and my own characteristic of adopting things that I like. From my young manhood and up to now I thought it was good that the Japanese were imitators and used it for themselves. I've done it myself. Japanese characters came from China; Buddhism came through China and they took it and made a better Buddhism than it was thought in China. They got Confucianism and taught it in Japanese schools. Karate is the same thing . . . Up to now, Japan wisely took the stand that it had to imitate others and it did well using that which was American or European . . . It is good for a backward country trying to come forth to imitate. But when you are imitating and you are at war, you have to do your own inventing.

The second was provided by the two Issei who left their wealth and possible high status in Japan for a different way of life in America. For them, the "future" has arrived. As one said:

The war was a big mistake. They didn't know anything about foreign countries. If they had known Americans here, they wouldn't have started the war. Forty or fifty years ago I went back to Japan for a short time and they had many mountains and hills. But they tried to do everything by hand. I told them, why don't you use machines? I used machinery here to make rice. Now they have beautiful highways and mountain tunnels. The Japanese people learned how to use machinery. America is the teacher and they now know what America is all about. Look at World War II. The head, Tōjō, never went to Europe or came here. Admiral Nomura came here and he didn't want war. The leaders must go to foreign countries. They have to go.

The old Issei vision of Japan's progress seems to be one that views progress not only as a good thing but also as being measurable only in terms of the standards established by other countries, most notably the *senshin koku*. Given their views on World War II, it may not be surprising that all Issei felt "Japan should still stay with the United States in politics and everything else." But they also felt that "now the Japanese must develop their own minds instead of imitating." As contradictory as this might seem, both are consistent with the view that progress is a good thing for Japan and with the Issei's own self-image that they are basically Japanese. They view themselves as something akin to fragments, to be sure, but by giving these two meanings to their image of Japan's progress, they seem to view themselves as being vicariously reunited with the evolving whole of Japan. Thus, the unique Japanese qualities and norms they see as eventually enabling Japan to turn the tables of imitation are almost identical to the ones they feel cannot be destroyed by the whole of America. As one Issei said, "If Japan keeps up some of its long-standing spirit, spirit which was instilled in them by the spirit of bushido, a sort of Spartan spirit of Greece, Japan has the possibility of growing much more than now . . . In order to develop their full capabilities and ambitions, they must be diligent and industrious, they must work under the spirit of bushido; no one gets anything without effort." Or as another put it in reference to being a Japanese in America: "If you have Japanese blood you are smart and you have the spirit of bushido. You always have it."

All the old Issei panelists also felt that Americans recognized that Japanese were "smart" and "industrious" people. Two went further and noted that "Americans say they [the Japanese] are too smart and the Americans have to worry about them." Along similar lines, one Issei said that "the Occupation army that went to Japan after the war found that the Japanese were civilized and better than any other people in Asia." Another, when asked what he thought most Americans saw in the label "Made in Japan," gave the following reply:

They think of cheap labor still, but not like before the war. Japanese products are much better made today. They are superior to products made in many other countries. Look at the cameras, color TVs, and Japan becoming the foremost shipbuilder in the world. But they know that Japan has been imitating all these things since they were so behind and had to do that. They accept them as imitations.

It is this tension, created from identification with Japan, on the one hand, and the uncertainty of how Americans view Japan, on the other, which contributes to the eventual recognition that a fragment is a fragment.

Our new Issei has many images of Japan similar to those of the old Issei. Owing, at least in part, to the differences in their ages (the old Issei were in their seventies and eighties, the new Issei in his forties) and the time of their departure from Japan, there are also variations and differences in their images. One of these differences stems from the self-images that the members of each fragment have in relation to the two wholes. For our new Issei, "Japan is becoming more and more a sentimental object for me. Once in a while my mind floats over there, but whatever I do now, I feel I am part of this soil and this country. At first I was like a small plant with little roots, and now I have a few more roots." There are also differences that flow from the way our new Issei sees himself in relation to the old Issei. As he said:

There is a Japanese-speaking community here which is closer to the Meiji era. This is my description. In Japan, they say, "Meiji is becoming further and further away." But when I came here I said it was becoming closer and closer to me. When they say that in Japan they mean that the good character of Meiji is getting farther away. But here you still find the bad elements of the Meiji era. The Issei are very clannish, and they brought over their feudal rivalries. They are based on feudal prefectures. That is why some Japanese congressmen said that the kenjinkai are the worst things and hurt their chances of being American. And people here didn't like to hear that.

Inasmuch as original members of fragments must contend with past fragments from Japan, the crucial question for our purposes is how the new fragment contends with the evolving whole of Japan.

To put it simply, the "future" has not arrived for our new Issei. He acknowledges Japan's progress but believes that Japan still must be taught by and learn from others. What he provides is an updated version of an old Issei theme: "What the Japanese should do now if they want to progress even more, I have tried to do since being in America." The emphasis now is placed on Japanese businessmen, tourists, and students who travel abroad, particularly to America, and then return to Japan where "they become experts on America; and the people believe them and are misled by them." This largely unfavorable view has many sides, all of which our new Issei sees as contributing to the noninvolvement or nonlearning attitude and behavior of Japanese who travel abroad. One contributing factor, he felt, was the stretch of Japanese-American communities along the Pacific coast that provided Japanese travelers and sojourners with the temptation "not to live an American way of life." Another evolved "around the difference between Americans and people from Britain" as compared to the Japanese:

When Americans go to Japan or anywhere else they try to experience the local customs. The British, on the other hand, were all over the world but kept their own customs, institutions, and other things. In many ways, Japanese are like the British. But in some ways they are not. They want to do things Americans do but don't know how. They still have customs from the feudal period like not expressing oneself too much.

A third factor, he believed, had its basis in preconceived attitudes toward the United States, which he felt were basically the images the Japanese people in general have developed over time about America:

Whoever comes from Japan, I can roughly divide into two groups. The first say, "Oh, everything is great." The second say, "Oh, I am disappointed." These two images are the same for all Japanese, who have had two images of America. The first was established by Dr. William Clark. He represented American freedom and democracy, the good images of the pioneer spirit and America's material prosperity. But at the same time, after the Meiji Restoration they got English textbooks in politics and economics and German military textbooks. And the British scientists talked about the bad taste of Americans. That is why many leaders followed the British. They came to talk negatively about America. Of course, this was not only in the

Meiji era. Some people come here too idealistic while others don't. I don't know which one is better for Japan. Very few people are objective observers. I remember a well-known scientist came here and I thought he couldn't do anything subjective. But when he was here he was as happy as a kid. He said that even Watts, a ghetto area, was beautiful. Even the journalists who come here. They should be objective. But unfortunately they are first Japanese and they don't change their images even if I present a different one.

All of these factors contribute to our new Issei's view that noninvolvement or nonlearning attitudes and behavior might defeat all purposes for traveling abroad: "I don't even know how some of them can conduct their business like that. I feel they are missing a lot of good things that are more important than trade." In contrast to the old Issei, he believed that the Japanese have not imitated or learned enough from other peoples. Instead they have remained fixed to their "own mind." Not surprisingly, it is the Japanese more so than others who must change: "The Japanese should try to think of and for an expanding world. We are all parts of the world community, which is something we couldn't say one hundred years ago. The world is becoming tightly knit, and people can now see Japan on the world map."

The Kibei

A Kibei, by definition, was born in America, returned to Japan for a considerable number of years, and later remigrated to the United States. In a general sense, the Kibei might be seen either as another fragment from the whole of Japan or as part of an old fragment that was reunited and later spun off from a changing whole. In both cases we are confronted with a set of questions that seemed unique for the Issei: What was the whole like when they spun off? How do they see the whole of Japan since being in America? And why are they fragments or fragments of fragments?

One Kibei panelist was born in Sacramento, another in Seattle. Both went with their parents to Japan during their adolescence and lived there during World War II. Both remigrated to America shortly thereafter. The significant characteristic that distinguishes our Kibei from the other panelists is the fact that they have lived approximately the same number of years in both Japan and America. This provided one Kibei with "the opportunity to look at Japan objectively and sympathize with them" and enabled the other "to feel closer to Japan than someone who hasn't lived there." This also led one Kibei to ponder: "Sometimes I think of my future as my children get older. Maybe my wife and I will be able to live—well, where will we be living? in America or Japan? . . . I can't see us moving back but we'll probably make more trips there."

The Kibei images of Japan tend to be more divided than those of the Issei. Like the Issei, they see "harmony" among the Japanese and certain traits and values that distinguish the Japanese from other people. But at the same time they are aware of the divisions, whether between urban and rural, traditional and modern, the "acceptable" and "not so acceptable" people, and the pro- and antinationalists. The Kibei also see Japan "after the war" somewhat as the Issei saw it, but their basis for comparison is not only their knowledge of the post- and prewar eras but also of the war period itself as they experienced it: where they were, what they were doing, what they saw then, and what they see now in those years. They also put a good deal of weight on this experience as a way of distinguishing themselves from other Japanese-Americans (and perhaps from all other people) and use this image of wartime Japan as one way of comparing America with Japan. As one Kibei said:

They came to the present age after being defeated by the power of materials. During the war, they said that for every two American soldiers only one Japanese was needed. That was proven wrong by the war. My wife comes from Japan and I think she has a common denominator with me. I have a half-brother here who was born and raised here, and I think his outlook is somewhat different than mine. It is both a difference in the outlook on life and the emphasis on the body or person. It is hard to understand and to make someone see what the difference is. A good example would be that I spent my formative years before the war in Japan and what the Meiji said we didn't question. It would be hard for someone to understand that if they didn't live it. It would be hard to grasp with your body and mind. Another example would be with Hitler's people and youth who seemed so loyal to Hitler, who was nuts. But to them it was the ultimate and they didn't question their loyalty to Hitler. In short, wartime Japan was frantic, but at that time in that whole atmosphere it seemed quite natural. It is this feeling you get from living there and not from reading. From being a part of that particular society.

And as our other Kibei said:

After the war—I left in 1954—even in Tokyo station there were a lot of ruins left from the war. I cannot picture the Japan I now see in newsreels. During the war everything was militaristic: clockwork and precision . . . I remember how my mother was treated during the war. Japanese people are different. I still can't help but look down at Japanese products and I don't have much faith in a lot of things I see in Japan. From the eighth grade, I was put in factories and in charge of small cannons; the finishing part. We also dug water holes to fight fires. And everything was primitive, even the cannon. In this huge factory the only machine that could make the cannon was an American-made lathe. And I think the Asian-American movement [predominantly Sansei in coalition with other Asian-American minorities] ties in with what the Japanese leaders were thinking, that is "Asia for Asians." My father went to China and he was part of a group trying to rebuild Asian countries. The purposes and goals were good but somehow that wasn't the way it worked out in the end. The problem was the government itself. I like this system in the United States when I compare the two.

The Kibei do not have a view of continuous progress for Japan, as do our old Issei. They acknowledge its achievements, to be sure, but they are also quite amazed that it has come this far in so short a period. Nor are they concerned about some correct or acceptable path succeeding generations in Japan should follow. Instead the dominant view they express centers around Japan composed of numerous divergent elements which, to a certain extent, are dialectically struggling with one another to create a semblance of harmony, but a harmony resulting from conflict rather than consensus. The wartime Japan our Kibei remember is far from dead and to them it occasionally shouts out to the world. As one Kibei said, "Look at Mishima. You can't say it [nationalism] is gone. It might be a minority, but it was amazing how young Japanese followed him to the end. Maybe there is only one out of a hundred or even one in a million. But I think in the future, no matter what, it will come back." At other times they see it reflected in Japan's phenomenal growth in the era of peace. One said: "I see the same seriousness and industriousness of the Japanese in war in the businessmen who come here from Japan. How they are totally involved in company work. They're always out. It is this willingness to do things: working ten hours a day. Of course, they are elites and maybe they are forced to do that."

The images based on their experiences in wartime Japan should not be unduly emphasized. The Kibei panelists also have images associated with prewar Japan and what they have seen and experienced in America since deciding to return. Both Kibei, like our new Issei, saw a Japan that was filled with many forms of prejudice—in terms of class, ethnicity, and social rank. But instead of directly relating this view to their harmony of conflict view of Japan, they relate it to their own experiences of returning to America. As one Kibei said:

When I arrived after the war, I was filled with apprehension. I was expecting the worst and having people call me a Jap. I didn't have much of that and before I knew it I was accepted in this society. I didn't think about it afterwards. I think this country is great. Now I am proud to be an American citizen in a country where aliens are tolerated. In Japan they look down on the Koreans and Chinese. When you compare that with the United States, the U.S. is much more open-minded and mature toward foreigners and aliens. Japan is a poor country when it comes to aliens. They are close-minded, intolerant, and sometimes inhuman. Japan needs a lot to learn. That lack of quality is stopping Japan from being the world leader. But this is the outstanding feature of this country.

And as another Kibei said:

After I came back, I was regarded as a foreigner, but I was treated like a human being with no harshness. Sometimes the Japanese will treat you as if you weren't there. But here the trust was there along with the kindness; and it wasn't a put-on. When you look at this country, there are all these racial problems and you might think that Japan is not the same. But there are many prejudices still there. I remember visiting one of my relatives in Niigata and they had several houses in the village. The Eta [a pariah or outcaste class in Japan] lived there and they were making baskets. I also remember Japan had many Koreans and they were part of the Japanese population, but they were looked down upon. At the same time, there is class prejudice from the "right" college idea to the Shitamachi [literally, bottom or lower town or village] in Tokyo where the lower-class people live.

One Kibei, like our Issei, also felt that "Japanese leaders do not look beyond their borders and are not sharing in the problems of Asia and the world." But the advice that our Kibei offer is also given to America. One said that "as a citizen of this country, one has the obligations of a citizen. You cannot possibly accept everything the government says, and you must be willing to criticize and oppose the government at times. One thing that Americans must be convinced about is that the materialistic way of life is not the only way but that there are other things in life." Or as the other Kibei said, "What the United States needs is more religion as compared to Japan where there is a lot. And in Japan, that means even going to an obutsudan [family shrine] even if you are a Christian."

Closely related to their prescriptions for Americans and Japanese are their images of how they think Americans view Japan. Somewhat like the Issei, they feel that "Americans are becoming more and more aware of the industrial capacity of Japan" and that "their outlook is changing from contempt to admiration of Japan's achievements." Perhaps due to the fact that the Kibei interviews were conducted before August 15, 1971, they also felt that "the American's outlook on Japan is changing, especially in the last five years with the exports she is sending over like Toshiba, Sony, and Toyota, whereas Europeans and others see Japan as threatening to their economies." At the same time, however, they felt "the ordinary American sees Japan as the country of myth, where lots of irrational things go on like students fighting politicians in broad daylight. It is the land of crazies. When Mishima committed hara-kiri, they thought that was typical of Japan. To the average American, Japan is the country of irrational, small people who are trying to compete with the giants. It is the land of cheap labor." Or as the other put it, "Americans see Japan as doing something she wasn't suppose to do without war, and they think she is just going for a ride." As we move to the Nisei and Sansei a much different emphasis in meaning and possible instrumental function becomes attached to how they feel America views Japan and how those attitudes, directly or tangentially, bear on them as Japanese in American society.

The Nisei

A Nisei cannot say that Japan is the "land of my birth." What he or she can say and what our Nisei panelists do say is that Japan is the "land of my ancestors" or the "land where my parents came from." Usually, when our Nisei utter either one of these two phrases, they open a treasure chest of personal memories that their parents related to them when they were young: how it was to live in a village community or to have participated in the Russo-Japanese War; what their parents' merchant status meant in Japan as opposed to distant relatives who were samurai; the serenity of Japan's natural landscape or the cultural arts and festivals of the nation; in short, what it was like to live in Meiji Japan. These phrases also bring back memories of the portrait of the emperor or of Mount Fuji which was displayed in the home, and what they felt their parents were trying to instill in or convey to them of Japanese customs, traditions, or cultural values. At the same time these phrases and the images that emerge from them also seem to lead to an important, common concern expressed by one Nisei in this way: "I see Japan as the land of my ancestors and, parenthetically, it is part of my ethnic or national identity that I have had to come to grips with somewhere along the way."

In viewing Japan as the "land of my ancestors," the Nisei rely on a combination of sources, some of which are derived from the fragment itself, others of which are not. These include not only what their parents wanted to transmit to them, but also the trips that nine out of the ten Nisei panelists have made to Japan as tourists or, in the case of three of them, two males and one female, with the United States Occupation forces. Also included are personal contacts with Japanese businessmen, artists, celebrities, government officials, tourists, and relatives who have come to America; what they see as distinctly Japanese in the Japanese-American community; and what they have read (in Japanese or English), seen, or heard about Japan via the media, their schooling in American public education and in Nihon gakuen (Japanese language school), movies, and other activities. At times, these different sources tend to reinforce each other and provide something more than just an image of Japan. As one Nisei described his trip to Japan in the 1930s:

My parents have a lot to do with my image of Japan. In my early years they told us historical incidents that took place in Japan and they made us appreciate the old Japan. When I went to Japan—the scenery, the old homes, the natural setting, and the Japanese gardens—they were all a reality now. It confirmed all that I had seen in books and heard from my parents. I could see these images emerging and I was sort of proud that I was Japanese because of the heritage I had. I now had an urge to learn the language, history, and culture. At least I have experienced that feeling of being Japanese. I found an identity. I knew I had an American cultural background, but I have more with Japan. My life is enriched that much more because of my parents' background. Americans, in many ways, made me feel that I was inferior, that my culture and I, myself, were backward and inferior. Now I thought differently.

At other times, these different sources tend to conflict or contradict each other and lead to a partial recognition that the Nisei are part of a fragment. As one Nisei said:

Earlier in my life, I received my impressions of Japan through my parents and school. A change has occurred over the years, but my general impressions have not changed that much. I think as we go along we are able to make more judgments on those basic impressions that we received earlier. After we acquire so much knowledge, we begin to draw our own conclusions and when we get feedback it either conforms or conflicts with both our earlier beliefs and the conclusions we have made. A good example would be that our parents came from a certain area of Japan where there might be a local custom that is not necessarily a custom of the whole country. More specifically, take the language. A lot of Nisei found out that Kagoshima or Hiroshima accent or dialect was not necessarily the same for the whole country.

It is, then, this collection of quite diverse sources, conflicting or reinforcing each other depending on time and circumstance, that forms the foundation of the Nisei's view of Japan.

The images they received from their parents are not entirely the same as the personal memories of what Japan was like at the time our old Issei left for America. It shows nothing of the impact of westernization on Japan but focuses more on the agrarian and village life that their parents experienced. It is a picture of farmers working in the rice paddies, samurai displaying the virtues of bushido, the Buddhist or Shinto temples, and the beauty of Japan's natural environment—in short, an "old, old," "traditional," and "positively Japanese" Japan that is not usually "projected to the world today" or that "few Americans really know, much less care about." Also included are the views that to be Japanese means "to be humble, courteous, patient, and having *enryo* (reserve)"; "to respect the conception of filial piety and to believe that the family is the cornerstone of Japanese life"; "to be quiet, reserved, and not aggressive"; "to have a feeling of superiority and not inferiority toward others"; "to have *shimaguni konjō* (island mentality)"; "to have all kinds of country-type superstitions about big monsters and things coming out from the water and eating you up"; "to be very intelligent, very handy with your hands, and to be skillful and creative"; "to have a love of nature"; "to be group-oriented and to have loyalty to more than self"; "to be paternalistic and fraternalistic"; and "to be religious." One descriptive term that was not uttered by our Nisei was "imitative." Some Nisei felt that what their parents were trying to communicate to them "made strong impressions on me throughout my life [and] I value these high principles of Japanese life," whereas others felt that "while we were growing up much of it was negated while we were trying to assimilate and be WASPish because we were more naive then and we thought that way." For those who fell into the latter category, most agreed with one Nisei who said: "In my formative years when I was deciding between whether I was Japanese or American, my parents always told me I was Japanese and I said American. I was in conflict. But now I think I am both." Most Nisei also felt that even today their parents and, to a large extent, the Issei generation as a whole still "carry the Meiji image of Japan in their minds" and "represent what is truly Japanese." They also felt that the Issei "take great pride in Japan's achievements since the war."

Our Nisei have other images of Japan that are not necessarily the product of their Issei upbringing. In the case of nine out of the ten, it is an image of Japan based on travel to the country, which provided at least one of them with the feeling that she was "closer to Japan than most Nisei." The one Nisei who had not been to Japan felt that "my image of Japan would differ from that of those who have visited it. My Japan is a fairyland Japan." One Nisei who went to Japan during the Occupation recalled:

When we were in Hokkaido and we used to go with the *hakujins* (Caucasians) and give chocolate to the children, it angered me when they thanked the *hakujins* and not me. It angered me to think that I should give chocolate to them simply because I was Japanese and not be thanked by them; this was thirty years ago. I have since grown up and matured and can see their impression. I am sure I wouldn't get that feeling if I went to Japan today.

Another Nisei, who went to Japan on a tour, said:

I've never seen any place as crowded as Tokyo. It was like a parade on Sundays. I thought it was amazing. The people I met were courteous. The only group that was rough was the taxi drivers. The amazing thing is that they don't have any dented fenders. The nightclubs were pretty rough as far as the money goes. They've got the b-girl thing worked out to an art. It is the best in the world, but it will probably hurt Japan in the long run. The amazing thing is that they do that to *kaisha* (company) people, too. I also went down to Kunigawa and I was impressed by how nature can twist the trees. Before I used to think of bonsai as distorted plants. But it was a duplication of nature. I'd like to see Japan capitalize on tourism. I think the government can do something about the sanitation. I found it hard to sit on that toilet [on the floor]. That's one of the things people worry about when they go on tours. That's something that Japanese can do and not me.

The Nisei leaders who visited Japan seemed to have acquired more than new knowledge about the country. The trip convinced many of them that the fragment of Japan their parents reflected and communicated to them still exists in modern Japan. For the Nisei, like our Kibei, Japan has at least two sides: the modern, postwar Japan of the urban areas, and the more "typical and traditional" Japan of the prewar era in the rural regions. At times, when this image of Japan's duality is placed against other possible sources of images, such as Japanese businessmen who come to America, another facet of the relationship between the fragment and the evolving whole of Japan is revealed. One Nisei made a sharp and insightful comment on this point:

I have some negative impressions of the Japanese when I think of the Japanese businessmen. This involves the older Nisei resentment toward them: it is something that is not spoken out. Basically, they have a condescending attitude toward Japanese-Americans. They are very class-conscious, and I feel that I in America and all Nisei are sons of immigrants and there is an unspoken word about the whole thing: their manners betray their real thoughts toward the Nisei and Sansei. These may be the shortcomings of the Japanese businessmen. When we talk culture you really have two areas to consider: one is prewar, and the other is postwar. I think the culture of the age groups is different. The young businessmen are disciplined but I think they have lost the culture and customs that we Nisei expect from them. We have received the customs of the prewar Issei, our parents. Our Issei parents left Japan forty or fifty years ago. These were the habits, customs, and lifestyles that they had known. In postwar Japan the really beautiful Japanese customs have become Americanized; even the language.

(In a later interview, however, this Nisei leader felt that the "older Nisei resentment" toward Japanese businessmen was due to a "lack of communication on the part of both parties more than anything else.")

Another revealing aspect of the relationship between the Nisei and the evolving whole of Japan centers around the set of impressions that come from increasing familiarity with Japanese products in American life: cars, radios, motorcycles, and TVs. One Nisei felt that these products had had a positive spillover effect for Japanese-Americans:

You don't even have to be Japanese to know about the impact of Japanese products—Suzuki, Sony, and so on. They are all household names. To my youngsters, who are eight, nine, ten, and twelve, Kawasaki and Suzuki are common names. They are not Japanese. It is part of their daily conversation. I think it is a very good thing and has a bearing on Japanese-Americans. To go back slightly, with the freer economic exchange, when they become household names they are no longer foreign but become part of our culture. Typhoon and other words used to be Japanese words but are accepted as English. Most of the economic products, when they become household names have an effect on the discrimination toward Japanese-Americans. When foreign-sounding names become household names, we are less fearful of the unknown. When these products become familiar, it has a great bearing on us as Americans.

Another Nisei, who was interviewed before August 15, 1971, foresaw a negative spillover effect.

For instance, look at this thing on the Vega,[9] and the whole trade thing. Everything was nice before but not any more. People are losing jobs. They talk about imports but not about the Volkswagens. Instead they talk about Datsuns and Toyotas. The motorcycle industry isn't that big, though, and was never really advanced. My guess is that the local American motorcycle industry sells more motorcycles. They are not hurting. The same thing is true with importing toys. It affects me in the sense that the Vega thing affects me and it is taking place in Los Angeles with the Buy America thing. As you look at the relationship between the United States and Japan changing from prewar to postwar, the attitudes toward Japanese change. Many writers when they look at us don't see any difference between us and the *kaisha* people. Many writers don't make this distinction. Their attitudes are affected by the times. If they are favorable toward Japan, then they are favorable toward us. If not, then it is the other way.

Some of our Nisei leaders also felt that the quality of Japanese products contributed to a feeling of pride. As one said:

My images of Japan have changed over the years in the sense that Japan in my early years was a more backward country. That everything made in Japan was cheap. But this has been completely changed with the electronic things like the television. They are superior to any in the world. The same with the transportation system in Japan. I have a great respect for the progressiveness of the Japanese people. The backwardness and inferiority have been eradicated from my mind. I take great pride in the things that are made in Japan. They give me a good feeling of pride.

These three short passages revealing the different meanings that our Nisei attach to Japanese products seem to have been glimpses of grander themes they foresaw in the interaction between themselves and the wholes of America and Japan. On the one hand, there was an idea shared by at least half the Nisei and expressed by one Nisei in the following manner: "We, as Nisei, can contribute Japanese culture, history, and ideas to America. We can make this contribution and more and more Nisei believe in this crusade." One Nisei translated this into a possible instrumental function for her image:

I am very proud that I am Japanese and I do feel that Japanese have a rich heritage. I feel proud that I can introduce this heritage to other people. As for myself, every year for Christmas I make my own cards and use a Japanese theme. In 1972 it was the "year of the rat" and so I used that as my theme. I have been doing this for some time now. I try to do as much as possible to introduce Japan to my friends, to show them how the Japanese people feel and the things they do. I feel that if they can profit by these things, I have done a little in helping the understanding between the two countries. I think by learning the cultural backgrounds of people we can become closer. Surely the world is becoming closer every day. I think we can work toward mutual understanding.

On the other hand, there was a theme expressed by the other half of our Nisei that recalled World War II and the evacuation. As one said: "The relationship between Japan and America definitely affects us. The living example is the evacuation. When things are going too well for Japan, racism toward Japanese-Americans is bad here." Or, as another said:

We are what other people say we are. Being visible Asians in America, we are not only representatives of ourselves but of Japan. We have to come to grips with it. We are caught in it. And we should recognize it and work it through. Years ago, I would have said that we should cut ourselves off and that physical similarities are not important. But now I realize that our destiny is tied with Japan, which comes from the Black struggle and how they are coming to grips with African culture and how they are trying to build one up.

Many Nisei leaders, thus, felt that, either through their own volition or the imposition of "what other people say we are," when "*hakujins* think of Japan they think of the Nisei," and "if Americans don't know the Nisei, they are naive and ignorant of Japan." Some of our Nisei also felt that "American views have changed over the years in that very few threatening or negative things have come out from Japan, but instead it is from China, [even though] there might be some connection between China and Japan in their minds"; others said that "most Americans see Japan and the Nisei in terms of the 'gook' thing carried over from the war"; while still others felt that "most servicemen who went to Japan during the Occupation would like to go back. I think they consider it the best place among the Asian nations."

Nisei views on whether Japanese or Americans should change their attitudes or behavior toward each other and the world parallel those of the Kibei. On the one hand, they believe that Japanese must change their ways. One Nisei said that "if the Japanese were better organized they wouldn't be short changed and exploited," while another said that "Japanese people as a whole think the white man is superior, and this shouldn't be the case." Some Nisei also "hoped that Japan will lend a hand to other countries in Asia in the future." On the other hand, many Nisei leaders felt that Americans should be learning from the Japanese: "If we want to preserve American business life, we must now pattern ourselves after the Japanese and reevaluate the rest of the world if we are to survive. We have been sitting back in our chairs and we are finding out that we are not that great, technologically and in other ways. The U.S. must know what other parts of the world are doing." Also, unlike the Issei, our Nisei felt America should remain aligned with Japan: "Japan is still a friend of the United States, and I think the U.S. would make a serious mistake if she should abandon Japan."

The Sansei

Japan, for our Sansei, is not only the "land of my ancestors" but also the "land of my grandparents" as well as "just another foreign country." One Sansei said he had a "strong psychological attachment to Japan like when I wore a meatball on December 7," while another claimed, "I don't have any closeness to Japan. I only have an intellectual and superficial attitude toward it, but no gut or emotional feeling. My real ties are to the Blacks, Chicanos, and Asians here." As we might expect, the Sansei panelists rely on an assortment of sources for their images, some which come from the fragment itself and others which do not. Many of these sources—such as American public and Nihon gakuen schooling, the media, relatives from Japan, movies, the Issei generation, Japanese businessmen, and the trips that four out of the twelve have made to Japan (two on academic fellowships, one to receive his Buddhist ministerial training, and another to participate in international kendo tournaments)—are similar to those of our Nisei. But the Sansei represent another part of the changing fragment and give or take quite different messages or meanings from many of these shared sources. Indeed, the Nisei as well as the Kibei become sources in themselves for Sansei images; and the fact that the Issei are an additional generation removed from them often places the issue of mutual communication in a new light. As one Sansei said: "My grandmother has only spoken Japanese. There hasn't been that much direct communication between us (because I don't speak Japanese), but there has been a feeling."

With the passage of time the fragment changes and becomes complex not only in itself but also in relation to the evolving wholes; and the creation of yet another generational unit which, in many respects, is different and considers itself to be different is a reflection of this process. This can be seen partly in the family backgrounds of our panelists who consider themselves to be Sansei. Some have Nisei parents "who were trying to get away from being Japanese and didn't pressure us into meeting other Japanese or going to Japanese [language] schools," and others have Nisei parents "who really believe in the idea of *Yamato-damashii* [Japanese spirit] and identify greatly with Japan." Some have Kibei parents, of whom one Sansei sorority officer said, "I sincerely think they have their hearts over there in Japan," while another felt that "my mother would like to go back, but my father wouldn't. He has emotionally cut himself off even though he retains Japanese culture." There is also one Sansei whose father belonged to the 442nd Regimental Unit, and whose mother is Italian; another whose father is Issei, "who snuck in through Mexico during the Gentlemen's Agreement," and whose mother is Kibei; and finally, one whose mother is Nisei, but whose father is Sansei. Most have also known their grandparents, whom one Sansei described as "my only reminders that I was Japanese or originally from Japan." Another felt that "my grandmother is very nationalistic. She is not an educated woman but she reads a lot. I asked her what she thought of the Vietnam War and she was anti-American and understood what it was all about." There was also one Sansei who said that his grandmother died in the Hiroshima holocaust. It is not surprising that the internal generational pathways and the external sources our Sansei rely on for their images provide information that is not confined solely to postwar Japan. Invariably, their images of Japan, like those of our Kibei and Nisei, tend to be divided. But the manner in which our Sansei paint these many sides of Japan, the meanings which they give and take from them, and indeed where they perceive themselves in relation to them are not the same as with our other generations.

Our Sansei, like our other generations, draw a distinction between what they believe Japan and the Japanese people once were or, in some respects, might still be and the progressive, westernized Japan of the postwar era. The Sansei image of this latter Japan, which they see as the image Japan projects to the world as a "business giant," includes the following views: it "borders on decadence: the people in the cities, the girls, and many of the actors who are trying to imitate the *hakujins*, especially girls with the blond hair, getting their eyes, noses, and breasts fixed and altered; and all those ads with Japanese girls clutching onto white guys"; "has a lot of avid businessmen who are quite gifted, but who are devoted to convenience and progress: two values that Buddhists do not share"; "has a student movement that turns me off with the same type of arrogance that you find with the white New Left here because they are in the majority and think and act like majority people do here"; "has a much too competitive social system where life is now a continual rat race"; "has a rigid class hierarchy that has replaced the old caste system"; and "has destroyed much of its beautiful natural scenery with highways, skyscrapers, and all the pollution from the industries." The vast majority of our Sansei also feel that *this* Japan is

"no different than what you would find here [in the United States]"
and "the one I do not think of when I view Japan and the Japanese
people." But most Sansei leaders believe that their parents and grandparents take a personal pride in this projected image of Japan's
progress and achievements in the postwar era.

All the Sansei panelists at the very most acknowledge the nation's
economic success but none vicariously participate in or identify with
its progress as do our other generations. Nor do they gain a feeling
of pride or even "superiority" from its achievements. Unlike the
other generations, many of our Sansei who are leaders in the Asian-
American movement offer strong radical perspectives on Japan's
role in Asia and the world. Japan to them is "the major U.S. puppet
in Asia" and its "nationalism of the war years has turned into the
rising militarism of today." They also feel that Japan, as a "business
giant" and "an imperialistic country with capitalistic ties to the
United States," "oppresses the Okinawan people from their rightful
claim for self-determinism," "exploits and oppresses the Southeast
Asian peoples," and "with the 10 percent surcharge on imported
products here [in the U.S.] will have to increase its trade and business
elsewhere and build a military to protect its interests." For the most
part, these are recent images and most said they had been developed
in the course of their participation in the Asian-American movement. Some said they "have mixed feelings about thinking of Japan
as an imperialistic country," while others simply stated, "I have a
lot of negative feelings about Japan's politics." Many also said that
they "have read and heard enough to be convinced that this is what
Japan is actually doing," while others confessed that "it is rhetoric
on my part because I haven't done any solid reading."

Our Sansei have other images of present-day Japan that are not
necessarily associated with their views of the modern, westernized
Japan. One such image involves the Japanese travelers and sojourners
who have come to America. Somewhat like one of our Nisei, the
majority of our Sansei felt that these visitors "look at us and treat us
like dirt," "don't think of us as Japanese but instead as Americans,"
and "could care less if they met us or not." Many of our Sansei
remembered that they "had fights with" or "were made fun of" and
"felt embarrassed by" newly-arrived immigrants and their children
or other Japanese from Japan when they were younger. Some said

they did so because "everyone else did it without really knowing why," while others said that "it was because our sense of inferiority was coming out." One Sansei who has been to Japan offered this observation, which comes closest to recognizing that the Sansei are indeed members of a fragment: "I think we can go a lot further if we said we weren't Japanese. I don't think we have admitted to ourselves that we aren't Japanese. It is evident that we don't like to meet people from Japan." But whether or not our Sansei are cognizant of their fragment status, they implicitly view themselves as such when they, like the other generations, draw distinctions between themselves and Japanese they have met from Japan. The list of "more or less" adjectives they use for this purpose runs the gamut from "reserved and restrained," "naive, straight, and disciplined," "unemotional," and "gracious and polite" to "happier," "aggressive," "outspoken," "feeling that they are superior," and "too westernized, but comically so." It might not be too surprising that when our Sansei make a distinction between themselves and the other generations, they utilize a similar "more or less" scale containing many of the same adjectives.

Our Sansei, like our Kibei and new Issei, have a set of images relating to the discriminatory practices toward minorities in present-day Japan. Unlike the other two generations, however, most Sansei panelists saw no difference in how minorities were treated in either country. As one said, "It is all based on the arrogance of being in the majority, which I align with the white people here and the way they treat minorities." At the same time, Sansei views are based on what they have seen or read and the "socialization I went through when I was little." As one Sansei put it:

My first exposure to these practices took place when I was thirteen and had Okinawan friends. My mother said that they were different and weren't really Japanese . . . I think the provincialism of the Japanese, the whole nationalism idea of thinking of themselves as a distinct race and really feeling that to be Japanese is to be the best causes this cultural and ethnic chauvinism among the Japanese. When I was in college I did a major investigation of Japanese society and I did a lot of reading on their attitudes and practices toward the Koreans, Okinawans, and Ainu. It is something that you have to investigate because it is something that Japanese don't talk about. But I guess my real knowledge of such practices and my truly negative feelings about them are not based on my reading but rather through understanding my parents' attitudes, those of my relatives, friends, and those who are familiar with Japan . . . My parents—and this is the main point—feel that a certain amount of discrimination is justified. My parents accept the fact that we are all equal, but they also believe that we must maintain a certain social distance from each other. It all symbolized the attitude that they (the Koreans, Okinawans, and so forth) are not all "Japanese" and therefore not that good.

Indeed, a good proportion of their negative views toward Japan revolves around "the idea of the Japanese being superior and being a distinct race [which] was drummed into me ever since I was small." Whereas the panelists of other generations, especially the old Issei and many Nisei, either accept the validity of this idea or are able to link it with Japan's progress, its exported goods, its unique cultural attributes, or their own personal identity, our Sensei do not. The words "nationalism," "superiority," and, to a certain extent, "distinctiveness" all seem to be associated with the Sansei views of the discrimination they see in Japan, with the experiences they have had at the hands of Japanese who have come to America, and in several respects with Japan's international posture. They differ from our new Issei and Kibei, who share their views on discrimination in Japan, in that most received their impressions from the fragment itself rather than from what they have seen in Japan, and most feel that larger wholes or majorities, be they in Japan or America, basically treat their minorities in a similar fashion.

The broadest picture our Sansei paint is one of Japan evolving into another America. Both wholes, in turn, are viewed negatively, as rather akin to Scylla and Charybdis. But instead of stopping here, our Sansei turn inward to the fragment and retrace its roots. Invariably, the Japan our Sansei relate to or view "when I think of Japan" is the rural, nonwesternized, and "real" Japan. Some see this Japan in samurai movies, others in what their grandparents communicated to them, and still others in what they have observed in the Issei generation. One described samurai movies in this manner.

I split Japan historically in terms of the contemporary class system and the old caste system. I relate to Japan in terms of its history. I look at rural and urban Japan and I can't relate to the urban. The rural Japan turns me on with its serenity . . . The influence of America is everywhere in the cities, and you find a lot of Japanese actors trying to be Humphrey Bogarts.

I relate to Toshio Mifune and the samurai because those were Japanese and they had an identity. The new ones are like James Bond . . . I would rather see a Japanese movie than an American one. To really see yourself as a person, as a human being—to love, care, and be brave. When I see samurai movies I see a characterization that is really human. We've never been depicted as such here. We are never seen as human beings.

For other Sansei, this Japan is reflected in their grandparents. As one said, "My real Japan comes from my grandparents and relatives and not from reading about it. When I was young my grandmother always celebrated Boy's Day—the dolls, flying kites, and the food. That's what I remember. [My grandparents] definitely feel that this is not their home country and definitely feel that Japan is . . . Their traditions, their manners, the way they act, and their moral values are Japanese." Still others saw it in the Issei generation. As one Sansei said: "I look through the Issei to see Japan. They speak the language, know the customs, foods, and rites. The Japan they are telling me about goes back to the pictures they show me." As similar as this might seem to the sources of our Nisei views, they differ in at least two respects: the sources .seem to provide and are given different meanings as they become filtered through the Sansei experience, and more important, the long-range aims of the two visions do not seem to be the same. Whereas many Nisei felt they could "contribute Japanese culture, history, and ideas to America," none of our Sansei expressed a desire for a similar crusade. Instead, the selection of this particular image of Japan is linked with the immediate goal of seeking a group identity (somewhat like our Nisei) that is defined on their terms, and a long-range vision of "building a culture and lifestyle that brings together the best of Japanese and American culture for ourselves and our children."

The Sansei preference for this Japan as opposed to its other aspects cannot be understood solely as an automatic, triggering "Hansen effect" of third-generation romanticism for the old country.[10] Some Sansei simply "like the old Japan, especially the countryside, because I have lived in the city all my life," while others prefer it "because it is the only one my parents and grandparents have told me about." But there are additional reasons. One Sansei kendo champion offered this observation:

The things that stood out in my mind when I went to Sacramento and Sutter's Fort were the historical artifacts and other things that were donated by the Native Sons and Daughters of the Golden West. I had a hard time relating to those things as a Japanese-American, especially after being at Tule Lake during the war. But when I went to Japan, I visited the shrines and temples and I could relate to those things. That's where my ancestors came from.

For many Sansei panelists, however, the preference for the old Japan centers around a collage of images they have of American society, of the other generations, and of United States-Japanese relations. Somewhat like our Nisei, but with a different emphasis, many Sansei felt that "Americans tend to think of Japanese-Americans as Japanese, which means that you could have come over yesterday for all they know or care." Or as one put it, "If you have a camera and go to Disneyland, they'll think you're a tourist. I don't think they look at us as Americans but instead as Japanese." Many Sansei also felt that "there is a great deal of anxiety among Japanese-Americans over Japan-America relations," or that "the economic thing should be interesting because if it goes too far then we're in trouble. I don't know to what degree, but it is consistent throughout our history: the image of Japanese-Americans depreciates and we become the objects of hostilities." The majority of our Sansei also believed that Americans have two fluctuating but distinct images of Japan: one that viewed it as "quaint, cute, and exotic" and another as being "threatening, dangerous, and competitive." In connection with these views, many Sansei spoke of meeting Japanophiles who "are really patronizing toward us," "expect us to know Japanese fluently," and "don't understand that we don't celebrate the emperor's birthday," and of meeting other Americans who "told me she didn't like Japanese because of Pearl Harbor," "called me a damn Jap," or "made me feel defensive and apologetic about what Japan is doing." Some Sansei, unlike any of the other generations, also felt that the Occupation had had some negative spillover effects for them as Japanese-Americans. One said, "The Blacks and Chicanos that went there with the service met the same kind of discrimination that they faced here except it was by Japanese," while a female Sansei provided this view:

I think there is an image of Japanese women: that whole catering to the man thing that affects me when I'm walking down the street and having white and Third World men make a lot of comments to me—racist comments—that's their image. I think those images are based on war experiences, especially the Occupation, and they think that we are the same here and look at us as the same and wanting us to sleep with them . . . It infuriates me in that they are not looking at me as a person but just as an object, an easy lay.

Our Sansei may prefer the old Japan, but they do not necessarily accept all its dimensions. Even though the majority of them felt that "the bond is stronger between the Issei and Sansei than it is between Nisei and Sansei," many of them said that "to relate to the Issei means to accept their chauvinism in terms of male and female roles," "to be prejudiced toward other minorities in a very extreme way," and "to accept a lot of the traditional values of Japan that I can't approve of." Or as another Sansei put it: "You can emulate and look back at the samurai background, the bushido idea, the readiness of cause, and so forth, but if you do so uncritically, then you are identifying with a class that cut down commoners. Indeed, if you relate to Japan, which Japan do you relate to?"

We have had a glimpse of how a panel of Japanese-American leaders and communicators in Los Angeles view various aspects and dimensions of the evolving whole of Japan from a number of windows within a changing fragment of that whole. We have seen the "future" that has arrived for our old Issei as well as the one that has not for our new Issei. We have glimpsed the Kibei vision of a multifaceted Japan in war and conflict, the Nisei crusade to bridge the gap of cultural understanding between the United States and Japan, and the Sansei view of Scylla and Charybdis. We have seen that our panelists are aware of the changing nature of the whole that is Japan even though they might not relate to the entire whole or to its changes. We have also seen the impact that Japan has had, does have, and may have on the lives of our panelists: from its exported goods, businessmen, samurai movies, and tourists to its relations with other countries and the United States. Contrasting these and other images from our inquiry with those of the other essays in this volume should provide us with clues as to whether or not they approximate those of other Japanese and Americans. Their images will also suggest additional topics for future inquiries and policy considerations.

One such topic deals with semantics. We have seen that our

panelists use a variety of words and phrases to describe the Japanese in Japan: their cultural attributes, behavioral patterns, and world views. Some of these words are cast in "more or less" statements and reflect the distinctions different generations within the fragment make between themselves and the evolving whole. Other words and phrases provide us with some insights into what our panelists consider to be distinctly Japanese characteristics and qualities. But if we closely examine their views, we will find that a number of somewhat disquieting or derogatory words such as "sly," "treacherous," "warlike," or "spiteful" have not been uttered. Indeed, we find that when similar adjectives such as "irrational," "dangerous," and "threatening" are used to describe the Japanese, they usually describe how our panelists feel Americans view Japan. What explanations might we offer for this? Do members of a fragment necessarily "know better" than to use such words in describing the whole? Are they consciously or unconsciously attempting to protect or perhaps to warn the whole? Are they attempting to preserve their own linkage with the whole? Or are they merely projecting their own views onto another whole? In addition to any explanations we might offer are the implications we might draw from them. What, in essence, does this tell us about being a Japanese in America? And what does this tell us about how Japanese-Americans view themselves in relation to the two wholes? The exceptions to this pattern are primarily our Sansei, who also use words such as "decadence," "arrogance," and "oppression" to describe modern Japan. What explanations might we offer for them? Does it follow from their negative views of both wholes, or does it reflect their movement inward within the fragment? Generally in the case of our panelists there seems to be a correlation between the views they attribute to Americans and the way they view themselves in relation to America and Japan. Our old Issei, for example, said Americans recognize that Japanese are smart, industrious, and imitative, an impression that would seem to reflect their view of themselves in relation to Japan's progress and the distinct Japanese characteristics they feel cannot be eradicated by America. The same might be said, in some respects, for our Nisei and Sansei, who view themselves as being entrapped in Japan-America relations.

Another topic deals with the question of boundaries. We have seen that our panelists refer to "old Nisei resentment" of Japanese businessmen and the "stronger bond" between Issei and Sansei. Cognitive boundaries such as these might be uncovered through an analysis of words and phrases. But to draw out some of the behavioral aspects that might be explored in future empirical works, an operational definition of boundaries is needed. Karl Deutsch defines boundaries as "marked discontinuities in the frequency of transactions and marked discontinuities in the frequency of responses—particularly, therefore, discontinuities in the degree of covariance." [11] If this definition were applied to the views solicited from our panelists (without regard to other factors), we might be inclined to say that there is an uneven or differential boundary between various generations of the fragment and the whole of Japan. To put it differently, there does seem to be a boundary between the fragment and Japan, but each generation places different numbers and types of shields between itself and the whole. In a general sense, this would suggest that if an old Issei were to "scratch" when Japan was "itching," he would probably do so before our new Issei, who in turn would do so before our Kibei, and in like fashion to our Nisei and Sansei. If we considered specific aspects of the boundary, we might find different response pattern sequences: our Kibei might respond before other generations when events such as Mishima's *seppuku* occur, while our Nisei might respond before others when a cultural awareness project is launched by Japan. In a similar manner, other boundary areas might be explored between the fragment and the United States, and within the fragment itself—historical situations such as the evacuation, mutual boundary situations between the fragment and the two wholes, and actual behavior patterns.

Some Concluding Remarks: The Turning Mirrors

We have mainly succeeded here in identifying questions that need more asking, more work that waits to be done. We have used "image" here to refer to stereotypes, perceptions, attitudes, opinions, propaganda creations, even policy orientations. This is perhaps as it has to be: we probably need a loose and ambiguous term to deal with such an inescapably loose and ambiguous subject. We are talking about those "pictures in our heads" of which Walter Lippman wrote many years ago, pictures or images we acquire from some particular history, exposure, education, experience.

The relation between "image" and "reality" is of course an old philosophic riddle. Every "reality" is made up of the sum of somebody's images; every "image" is part of someone's reality. Images, moreover, appear in the eye of the beholder. Who, then, is beholding, and who is being beheld, when, where, in what circumstances, under what light, at what angle? These old questions are always new—they even have a new Japanese name, the Rashomon approach. They have to be asked in every particular case and more than once in time, for the pictures in our heads are moving pictures, always the same and always changing. It was one purpose of the essays prepared for this volume to look at certain matters or events as they appeared through two windows on the world, Japanese and American, at a given time. I think we have shown that more remains to be more rigorously done along these promising lines.

There is the question, so pointedly raised by Nagai Michio, of the relation between image-of-others and images-of-self. There is the relation between images and events or actualities, as experienced by participants, as discovered from afar through the prisms of this or that form of communication, this or that propaganda device or manipulation. There is a central issue of the relationship of images to the making of policy. How do policymakers, like the Japanese navy planners described by Miwa Kimitada, bent on deciding issues of war and peace, sort out their own images and their own grasp of the realities? What pictures in the heads of American policymakers led to the American disaster in Vietnam? These questions can be explored, I believe, only as they appear in specific cases, in the tracing of all the interacting elements—rational and irrational—as they come together in events in a particular place at some particular time.

In my own inquiries into some of these matters, I have been particularly struck by one finding, by the fact that we tend to hold our images of other peoples and cultures in pairs, jostling pairs of coupled pluses and minuses, favorable and unfavorable images that appear, disappear, and reappear at different times, displacing each other at the call of political circumstance. Recent events have given us some spectacular examples of this process in connection with the reopening of relations between the United States and China. This major policy shift, taking place for a whole set of cogent reasons on both sides, set in motion a great turning and moving, images shifting as in a revolving column of mirrors under moving lights. The powerfully negative images of China and the Chinese that had dominated the center of the stage in American thinking about China for some twenty years began to turn away, to recede into the darkness backstage, and to be displaced as the mirrors swung by the highly positive views that had been quite out of view all this time but now came sweeping back to serve the needs of the new circumstances.

I have written elsewhere in some detail of this matter[1] and would like to remark here only for our present purposes that this process includes not only the mutual displacement of favorable and unfavorable images, but often also the transfer of these views from one object to another, again as political needs dictate. A peculiarly dramatic and explicit illustration of both the displacement and the transfer appears in a Gallup poll in which Americans have been asked to select adjectives which seem to them to describe various other peoples. Crude and unsubtle as such data might be, the showing of this poll is especially illuminating because the Gallup organization has been taking and retaking it at intervals over the last thirty years or more. The results illustrate graphically how an American sample has distributed and redistributed sets of adjectives among the Chinese, the Japanese, the Germans, and the Russians, all of whom have figured in the trapeze-like swing of relationships and alliances with the United States during these decades. The full list of countries has not always been consistently included in these polls, unfortunately, but there are enough of them to show how readily we change our views and transfer qualities from one people to another when conditions suggest or require it.

The following sets of percentages relating to the Chinese and the Japanese are taken from a sampling made in 1942, just after Pearl Harbor when the Chinese had become our heroic allies and the Japanese our attacking foes, again in 1966, when the Chinese had long since become the foe and Japan the ally, and most recently again—though regrettably not about the Japanese this time—in March 1972, just after President Nixon's trip to Peking. The selection of adjectives went as follows:

CHINESE

	1942	1966	1972
Hardworking	69	37	74
Honest	52	—	20
Brave	48	7	17
Religious	33	14	18
Intelligent	24	14	32
Practical	23	8	27
Ignorant	22	24	10
Artistic	21	13	26
Progressive	14	7	28
Sly	8	20	19
Treacherous	4	19	12
Warlike	4	23	13
Cruel	3	13	9

JAPANESE

	1942	1966
Treacherous	73	12
Sly	63	19
Cruel	56	9
Warlike	46	11
Hardworking	39	44
Intelligent	25	35
Brave	24	17
Religious	20	18
Progressive	19	31
Artistic	19	31
Ignorant	16	4
Practical	9	17
Honest	2	9

We see from this that in 1942 the Chinese were seen by most as hardworking, honest, brave, religious, and intelligent, in that order. Other qualities often attributed to them in the past—treacherous, sly, cruel—all appear this time, in that order, at the top of the list for the Japanese. By 1966, these sets of plus and minus attributions were reversed. Now the Chinese were seen as hardworking, ignorant, warlike, sly, and treacherous and the Japanese had become hardworking, artistic, intelligent, progressive. In March 1972, another spectacular reversal in the sample's view of the Chinese had taken place. From 8 to 5 negative, the balance had shifted to 3 to 1 positive. Once more the positive adjectives led the list for the Chinese, now again hardworking, intelligent, progressive, artistic, honest, practical.

A closer look at some of these adjectives will tell us more about how these views are held and how they move. Consider "hardworking," a universal stereotype of the Chinese based on a thousand different glimpses of the Chinese actuality, tillers in the fields, pullers and carriers of burdens. This reality is so powerful that although "hardworking" is clearly a favorable quality in American eyes, it leads both the favorable and the unfavorable lists. But whereas in 1942, a broad 69 percent credited our Chinese friends with this admirable trait, in 1966 it was granted to our Chinese foes by a much more grudging 37 percent, while in 1972 it zoomed back to an admiringly impressed 74 percent. It is worth noting that not even at their most negative were the Chinese often seen as "lazy"; the American sample could let go much more easily on "honest." This strongly established old stereotype about the Chinese drew a strong 52 percent in 1942, disappeared completely—to less than 1 percent—in 1966 and rebounded to a more substantial—yet still tentative—20 percent in 1972. The same steepness occurs in the gyrations on "progressive," from 14 percent in 1942 down to 7 percent in 1966 and up to 28 percent in 1972. On the other hand "sly" fluctuated more cautiously, moving from 8 percent in favorable 1942 up to 20 percent in unfavorable 1966, and quivering back a stroke to 19 percent in 1972, while "treacherous" moved from 4 percent to 19 percent and subsided to a somewhat more relaxed but still watchful 12 percent in 1972.

These adjectives carry more valence than substance. The differences among these fluctuations even suggest some of the tentativeness of the change in direction of bias. Not many in the Gallup example could say why they see or do not see the Chinese as "honest" or explain what is meant in this context by "progressive." "Sly" and "treacherous" are of course variants on those old attributions of mystery, deviousness, and inscrutability which came long ago out of the common ignorance—and therefore sometimes fear—of these remote, different, unfathomable Orientals.

A somewhat sharper probe comes, however, with the adjective "cruel," a quality, as I have pointed out, deeply etched among the American images of the Chinese. It was rooted for earlier generations in accounts of Chinese torture—the water treatment, the thousand cuts, the killing of Christians by Boxer rebels in 1900—which somehow made the Chinese more cruel than the rack and the burning of Christians had ever made the Europeans. It also came out of the need to explain why Chinese could endure hardship or pain—the two became interchangeable—as no European, especially the kind of European who came to China, thought *he* could. From this came the idea of a uniquely peculiar Chinese nervelessness. Later the image and the reality of millions of Chinese dying of famine, flood, or in war, unheeded and uncared for, became an extension of this idea. All together, these helped produce the notion of subhumanness, of disregard for human life, that made Western indifference to these conditions tolerable and justified their behavior.

Under the rosy light of 1942, the view of the Chinese as "cruel" could fade back—it fell to 3 percent in Gallup's sample—and be replaced by the quite new view of the Chinese as "brave" (56 percent). The cruelty passed intact to the Japanese (56 percent). Wanton depredations by the Japanese army in China and at that moment in the Philippines and Southeast Asia made this no fictive transfer. By 1966, however, the Chinese had regained their cruel character to the extent of 13 percent of Gallup's sample, and the Japanese had shed it, down to 9 percent. In March 1972, the number who saw the Chinese as cruel had fallen to 9 percent. Such movements, it should be clear, are now always the flitting passages of fiction or fantasy, but also in some degree show what we do with the realities that flicker too among all these revolving images and moving lights.

Unfortunately, the 1972 poll did not show what changes might have taken place meanwhile in the images of the Japanese. Certain tensions had begun to develop in Japanese-American relations as Japan began to reappear as a great power in its own right and especially as a competitor in trade and monetary affairs. But there was nothing in this yet to suggest any shift in relationship violent or threatening enough to begin producing any shift or transfer of attributes between the Chinese and Japanese as had happened in the past. Yet it was striking how powerfully the logic of even the possibility of this shift asserted itself. The maximum TV coverage in the weeks building up to the presidential trip to China included the re-screening of dozens of film and TV documentaries made at various times in the past about events in China. Some of these were made during World War II, some afterward. The viewer was exposed in a short time to all the successive biases and emotions that have been part of this crowded history, sometimes stumbling over each other in hastily re-edited versions made up for new showing at this new time. But unavoidably most vivid of all were the sequences that brought back the scenes of the Japanese war in China, in the 1930s when China shuddered alone under massive Japanese blows, and during the 1940s, when it was America's war against Japan as well. Night after night, American living room screens quivered with scenes of the merciless Japanese bombing and shelling of Chinese cities and towns, the pitiless descent of Japanese soldiery on conquered populations, the Japanese rape of Nanking in 1937. These films could not but powerfully stir the memories of adults who had shared some part of the experience when it took place. Most assuredly, they made brand new scratches on the minds of the young.

But how strong this impact was, how deep those scratches, we cannot really say without having made some systematic effort to inquire into it, and I do not know if any such research has been undertaken. The "window on the world" through which we see most of what we see of others has become everyone's living room screen. No one can doubt that the television medium is more powerful than any other that has ever shaped the pictures of things and people that we carry in our heads. Television has widened communication in unprecedented ways. George Gallup reported that 98 percent of his sample had heard or read of the presidential journey to China, "the highest awareness score for an event in the thirty-seven years of the Gallup Poll's existence." Much of the effect of this new medium spreading on a global scale may well be and remain beyond calculation. Yet it is clear that it has its own limits and deformations. Television multiplies coverage, but it also saturates. It probably shortens the halflife of any effect. It narrows the attention span. The sheer quantity of it makes it indigestible and there is so much of it that is fantasy or fiction or just plain false, as in the case of political propaganda or advertising against which some large part of almost any audience instinctively stiffens itself. More to the point, in our present context, television blurs the line between the actual and the pseudoreal and the phony. As in the case of the actuality films of Vietnam war happenings, one might well ask not only what the viewing audience took in from these old films but also what it retained from all that it saw. Scenes of violence especially lend themselves to a response of rejection of the real as unreal or vice versa. We just do not know enough about this to do anything but guess the effect of the saturation exposures about China and Japan on American viewers at the time of the Nixon trip to China. Farther along the line, at new turnings, future researchers may have more to tell us about it.

In any case, the process of image-changing and image-making still waits on indecisive events. The Chinese-American policy shift itself, for all the wave-making and pro-Chinese faddism it generated in the United States, remains limited, tentative, its future unclear. Japan, forced to move toward some new place in the still unformed new scheme of things, remains a "friend" and "ally"—albeit an increasingly important competitor—of the United States. The further effect on policy behavior of the pictures of China and Japan in the heads of America's policymakers remains to be seen.

Meanwhile let me add a reminder that this phenomenon of the transfer of images and attributed qualities from friend to foe and back again is not at all confined to those inscrutable Orientals whom, as they used to say, we could not tell apart anyway. The same polls quoted here and much other evidence show how Americans in similar fashion transferred monsterhood and other assorted negative characteristics from Stalin and the Russians to Hitler and the Germans after Stalin stopped being Hitler's ally and became ours, and then back again from the now-friendly Germans to the now-hostile Russians when the cold war followed the hot. Indeed, it was difficult during the time of the Nixon trip to Peking not to see the resemblance between the way "Good Old Joe" Stalin of 1941–45 emerged from behind the visage of the mass purger-murderer Stalin of the previous years, and the way the features of a new good old Chou, En-lai that is, turned up, formidably charming and clever and straightforward, from behind the mask of that other Chou, formidably hypocritical, shrewd, and devious, of only a few weeks or months before. The role change being still so tentative, its future so uncertain, both appearances in this case remained in view. No one could be sure when the "real" Chou En-lai or the "real" Chinese would step forth.

For some time then, it seems, the turning column of mirrors will turn slowly, and all the pluses and minuses and *all* the contending images of *all* the actors in these dramas will stay somewhere in view.

Contributors, Notes, and Index

Contributors

PRISCILLA A. CLAPP is a research associate, Brookings Institution, where she is codirector of a project on the politics of U.S.-Japanese relations. She is coeditor of *United States-Japanese Relations: The 1970's* (1974).

NATHAN GLAZER is professor of education and social structure, Harvard University, and coeditor of *The Public Interest*. His recent publications include *America's Ethnic Pattern: A New Phase?* (1975), *Ethnicity: Theory and Experience,* which he co-edited with Daniel P. Moynihan (1975), and "Social and Cultural Factors in Japanese Economic Growth" (to be included in a book on Japanese economic growth, edited by Hugh Patrick and Henry Rosovsky).

MORTON H. HALPERIN is research director of "the project on information, national security, and constitutional procedures," Twentieth Century Fund. He is the editor of *Bureaucratic Politics and National Security* (1972), and coeditor of *Readings in American Foreign Policy: A Bureaucratic Perspective* (1973) and *U.S.-Japanese Relations: The 1970's* (1974).

NEIL HARRIS is professor of history, University of Chicago. His recent publications include *The Land of Contrasts, 1880–1901* (1970), "Four Stages of Cultural Growth: The American City" (Indiana Historical Society Lectures, 1972), and *Humbug: The Art of P. T. Barnum* (1973).

AKIRA IRIYE is professor of history, University of Chicago. His publications include *Pacific Estrangement: Japanese and American Expansion, 1897–1911* (1972), *The Cold War in Asia: A Historical Introduction* (1974), and *From Nationalism to Internationalism: U.S. Foreign Policy Before 1914* (forthcoming).

HAROLD R. ISAACS is professor of political science, Massachusetts Institute of Technology, and the author of a long list of studies including *Scratches on Our Minds: American Images of China and India* (paperback title: *Images of Asia,* 1973), *The New World of Negro Americans* (1964), *India's Ex-Untouchables* (1965), *American*

Jews in Israel (1967), and *Idols from the Tribe: Group Identity and Political Change* (1975).

SHUNSUKE KAMEI is associate professor of literature, University of Tokyo, and the author of *Yone Noguchi: An English Poet of Japan* (1965), *Kindai bungaku ni okeru Whitman no unmei* (Walt Whitman in modern literature, 1970), and *Nationalism no bungaku: Meiji no seishin no tankyū* (Literature of nationalism: an inquiry into the mind of the Meiji era, 1971).

HIDETOSHI KATŌ is professor of sociology at Gakushūin University and at the East-West Communication Institute, Honolulu. He is the author of numerous articles and books including *Ningen kankei* (Human relations, 1971) and *Hyakka jiten sōjūhō* (How to make use of encyclopedias, 1973).

KIMITADA MIWA is professor of history, Sophia University Institute of International Relations, and the author of *Matsuoka Yōsuke* (1971) *and Nichi-Bei kankei no imeiji to kōzō* (Images and structure of Japanese-American relations, 1974).

MICHIO NAGAI was professor of sociology at Tokyo Institute of Technology before joining the *Asahi shimbun* as editorial writer in 1970. In December 1974 he was appointed minister of education in the cabinet of Prime Minister Miki. He has written, edited, and translated many books including *Nihon no daigaku* (Higher education in Japan, 1965), *Daigaku no kanōsei* (Possibilities of the university, 1969), *Kindaika to kyōiku* (Modernization and education, 1969), and the translations of books by Talcott Parsons (1962) and Thomas Hobbs (1971).

DON TOSHIHIAKI NAKANISHI is completing his doctoral dissertation for Harvard University on minority groups in the context of international politics. He is a graduate associate for the Center for International Affairs, Harvard University, publisher of *Amerasia Journal,* and coeditor of *Roots: An Asian American Reader,* volume 2.

TAKEO NISHIJIMA is a member of the editorial board, *Asahi shimbun.*

SHŌICHI SAEKI is professor of literature, University of Tokyo, and the author of *Amerika bungakushi* (History of American literature, 1969), *Uchi to soto karano Nippon bungaku* (Japanese literature from within and without, 1969), *Nipponjin no jiden* (Autobiography in Japan, 1973), and *Nippon no watakushi o motomete* (In search of the Japanese ego, 1973).

Notes

1. INTRODUCTION, BY AKIRA IRIYE

1. Saitō Makoto and Sigmund Skard, eds., *Sekai ni okeru Amerika zō* (How the world looks at America; Tokyo, Nan'undō, 1972).

2. Durand Echeverria, *Mirage in the West* (Princeton: Princeton University Press, 1957), pp. 281, 282.

3. Christopher Lasch, *The American Liberals and the Russian Revolution* (New York: Columbia University Press, 1962), pp. 26, 218.

4. Peter G. Filene, *Americans and the Soviet Experiment* (Cambridge, Mass.: Harvard University Press, 1967), pp. 17, 153.

5. Carl P. Parrini, *Heir to Empire: United States Economic Diplomacy, 1916–1923* (Pittsburgh: Pittsburgh University Press, 1969), pp. 10, 88. Other books mentioned in this paragraph include William Appleman Williams, *The Roots of the Modern American Empire* (New York: Random House, 1969); Lloyd C. Gardner, *Economic Aspects of the New Deal Diplomacy* (New Brunswick, N.J.: Rutgers University Press, 1964); N. Gordon Levin, *Woodrow Wilson and World Politics* (New York: Oxford University Press, 1969); Gabriel Kolko, *Politics of War* (New York: Knopf, 1969); Richard Freeland, *The Truman Doctrine and the Origins of McCarthyism* (New York: Knopf, 1972); and Bruce Kuklick, *American Policy and the Division of Germany* (Ithaca: Cornell University Press, 1972).

6. Hiroshi Wagatsuma, "Problems of Cultural Identity in Modern Japan," paper prepared for Burg Wartenstein Symposium No. 51, New York, 1970, p. 1.

7. Kamei Shunsuke, *Kindai bungaku ni okeru Whitman no unmei* (Walt Whitman in modern literature; Tokyo, Kenkyūsha, 1970); the same author's *Nationalism no bungaku* (The literature of nationalism; Tokyo, Kenkyūsha, 1971).

8. By far the most ambitious collaborative effort by Japanese scholars has been the three-volume publication, *Nihon to Amerika: Hikaku bunka-ron* (Japan and America: Essays in comparative culture; Tokyo, Nan'undō, 1973), edited by Saitō Makoto, Homma Nagayo, and Kamei Shunsuke. Each volume contains seven or eight essays that deal with various topics in Japanese-American cultural relations.

9. Address by Francis M. Huntington Wilson, Baltimore, May 4, 1911, Huntington Wilson Papers, Ursinus College, Collegeville, Pa.

10. On the transference of the economistic ethos from America to Japan see the highly impressionistic but insightful essay by James Sterba, "The Japanese Pattern: The Yen Is Mightier than the Sword," *New York Times Magazine,* October 29, 1972.

11. George C. Perkins, "The Competition of Japan," *Overland Monthly* 28:393-403 (October, 1896).

12. Paolo E. Coletta, *William Jennings Bryan, I, Political Evangelist* (Lincoln, Neb.: University of Nebraska Press, 1964), pp. 262-264.

13. Among the best recent studies of Japan's Western learning are Hirakawa Sukehiro, *Wakon yōsai no keifu* (The tradition of "Japanese spirit and Western learning"; Tokyo, Kawade shobō, 1971); and the eight-volume *Kōza hikaku bungaku* (Studies in comparative literature; Tokyo, Tokyo University Press, 1973-1974), edited by Haga Tōru, Hirakawa Sukehiro, Kamei Shunsuke, and Kobori Keiichirō.

2. ALL THE WORLD A MELTING POT? JAPAN AT AMERICAN FAIRS, 1876–1904, BY NEIL HARRIS

1. Clay Lancaster, *The Japanese Influence in American Architecture* (New York: W. H. Rawls, 1963). The book contains the best account of Japanese participation at American fairs.

2. Scholarly literature on the fairs is sketchy. The best survey is Kenneth W. Luckhurst, *The Story of Exhibitions* (London and New York: Studio Publications, 1951). The Crystal Palace has received more attention than any subsequent exhibition, although every international fair published at least one authoritative (and usually multivolume) history. Merle Curti, "America at the World's Fairs, 1851-1893," *American Historical Review* 55:833–856 (June 1950), is one of the few recent articles. For more bibliography and an essay on the bibliographical problems and opportunities for writing the history of fairs see Richard D. Mandell, *Paris 1900: The Great World's Fair* (Toronto: Univ. of Toronto Press, 1967), pp. 122-139.

3. Luckhurst, *Story of Exhibitions,* pp. 220-221, presents a tabular survey of exhibition costs, attendance, and so forth.

4. For a concise history of the Centennial Exhibition see Edward C. Bruce, *The Century: Its Fruits and Its Festival* (Philadelphia, 1877). The multivolume *United States Centennial Commission. International Exhibition. 1876* (Washington, D.C., 1880) contains massive amounts of information. James D. McCabe, *The Illustrated History of the Centennial Exhibition* (Philadelphia, Chicago, St. Louis, 1876) is helpful. A bibliography of material on the centennial can be found in Julia

Finette Davis, "International Expositions, 1851-1900," in William B. O'Neil, ed., *The American Association of Architectural Bibliographers, Papers* 4:47-130 (1967). The most recent study of the Centennial Exhibition is John Maass, *The Glorious Enterprise: The Centennial Exhibition of 1876 and H. J. Schwarzmann, Architect-in-Chief* (Watkins Glen, N.Y.: American Life Foundation, 1973). Finally, see the provocative essay on three American exhibitions by John G. Cawelti, "America on Display: The World's Fairs of 1876, 1893, 1933," in Frederic Cople Jaher, *The Age of Industrialism in America: Essays in Social Structure and Cultural Values* (New York: Free Press, 1968), pp. 317-363.

5. Bruce, *The Century,* p. 65.

6. This account is based on *International Exhibition, 1876. Official Catalogue of the Japanese Section* (Philadelphia, 1876).

7. *United States Centennial Commission. Report of the Director General* (Washington, D.C., 1880), I, 54.

8. Ibid., p. 369.

9. *New York Times,* February 4, 1876, p. 1. For similar reactions see Scrapbook of Centennial Clippings, Historical Society of Pennsylvania (hereafter cited as HSP Scrapbook), p. 24; and *Philadelphia Graphic,* February 3, 1876.

10. W. D. Howells, "A Sennight of the Centennial," *Atlantic Monthly* 38:97 (July 1876).

11. "Characteristics of the International Fair," ibid., p. 91.

12. Ibid., p. 89.

13. J. S. Ingram, *The Centennial Exposition* (Philadelphia, 1876), pp. 559-560, gives a clear description of the Japanese arrangement in the main building.

14. McCabe, *The Centennial Exhibition,* p. 446.

15. "Characteristics of the International Fair," *Atlantic Monthly* 38:90 (July 1876).

16. HSP Scrapbook, p. 58.

17. Bruce, *The Century,* p. 141.

18. HSP Scrapbook, p. 92.

19. *New York Times,* June 24, 1877, p. 6.

20. "The Japs' Handiwork," HSP Scrapbook.

21. Bruce, *The Century,* p. 80.

22. HSP Scrapbook, p. 58.

23. Bruce, *The Century,* p. 141.

24. Ingram, *The Centennial Exposition,* p. 560.

25. [Marietta Holley,] *Josiah Allen's Wife as a P. A. and P. I. Samantha at the Centennial* (Hartford, Conn., 1878), pp. 440-445.

26. Ibid., p. 444.

27. "Characteristics of the International Fair," *Atlantic Monthly* 38:91 (July 1876).

28. "Characteristics of the International Fair," *Atlantic Monthly* 38:733 (December 1876).

29. For a discussion of Japanese appeals to American eclecticism see Lancaster, *The Japanese Influence,* p. 62.

30. Charles Wyllys Elliott, "Pottery at the Centennial," *Atlantic Monthly* 38:576 (November 1876).

31. "Japanese Art," *New York Times,* June 24, 1887, p. 6.

32. *Philadelphia Bulletin,* July 2, 1875.

33. Bruce, *The Century,* pp. 244-245.

34. *Samantha at the Centennial,* pp. 444-445.

35. Bruce, *The Century,* p. 244.

36. HSP Scrapbook, p. 92.

37. Carl T. Western, *Adventures of Reuben and Cynthy at the World's Fair. As Told by Themselves* (Chicago, 1893), p. 101.

38. HSP Scrapbook, p. 92.

39. See Lafcadio Hearn, *Occidental Gleanings: Sketches and Essays Now First Collected by Albert Mordell* (Freeport, N.Y.: Dodd, Mead and Company, 1967), II, 209-240. Half a dozen of Hearn's articles are reprinted in this collection.

40. Good accounts of the Columbian Exposition can be found in Hubert Howe Bancroft, *The Book of the Fair,* 2 vols. (Chicago, 1894); D. H. Burnham, *World's Columbian Exposition: The Book of the Builders* (Chicago, 1894); H. N. Higginbotham, *Report of the President* (Chicago, 1898); R. Johnson, ed., *History of the World's Columbian Exposition,* 4 vols. (New York, 1897).

41. Gōzō Tateno, "Foreign Nations at the World's Fair," *North American Review* 156:33–43 (January 1893).

42. "Unpacking Art Exhibits," *Harper's Weekly* 37:355 (April 15, 1893).

43. "The World's Japanese Exposition: The Japanese Village," *Harper's Weekly* 37:259 (March 18, 1893).

44. Lancaster, *The Japanese Influence,* p. 83. Lancaster presents a detailed description of the Hō-ōden.

45. *The Official Directory of the World's Columbian Exposition* (Chicago, 1893).

46. H. D. Northrop, *The World's Fair as Seen in One Hundred Days* (Philadelphia, 1893), p. 508. See also Mrs. Mark Stevens, *Six Months at the World's Fair* (Detroit, 1895), p. 54.

47. Northrop, *The World's Fair,* p. 582.

48. Ibid., p. 591.

49. *Harper's Weekly* 38:1023 (October 28, 1893).

50. [Marietta Holley,] *Samantha at the World's Fair. By Josiah Allen's Wife* (New York, London, Toronto, 1893), p. 402.

51. Ibid., p. 405.

52. Ibid., pp. 594-595.

53. Denton J. Snider, *World's Fair Studies* (Chicago, 1895), p. 230. Snider was an American Hegelian; his book is one of the most interesting interpretations of the White City published at the time.

54. H. G. Cutler, *The World's Fair: Its Meaning and Scope* (Chicago 1892), p. 286. This book was published before the fair opened and was designed to publicize the forthcoming exhibition.

55. Mrs. D. C. Taylor, *Halcyon Days in the Dream City* (n.p., n.d.), pp. 35, 42.

56. Julian Hawthorne, *Humors of the Fair* (Chicago, n d.), p. 93.

57. Cutler, *The World's Fair,* p. 281. This, of course, was an exaggeration.

58. The figures can be found in Higginbotham, *Report of the President.*

59. Tudor Jenks, *The Century World's Fair Book for Boys and Girls* (New York, 1893), p. 144.

60. Western, *Adventures of Reuben and Cynthy,* p. 100.

61. "Quondam," *The Adventures of Uncle Jeremiah and Family at the Great Fair* (Chicago, 1893), p. 100. Other writers used the metaphor of reversing the direction of missionaries from East to West. See *Samantha at the World's Fair,* p. 594.

62. Bancroft, *The Book of the Fair,* I, 222.

63. *Official Directory of the World's Columbian Exposition,* p. 133.

64. Joseph Kirkland and Caroline Kirkland, *The Story of Chicago* (Chicago, 1894), II, 135.

65. Snider, *World's Fair Studies,* pp. 229-230.

66. Ibid., p. 231.

67. William Elroy Curtis, *The Yankees of the East: Sketches of Modern Japan* (New York, 1896, 1906), p. 561.

68. A. Herbage Edwards, *Kakemono, Japanese Sketches* (Chicago: A. C. McClurg, 1906), p. 209.

69. Gōzō Tateno, "Foreign Nations at the World's Fair," p. 43.

70. See, for example, the editorial, "The Japanese Indemnity Fund," *Harper's Weekly* 20:143 (February 19, 1876). The money was paid back in 1893.

71. The history of the Japanese effort is described in Hajime Hoshi, *Handbook of Japan and Japanese Exhibits at World's Fair* (St. Louis, 1904); and Isaac F. Marcosson, "Japan's Extraordinary Exhibit," *The World's Work* 8:5146-5153 (August 1904). This entire issue of *The World's Work* was devoted to the fair. See also *The Exhibition of the Empire of Japan. Official Catalogue* (St. Louis, 1904).

72. For the St. Louis fair see *The History of the Louisiana Purchase Exposition* (St. Louis, 1904), a profusely illustrated book; and David R. Francis, *The Universal Exposition of 1904,* 2 vols. (St. Louis, 1913). Francis was the president and leading spirit of the exposition.

73. Plans showing the comparative size of American expositions can be found in G. H. Edgell, *The American Architecture of To-day* (New York and London: Scribner's, 1928). p. 52.

74. Baron Hirata Tōsuke, minister of agriculture and commerce, was the president of the commission; Tejima Seiichi was commissioner general.

75. Lancaster, *The Japanese Influence,* pp. 155-156.

76. *The World's Work* 8:5061 (August 1904).

77. The figures are printed in Francis, *The Universal Exposition,* 1, 580-589.

78. [Marietta Holley,] *Samantha at the St. Louis Exposition. By Josiah Allen's Wife* (New York: G. W. Dillingham, 1904), p. 239.

79. Ibid., pp. 91-92.

80. Ibid., p. 242. This was certainly Samantha's most enthusiastic reaction to any of the three exhibitions Marietta Holley published books about.

81. Marcosson, "Japan's Extraordinary Exhibit," p. 5153.

82. "Lights and Shadows at the St. Louis Exposition," *The Nation* 79:175 (September 1, 1904).

83. Mabel Loomis Todd, "The Louisiana Exposition," *The Nation* 78:511 (June 30, 1904).

84. Francis, *The Universal Exposition,* I, 359. There also appeared highly sophisticated discussions of Japanese art efforts, the product, in part, of years of writing and lecturing by men such as Ernest Fenollosa. See, for example, Charles H. Caffin, "The Exhibit of Paintings and Sculptures," *The World's Work* 8:5179-5184 (August 1904).

85. "Is Japanese Progress Changing Japanese Character" *The World's Work* 8:4726-4727 (May 1904).

86. "Japan and the Jingoes," *The Nation* 79:254-255 (September 29, 1904).

87. "Japan's Rising Influence Won by War," *The World's Work* 8:4948 (July 1904). See also the interesting comments in "The Spirit of New Japan," *Harper's Weekly* 58:1982 (December 24, 1904), where the ironies of military success as a device to gain world attention are canvassed. "We may be certain that the surface hardness which the fierce contests of material life have imposed upon Japan are for a time only," *Harper's* concluded, "and that, once her national well-being is assured, the old beauty and idealism will once more shine through." In its own way, therefore, *Harper's* also was worried about the effects of modernization in changing the distinctive character of old Japan. See also "The Japanese Spirit," *The World's Work* 7:4837 (June 1904), in which the writer argues that the new spirit demonstrated by the Japanese will be present in whatever enterprises they undertake, even after the war is over. Many American journals, overwhelmingly sympathetic to the Japanese side, were at pains to counter the Yellow Peril argument that Russians and others were propagating.

88. "Japan: A Paradox in Education," *The Nation* 78:327 (April 28, 1904).

89. Quoted in Barbara Solomon, *Ancestors and Immigrants: A Changing New England Tradition* (Cambridge, Mass.: Harvard University Press, 1956), pp. 57-58.

90. These included William James, Emily Balch, Jane Addams, and Charles William Eliot. See ibid., chap. 9.

3. THE SACRED LAND OF LIBERTY: IMAGES OF AMERICA IN NINE-TEENTH CENTURY JAPAN, BY SHUNSUKE KAMEI

1. Francis L. Hawks, comp., *Narrative of the Expedition of an American Squadron to the China Seas and Japan . . . under the Command of Commodore M. C. Perry* (Washington, D.C., 1856; facsimile edition, New York: AMS Press—Arno Press, 1967), p. 248.

2. Ishii Kendō, ed., *Ikoku hyōryū kitan-shū* (Collection of castaways' strange stories about strange countries; Tokyo, Shin Jinbutsu Ōrai-sha, 1971).

3. Joseph Heco, *The Narrative of a Japanese* (Tokyo, 1892-95?; facsimile edition, San Francisco: American-Japanese Publishing Association, n.d.), II, 90 and throughout.

4. Collected in Nichi-Bei Shūkō Tsūshō Hyakunen Kinen Gyōji Un'eikai, ed., *Man'en gannen ken-Bei shisetsu shiryō shūsei* (Historical materials on the 1860 mission to the United States, 7 vols.; Tokyo, Kazama Shobō, 1960-61). Muragaki Norimasa's diary, which is not included there, is printed in several books, among them Nichi-Bei Kyōkai, ed., *Man'en gannen daiichi ken-Bei shisetsu nikki* (Diary of the first Japanese embassy to the United States, 1860; Tokyo, 1918).

5. Collected in Yamaguchi Takayuki and others, eds., *Nihon shisō taikei* (Masterpieces of Japanese thought, vol. 55; Tokyo, Iwanami Shoten, 1971).

6. Kimura Ki, *Nichi-Bei bungaku kōryū-shi no kenkyū* (A History of Japanese-American literary relations; Tokyo, Kōdan-sha, 1960), p. 217.

7. Mori Arinori, *Life and Resources in America* (Washington, D.C., 1871), pp. 298-299.

8. Ibid., p. 13.

9. In Ōkubo Toshikane, ed., *Meiji bungaku zenshū 3: Meiji keimō shisō shū* (Complete works of Meiji literature, 3: Ideas of enlightenment in the Meiji era; Tokyo, Chikuma Shobō, 1967).

10. *Kokumin no tomo* (The Nation's companion), no. 14 (January 20, 1888). *Kokumin no tomo,* a liberal magazine that discussed current affairs, was published by Tokutomi Sohō and was strongly influenced by the American magazine *The Nation.*

11. Kamei Shunsuke, *Yone Noguchi: An English Poet of Japan* (Tokyo: The Yone Noguchi Society, 1965).

12. Recorded in *Beishi taiwa-sho hachi-satsu* (Conversations with the American embassy in eight volumes), quoted in Saha Wataru, ed., *Uemura Masahisa to sono jidai* (Uemura Masahisa and his times; Tokyo, Kyōbunkan, 1937-41), I, 179.

13. Katsumoto Seiichirō, ed., *Tōkoku zenshū* (Collected writings of Tōkoku; Tokyo, Iwanami Shoten, 1950-55), III, 198-202.

14. A Heathen Convert [Uchimura Kanzō], *How I Became a Christian* (Tokyo, 1895), pp. 91-92.

15. Ibid., pp. 103-104.

16. *Yorozu chōhō* (All the morning news), May 8, 1913.

4. JAPAN AS A COMPETITOR, 1895–1917, BY AKIRA IRIYE

1. *Arena* 20: 647-657 (November 1898).

2. *North American Review* 163:144-155 (August 1896).

3. *Contemporary Review* 71:53-62 (January 1897).

4. *Overland Monthly* 28:82-93 (July 1896).

5. *Overland Monthly* 28:393-403 (October 1896).

6. Ohara Keishi, ed., *Nichi-Bei bunka kōshō-shi: Tsūshō sangyō hen* (A history of cultural relations between Japan and the United States: International trade and industry; Tokyo, Yōyōsha, 1954), p. 19.

7. See notes 4 and 5 above.

8. Richard Austin Thompson, "The Yellow Peril, 1890-1924," Ph.D. dissertation, University of Wisconsin, 1957, p. 110.

9. Archibald Cary Coolidge, *The United States as a World Power* (New York: Macmillan, 1909), pp. 64, 74, 75, 352.

10. Newlands to Dickerson, February 3, 1909, State Department Archives, 12622/119.

11. Thorne to Roosevelt, December 28, 1907, ibid., 1797/431.

12. Hans to Roosevelt, January 1, 1908, ibid., 2542/275.

13. Rainsberger to Taft, February 15, 1908, War Department Archives, Record Group 94.

14. Judge to War Department, June 22, 1910, ibid.

15. McKay to Taft, July 15, 1907, ibid.

16. Root to Metcalf, October 27, 1906, State Department Archives, 1797/13.

17. Jones to Fort Worden, March 13, 1908, War Department Archives, Record Group 165; Liggett memorandum, March 27, 1911, ibid.

18. General Staff to military attachés, December 3, 1910, and their reports, ibid.

19. Sames to Alexander, August 7, 1907, War Department Archives, Record Group 94.

20. Roberts to War Department, January 5, 1911, ibid.

21. Frederick memorandum, November 3, 1910, War Department Archives, Record Group 165.

22. Learnard memorandum, Army War College, 1913-1914, ibid.

23. Calhoun to Knox, 1911, State Department Archives, 893.00/1244.

24. Story's preface to Homer Lea, *The Valor of Ignorance* (New York: Harper 1909), p. xxi.

25. Ibid., pp. 161, 187.

26. Wilson to Root, July 6, 1907, State Department Archives, 1797/385-386.

27. Castle to Rossiter, December 5, 1906, ibid., 2542/11.

28. War College Division memorandum, February 25, 1916, War Department Archives, Record Group 165.

29. Bliss memorandum, February 14, 1910, and accompanying documents, ibid., Record Group 94.

30. Swift to chief of staff, December 7, 1907, ibid., Record Group 165.

31. Memoranda on these matters are included ibid.

32. War Plan Orange, May 19, 1913, War Department Archives.

33. *Contemporary Review* 71:53-62 (January 1897).

34. Alfred Thayer Mahan, *The Problem of Asia* (Boston, 1900), pp. 158-159.

35. Straight to Rockhill, May 8, 1907, State Department Archives, 551/46-47.

36. Wilson memorandum, March 6, 1908, ibid., 551/92.

37. Thomas F. Millard, *America and the Far Eastern Question* (New York: Scribner's, 1909), p. 21.

38. Cited in *Public Opinion* 28:74 (June 21, 1900).

39. *Independent* 52:1655 (July 12, 1900).

40. Phillips to Wilson, February 14, 1908, State Department Archives, 2321/19-20.

41. Millard, *The Far Eastern Question,* pp. 12-13, 59, 361.

42. Joseph King Goodrich, *The Coming China* (Chicago: A. C. McClurg, 1911), pp. 2-3, 164, 166, 206.

43. Ibid., pp. 224-225.

44. *Journal of the American Association of China* (Shanghai) 2.6:35 (July 1908).

45. Millard, *The Far Eastern Question,* p. 319.

46. Bash to Taft, December 18, 1905, William Howard Taft Papers, Library of Congress, Washington, D.C.

47. Arthur H. Smith, *China and America Today* (New York: F. H. Revell, 1907), pp. 215-216.

48. Ibid., p. 212.

49. Mitchell memorandum, January 2, 1912, War Department Archives, Record Group 165.

50. Millard, *The Far Eastern Question,* pp. 59, 353.

51. Seoane memorandum, October 28, 1911, War Department Archives.

52. Goodrich, *The Coming China,* pp. 227-228.

53. Halstead to Taft, May 10, 1905, Taft Papers.

54. Wilson to Root, March 15, 1906, State Department Archives, Japan Dispatches.

55. William Graham Sumner, *Folkways* (New York: Ginn and Co., 1906), p. 91; Millard, *The Far Eastern Question,* p. 59.

56. On the theme of Anglo-American cooperation see Bradford Perkins, *The Great Rapprochement* (New York: Atheneum, 1968).

57. Hoyt to Adee, September 10, 1907, cited in Michael Hunt, "Frontier Defense and the Open Door: Manchuria in Chinese-American Relations, 1895-1911," Ph.D. dissertation, Yale University, 1971, pp. 251-252.

58. Ernest Hugh Fitzpatrick, *The Coming Conflict of Nations* (Springfield, Ill.: H. W. Bokker, 1909), pp. 164-165, 197, 285.

59. Wilson to Knox, January 20, 1910, Francis M. Huntington Wilson Papers, Ursinus College, Collegeville, Pa.

60. Grey to Durand, January 2, 1906, Foreign Office Archives, Public Record Office, F.O. 800/81.

61. Durand to Grey, January 26, 1906, ibid.

62. Jordan to Grey, June 11, 1908, ibid., F.O. 350; Jordan to Grey, June 28, 1909, ibid., F.O. 500-544.

63. Grey to Jordan, August 13, 1909, ibid.

64. *Outlook* 110:121 (May 19, 1915).

65. *Current History* 59:152-153 (September 1915).

66. Cited in Cedric C. Cummins, *Indiana Public Opinion and the World War, 1914–1917* (Indianapolis: Indiana Historical Bureau, 1945), p. 18.

67. Cited in Ian H. Nish, *Alliance in Decline: A Study in Anglo-Japanese Relations, 1908–23* (London: University of London Press, 1972), p. 224.

68. *Outlook* 117:200 (October 10, 1917).

69. *Independent* 91:501 (September 29, 1917).

70. *Asia* (December 1917), p. 792.

71. *Nation* (November 15, 1917), p. 528; *New Republic* (November 30, 1917), p. 31.

72. Wilson memorandum, n.d. [1917], Huntington Wilson Papers.

73. Arnell to Straight, January 28, 1909, Willard Straight Papers, Cornell University, Ithaca, N.Y.

74. See Sondra R. Herman, *Eleven Against War: Studies in American Internationalist Thought, 1898–1921* (Stanford: Stanford University Press, 1969); Warren F. Kuehl, *Seeking World Order: The United States and International Organization to 1920* (Nashville: University of Tennessee Press, 1969).

5. IMAGES OF THE UNITED STATES AS A HYPOTHETICAL ENEMY, BY SHŌICHI SAEKI

1. Cited in the bibliography compiled by Inō Dentarō, "Meiji ikō ni okeru sensō jiraiki no ryūkō to shōchō" (War scare stories in Japan after the Meiji era), in *Kokugakuin Daigaku kiyō* (Proceedings of Kokugakuin University, vol. 7; Tokyo, 1969).

2. Mizuno Hironori, *Tsugi no issen* (The next war; Tokyo, Kōdansha, 1914), p. 59.

3. Payson J. Treat, *Japan and the United States* (Stanford: Stanford University Press, 1928), p. 258.

4. This title was kept in the American edition, but it was the second chapter. The first chapter, "The Heritage of New Japan," was mainly devoted to a historical review of the cultural heritage of the Edo period and thus would not have been particularly enlightening for Japanese readers. This might have been why Murakawa eliminated it in the Japanese version. At the same time, he might have wished to emphasize the theme "Peace and Friendship" by placing it at the beginning of the Japanese edition.

5. Treat, *Japan and the United States,* p. 16.

6. Preface to the Japanese translation, *Nichi-Bei gaikōshi* (A history of diplomatic relations between Japan and the United States; Tokyo, Yūbunkan, 1922), p. 3.

7. Ibid., p. 4.

8. Hirata Shinsaku, *Ware moshi tatakawaba* (If we fight; Tokyo, Kōdansha, 1933), p. 2.

9. Ibid., pp. 11-13.

10. Ibid., p. 162.

11. Ishimaru Tōta, *Nichi-Bei hatashite tatakau ka* (Will Japan and the United States fight? Tokyo, Shunjūsha, 1932), p. 4.

12. Kiyosawa Kiyoshi, *Amerika o hadaka ni su* (Naked America; Tokyo, Chikura Shobō, 1930); Kimura Ki, *S.O.S. no Amerika* (America in distress; Tokyo, Chikura Shobō, 1932); Yamauchi Kazuo, *Tenraku Amerika no zembō* (America in decline; Tokyo, Takase Shobō, 1933).

13. Kimura, *S.O.S. no Amerika,* pp. 1-2.

14. Yamauchi, *Amerika no zembō,* pp. 1-2.

15. Kiyosawa, *Amerika o hadaka ni su,* p. 180.

16. Ibid., p. 4.

6. JAPANESE IMAGES OF WAR WITH THE UNITED STATES, BY
KIMITADA MIWA

1. Donald Keene has masterfully pointed out such psychological tensions prevalent among Japanese writers in "Japanese Writers and the Greater East Asia War," *Journal of Asian Studies* 23:209-225 (February 1963). Imai Seiichi made a similar observation in "Unmei no sono asa" (That fateful morning), *Shōwa shi no shunkan* (Moments of truth in Showa history) 2:30–31 (Tokyo, Asahi Shimbunsha, 1966).

2. This song begins with the words, "The old America where the Statue of Liberty once stood has perished." See *Kokumin shimbun,* June 8, 1924, evening edition.

3. Tsurumi Kazuko, *Nihonjin to kōkishin* (Japanese curiosity: A theory of the stratified system; Tokyo, Kōdansha, 1972), pp. 114–155.

4. Kimitada Miwa, "Crossroads of Patriotism in Imperial Japan," Ph.D. dissertation, Princeton University, 1967, pp. 400–411.

5. Strong criticism by an army officer of the navy's irresponsible chauvinism was expressed in a recent conversation by Lieutenant General Suzuki Teiichi, who was president of the Cabinet Planning Board on the eve of Pearl Harbor. See *Suzuki Teiichi shi danwa sokki roku* (A record of interviews with Suzuki Teiichi) 1:160 (Tokyo, Tokyo Daigaku Nihon Kindai Shiryō Kenkyūkai, 1971). Another example of the army's criticism of the navy is found in Satō Kenryō, *Tōjō Hideki to Taiheiyō sensō* (Tōjō Hideki and the Pacific War; Tokyo, Bungei Shunjūsha, 1960), pp. 215–216. Satō points to Admiral Yamamoto Isoroku directly.

6. For the Orange Plan and Japanese responses to it see Bōeichō Senshi Shitsu (National Defense Agency, Military History Office), ed., *Daihon'ei rikugumbu* (Imperial Headquarters, Army department) 1: 157 (Tokyo, Asagumo Shimbunsha, 1967). See also another volume in the same series, *Kaigun gunsembi* (Naval armaments and preparations for war) 1:143–146 (1969).

7. Interview with Ōi Atsushi, November 13, 1970. Ōi, formerly an Imperial Navy staff officer, said that one Anglophile among high-ranking naval officers had once gone so far as to refer to Great Britain as "our fatherland."

8. Gaimushō Hyakunen-shi Hensan Iinkai, ed., *Gaimushō no hyakunen* (One hundred years of the Foreign Ministry) 1:832–833 (Tokyo, Hara Shobō, 1969).

9. After the Washington Conference, whenever Japanese-American relations became tense, many books aiming at winning public support for naval expansion programs were written by officers of the Imperial Navy. An overwhelming majority of such books were published by the Yushukai, a public relations organization of the navy. *Beikoku kaigun no shinsō* (A true picture of the U.S. navy) is one of its publications. This book, which came out in November 1936, consists of page after page of often technical arguments to make the point that the Japanese navy should be enlarged. One chart purported to show that whenever the material strength of a navy has been inferior, no naval engagement has been won. The book contained an introduction by Takahashi Sankichi, then vice-chief of the Navy General Staff. It was reviewed by Tokutomi Sohō in the August 28, 1933, issue of the Osaka *Mainichi shimbun.* The book, Tokutomi wrote, presented a "true

picture," on the basis of which he warned the Japanese that American naval policies were indeed directed against Japan.

10. William L. Neumann, *America Encounters Japan: From Perry to MacArthur* (Baltimore: The Johns Hopkins Press, 1963), p. 1.

11. Yabe Teiji, *Konoe Fumimaro,* 2: 420 (Tokyo, Konoe Fumimaro Denki Hensan Kankō-kai, 1952).

12. Quoted in Yoshii Hiroshi, *Shōwa gaikō shi* (A diplomatic history of the Showa period; Tokyo, Nansō Sha, 1971), p. 198.

13. Interviews with Suekuni Masao, November 30, 1970, and March 24, 1972. Suekuni was an adjutant on the Navy General Staff when Nagano was its chief.

14. The international environment in the mid-nineteenth century had produced a division of opinion in Japan. One common factor was a sense of the urgent need to develop a national defense. Some believed that opening the country for modernization was indispensable to prepare Japan for vindicating the national honor in a future war against the United States, while others maintained that national survival could be assured only through maintenance of the policy of seclusion and exclusion. Yamamoto's views seem to have approached the former, while Nagano's were closer to the latter.

15. Suekuni interviews. Also interviews with Sekino Hideo, October 22, 1970, and with Takuma Rikihei, November 30, 1970. See also Takuma Rikihei, "Kaigun Heigakkō no kyōiku" (Education at the Naval Academy), *Tōgō* 36:10-13 (October 1970).

16. Kiba Kōsuke, *Nomura Kichisaburō* (Tokyo, Nomura Kichisaburō Denki Kankōkai, 1961), p. 230.

17. Sekino interview. Sekino was one of the cadets.

18. Takuma interview.

19. Sekino interview. This new image of America was to become predominant in Japanese minds later in the 1930s. See, for example, the article by Takada Ichitarō, a staff reporter of the *Tōkyō nichi nichi shimbun,* in the September 1, 1932, issue of *Ekonomisuto* (The economist), pp. 30-33. Commenting upon an article entitled "Capone for President" in an American political journal, Takada said that it was an odd idea but was representative of American cynicism. He concluded that American democracy was bankrupt.

20. Interview with Akimaru Jirō, December 5, 1970. Also Akimaru Jirō, "Keizai sen kenkyū han shimatsu ki" (A note on the Economic Warfare Research Group), *Wakamatsu,* no. 32: 4-5 (April 1, 1964). *Wakamatsu* is the alumni magazine of the Army Intendant School.

21. They were Arisawa Hiromi, of Tokyo Imperial University, who was to study Britain and the United States; Miyagawa Minoru, Rikkyō University, the Soviet Union; Takemura Tadao, Keiō University, Germany and Italy; Nawa Ken'ichi, Yokohama Specie Bank, Southeast Asia; Nakayama Ichirō, Tokyo Higher School of Commerce, Japan; and Rōyama Michio, Tokyo Imperial University, and Kinoshita Hanji, Tokyo College of Education, general political affairs. Except for Akimaru, the only person from the Army Ministry was an accountant.

22. Akimaru, "Shimatsu ki," p. 5. See also Arisawa Hiromi, *Gakumon to shisō*

to ningen (Scholarship, ideology, man; Tokyo, Mainichi Shimbunsha, 1957), pp. 187–189.

23. Mr. Akimaru gave me some of these materials when I interviewed him in December 1970. I would like to take this opportunity to express my sincere gratitude to him.

24. The copy of Einzig's book in the Akimaru materials was a Japanese translation published by Hakuyōsha in September 1941. According to the translator's preface another translation had already appeared from a different publisher in the same year. It appears to have been a controversial book. In March 1941 Akimaru himself produced a mimeographed interim report entitled "Keizai sensō no hongi" (Fundamentals of economic warfare). This was the first report by the economic research group. The report contains a few references to the Einzig work, as does Akimaru's "Shimatsu ki." Akimaru also quotes frequently from Stephen Possony, *Tomorrow's War: Its Planning, Management, and Cost* (1939), and Otto Korfes, *Grundsätze der Wehrwirtschaftslehre* (1936), to make the point that in modern warfare a nation's military capability is completely predicated upon its economic power and that economic power in fact decides the ultimate outcome of a war.

25. Takahashi Masae, *Shōwa no gumbatsu* (Shōwa military cliques; Tokyo, Chūōkōronsha, 1969), pp. 231–232.

26. Iwakuro Hideo, "Heiwa e no tatakai" (The struggle for peace), *Bungei shunjū* (August 1966), p. 237.

27. Ibid., p. 238.

28. Ibid., pp. 238–240.

29. Interview with Sanematsu Yuzuru, November 27, 1970. According to Sanematsu, who was naval attaché at the Japanese embassy in Washington at the time, the army attaché did not personally collect information but relied almost exclusively on what he obtained from a Nisei employee. According to Endō Takekatsu (interview, December 17, 1970), Shinjō's investigation was based entirely upon data given him by the representatives of Japanese trading companies in the United States. It may be inferred that Tōjō was aware of this and decided that Iwakuro's report was not to be taken seriously.

30. Akimaru, "Shimatsu ki." See also Arisawa, *Gakumon,* p. 190.

31. Arisawa, *Gakumon,* p. 191.

32. The beginning of a dualistic thinking about justice and order in international society is a topic deserving of full investigation. I have suggested a few related historical developments in my book, *Nichi-Bei kankei no ishiki to kōzō* (The structure and images of Japanese-American relations; Tokyo, Nansōsha, 1974), pp. 41–60.

33. Maida Minoru, *Taiheiyō mondai* (Pacific problems), vol. 1 of *Dai-ni Asahi jōshiki kōza* (The second Asahi Common Sense Lecture series; Tokyo, Asahi Shimbunsha, 1929), p. 244.

34. Ibid., p. 246.

35. Ibid., pp. 247–248.

36. Inahara Katsuji, *Gaikō dokuhon* (Reader in diplomacy; Tokyo, Gaikō Jihō Shuppanbu, 1927), p. 260.

37. *Ekonomisuto* (December 15, 1931), p. 23.

38. Ibid. (April 1, 1932), p. 72.

39. For a variety of Pan-Asianist thought see Miwa Kimitada, "Ajiashugi no rekishi teki tenkai" (Historical development of pan-Asianist thought in Japan), in Hirano Ken'ichirō, ed., *Nihon bunka no henyō* (The transformation of Japanese culture), vol. 4 of *Nihon shakai bunka shi* (A social and cultural history of Japan), forthcoming from Kōdansha, Tokyo.

40. *Tōyō keizai shimpō,* October 28, 1939, pp. 13–14.

41. Ibid, January 18, 1941, p. 6.

42. Ibid, February 8, 1941, p. 28.

43. Ibid., August 23, 1941, p. 4. For a further example see *Ekonomisuto* (July 28, 1941), pp. 9–12, where Inahara sought to expose the hypocritical nature of Anglo-American pacifism. In another issue (January 20, 1941, pp. 12–13) Takada Ichitarō, a graduate of the University of Washington then on the staff of the Mainichi Press, declared the United States had entered the war with the passage of the Lend-Lease Act, which became law on March 11, 1941. In the issue of January 6 (p. 22), Taguchi Yoshihiko, professor of economics at Kyoto Imperial University, remarked that in reality the British and American governments were no longer democracies and their economies were not free.

44. *Tōyō keizai shimpō,* November 22, 1941, p. 3.

45. Ibid., November 29, 1941, p. 4.

46. Ibid., November 13, 1941, p. 10.

47. Ibid., November 2, 1941, p. 7.

48. This article was originally published in the December 15, 1918, issue of *Nihon oyobi Nihonjin* (Japan and the Japanese). An English translation was printed in the Shanghai periodical *Millard's Review* on January 11, 1919, as Konoe sailed for France. An accompanying editorial regretted that such an opponent of pacifism should be a member of the Japanese delegation. See Kimitada Miwa, "Japanese Opinions on Woodrow Wilson in War and Peace," *Monumenta Nipponica* 22. 3–4:382–383 (1967). See also Miwa Kimitada, *Matsuoka Yōsuke* (Tokyo: Chūōkō-ronsha, 1971), pp. 59–62.

49. In 1912 Konoe made an "ideological" decision of his own by transferring from Tokyo Imperial University to Kyoto Imperial University. Departing from the statist orthodoxy of Professor Inoue Tetsujirō, he adopted the progressive-to-revolutionary social ideas best expressed by the Marxist economist Kawakami Hajime. See Yabe, *Konoe* 1:60 (1951); Oka Yoshitake, *Konoe Fumimaro* (Tokyo, Iwanami Shoten, 1972), pp. 7–8.

50. In "Ajiashugi no rekishi teki tenkai" I have argued that in some instances Marxists became pan-Asianists when they were forcefully confronted with Japanese nationalism. The concept of "class warfare" was applied to relations between states and, when combined with ideas of Asian liberation and Japanese racist nationalism, evolved into an ideology of Asian liberation from the yoke of Western imperialism.

51. Miwa, "Japanese Opinions on Wilson," p. 383.

52. *Liberty* (September 14, 1935), pp. 44–47. The influence of this article was far-reaching. House attempted to demonstrate that the Japanese self-image which

had earlier been implanted in the United States was later reaccepted by Americans as correct. For the Japanese, who customarily deferred to Western thought, this reconfirmation of the "have-not" nation thesis must have suddenly endowed it with an aura of respectability and made it increasingly appear a feasible interpretation. Narita Atsushi's article, "Sekai no keizai kattō to shokuminchi shigen saibumpai mondai" (Worldwide economic struggles and the redistribution of colonial resources), which appeared in *Ekonomisuto* (November 11, 1935), p. 29, is an example. Narita praised House's fairness and wrote optimistically of Japan's future.

53. Fumimaro Konoye, "How to Secure Lasting Peace," *Liberty* (December 7, 1935), p. 31.

54. Yabe, *Konoe* 1:254–276.

55. Ibid., p. 36.

56. Waldo H. Heinrichs, Jr., *American Ambassador: Joseph C. Grew and the Development of the United States Diplomatic Tradition* (Boston: Little, Brown, 1966), p. 317.

57. Chihiro Hosoya, "Japan's Decision for War in 1941," *Peace Research in Japan, 1967* (Tokyo, 1968), p. 50.

58. Nakamura Takafusa and Hara Akira, eds., *Gendai shi shiryō* (Source materials on contemporary history) 43:27 (Tokyo: Misuzu Shobō, 1970). See also Nakamura Takafusa, *Senzen-ki Nihon keizai seichō no bunseki* (An analysis of prewar Japanese economic growth; Tokyo, Iwanami Shoten, 1971), pp. 260–261. In 1927 Okada, as a student at the Army War College, was enthusiastically drawn to one of his instructors, Colonel Ishiwara Kanji, renowned for his deterministic view of a final war that was coming between Japan and the United States. See Tsunoda Jun, ed., *Ishiwara Kanji shiryō: Sen shi hen* (Writings of Ishiwara Kanji: The history of war; Tokyo, Hara Shobō, 1968), p. 44.

59. Yabe, *Konoe* 2:385. See also Robert J. C. Butow, *Tojo and the Coming of the War* (Stanford: Stanford University Press, 1969), p. 267.

60. Sambō Hombu (Army General Staff), ed., *Sugiyama memo* (Liaison Conference records of Chief-of-Staff Sugiyama) 1:360 (Tokyo: Hara Shobō, 1967). For another translation of this passage see Nobutaka Ike, ed. and trans., *Japan's Decision for War: Records of the 1941 Policy Conferences* (Stanford: Stanford University Press, 1967), p. 147.

61. Yoshii, *Shōwa gaikō shi,* p. 163. Yoshii strongly supports the interpretation that Suzuki's assessment of the "material strength" of Japan contributed a great deal to the bellicose arguments.

62. Miyamoto Takenosuke, "Kokumin shiki no sakkō" (Rejuvenation and reinforcement of the national spirit," *Ekonomisuto* (September 1, 1941), p. 32.

7. FROM RUTH BENEDICT TO HERMAN KAHN: THE POSTWAR JAPANESE IMAGE IN THE AMERICAN MIND, BY NATHAN GLAZER

1. Hadley Cantril, ed., *Public Opinion, 1935–1946* (Princeton: Princeton University Press 1951), pp. 265–266.

2. Hazel Gaudet Erskine, "The Polls; Exposure to International Information," *Public Opinion Quarterly* 27. 4:658–662 (Winter 1963).

3. Hiroshi Kitamura, *Psychological Dimensions of U.S.-Japanese Relations,* Occasional Papers in International Affairs, No. 28 (Harvard University, Center for International Affairs, August 1971).

4. Kitamura, *Psychological Dimensions,* pp. 23–24.

5. Harold Isaacs, *Scratches on Our Minds* (New York: John Day, 1958), pp. 107–108.

6. Ibid., p. 216.

7. All figures from *Japanese Studies in the United States,* a report on the state of the field, present resources, and future needs, prepared by the Social Science Research Council–American Council of Learned Societies Joint Committee on Japanese Studies, February 1970.

8. Charles E. Hamilton in *Journal of Asian Studies* 17.4:629–630 (1958).

9. Edwin O. Reischauer, *Japan Past and Present* (New York: Alfred A. Knopf, 1946), p. 8.

10. Edwin O. Reischauer, *Japan: The Story of a Nation* (New York: Alfred A. Knopf, 1970), p. 8.

11. Reischauer (1946), p. 179.

12. Reischauer (1970), p. 208.

13. Reischauer (1946), pp. 184–185.

14. Reischauer (1970), p. 216.

15. Reischauer (1970), pp. 182–183.

16. In Robert J. C. Butow, *Tojo and the Coming of the War* (Stanford: Stanford University Press, 1961), pp. 463–464.

17. Reischauer (1946), pp. 54–55.

18. Reischauer (1946), p. 191.

19. Reischauer (1970), p. 242.

20. Ruth Benedict, *The Chrysanthemum and the Sword* (Boston: Houghton Mifflin, 1946), pp. 1–2.

21. Ibid., p. 1.

22. Reischauer (1946), p. 94.

23. Zbigniew Brzezinski, *The Fragile Blossom* (New York: Harper and Row, 1972), pp. 6–7.

24. Ibid., p. 3.

25. Ibid., p. 16.

26. Robert Guillain, *The Japanese Challenge* (Philadelphia: Lippincott, 1970), p. 33.

27. Herman Kahn, *The Emerging Japanese Superstate: Challenge and Response* (Englewood Cliffs, N.J.: Prentice-Hall, 1970), p. 25.

28. Benedict, *The Chrysanthemum and the Sword,* pp. 172–173.

29. Shūichi Katō, "Japanese Writers and Modernization," in Marius Jansen, ed., *Changing Japanese Attitudes Toward Modernization* (Princeton: Princeton University Press, 1965), pp. 443–444, as quoted in Brzezinski, *The Fragile Blossom,* p. 15.

30. Brzezinski, *The Fragile Blossom,* p. 16.

31. Benedict, *The Chrysanthemum and the Sword*, p. 86.

32. Ibid., pp. 314–316.

33. Brzezinski, *The Fragile Blossom*, p. 35.

34. Herbert Passin, "The Future," in Herbert Passin, ed., *The United States and Japan* (Englewood Cliffs, N.J.: Prentice-Hall, 1966), p. 146, as quoted in Brzezinski, *The Fragile Blossom*, p. 12.

35. Brzezinski, *The Fragile Blossom*, pp. 13–14.

36. Kahn, *The Emerging Japanese Superstate*, pp. 39–40.

37. Theodor Adorno and his associates in *The Authoritarian Personality* (New York: Harper, 1950) see prejudice as deeply anchored in personality needs; Gordon Allport, in *The Nature of Prejudice* (Cambridge, Mass.: Addison-Wesley, 1954), while not insisting on prejudice as based necessarily in personality needs, does emphasize its role in organizing perception, knowledge, and experience dynamically so that the prejudice can be maintained.

38. Note in this connection the interesting article by Etō Jun in *The Japan Interpreter* 3.1:63–75 (Winter 1973), "Japan's Shifting Image," where he argues the dangers of an image which asserts "the Japanese are just like us," when it turns out they are not like us. His position is that differences do not necessarily spell conflict nor similarities harmony, and whether other nations are the same or different, good relations may still be promoted and exist between them.

39. Johannes Hirschmeier, in an oral comment on the presentation of part of this essay in the summer of 1973 at Nagoya, argued that the American image of Japan, too, has its positive as well as its negative aspects. Thus, for example, even the view of Japan as paradoxical and alien has its positive side—the fascination with Japan and all things Japanese that has been a major characteristic of Western reactions to Japan for generations. Clearly certain aspects of the American image of Japan as developed here do partake of this double character. Thus the Japanese were seen in World War II as cunning and tricky; they are seen today as intelligent and ingenious. Are these really opposites? They are rather difficult evaluations of something that, at a deeper level, refers to the same thing. Cunning and intelligence in any case exclude dullness, and trickiness and ingeniousness exclude stolidity. Similarly there is a positive side to instability: willingness to change and adapt. And a positive side even to unpredictability: willingness to change and adapt in new and unexpected ways. (Consider the Japanese reaction to their defeat in 1945 and the Arab nations' reaction to theirs in 1967). Even incomprehensibility may have a positive side, when one considers that the ingeniousness of the adaptation might astound in its unexpectedness. As experts on international relations in a nuclear age have pointed out, unpredictability and incomprehensibility also have their advantages in that context: if an opponent does not know how you will react, it may make him more cautious and give you some advantages.

While Dr. Hirschmeier's point is well taken, I am not fully persuaded, and it is still my feeling that the American image of Japan tends more easily to take the negative than the positive form. And, as in the text, I would argue the same with the American image of India. The American image of China would be an example of an image that tends more easily to take positive forms, as demonstrated in the incredible rapidity of the change of 1972.

8. POSTWAR JAPANESE EDUCATION AND THE UNITED STATES, BY MICHIO NAGAI AND TAKEO NISHIJIMA

1. *Asahi shimbun,* October 4, 1945.
2. September 9, 1945, broadcast entitled "An Announcement to Young Students." See also Maeda Tamon, *Sansō seishi* (Meditations at a cottage; Tokyo, Haneda Shoten, 1947), p. 48.
3. "Sengo kyōiku seido kaikaku no igi" (The meaning of postwar educational reform), *Ekonomisuto* (Mainichi Shimbunsha, November 1965), p. 84.
4. Muchaku Seikyō, *Shisō no kagaku jiten* (Encyclopedia of the history of ideas; Tokyo, Shisō no kagakusha, 1969), p. 661.
5. Saitō Kihaku, *Saitō Kihaku zenshū* (Complete works of Saitō Kihaku; Tokyo, Kokudosha, 1971), 12:216.
6. Mizuno Shigekazu, *Hadaka no kyōshi* (The naked teacher; Tokyo, Tokuma Shoten, 1967), p. 63.
7. Murata Eiichi, *Sengo kyōiku ron* (Essays on postwar education; Tokyo, Shakai Hyōronsha, 1970), p. 19.
8. Hidaka Rokurō, *Kyōiku ron shū* (Essays on education; Tokyo, Hitotubashi Shōbō, 1970, p. 15.
9. Kanazawa Kaichi, *Aru shōgakkōchō no kaisō* (Reminiscences of a grade school principal; Tokyo, Iwanami Shoten, 1967), p. 59.
10. Maruki Makiomi, testimony at the "textbook trial" of Ienaga Saburō (Tokyo, Sōgō Tosho, 1968).

9. AMERICA AS SEEN BY JAPANESE TRAVELERS, BY HIDETOSHI KATŌ

1. See the discussion of *miyage* in Hayashiya Tatsusaburō and others, *Nihonjin no chie* (The wisdom of the Japanese; Tokyo, Chūōkōronsha, 1962).
2. European intellectuals such as Michel de Montaigne traveled across Europe with ease and had contacts with scholars of each country as early as 1580. See Ernest S. Bates, *Touring in 1600* (Boston: Houghton Mifflin, 1911).
3. Minakami Takitarō, a novelist, wrote in 1917 that when his ship docked at Kobe upon his return from Europe, he was immediately surrounded by newspaper reporters and editors asking about recent trends in art and literature in Europe. See his "Shimbunkisha o nikumu no ki" (On the arrogance of newspaper reporters), in *Daiichi kaigara tsuihō* (Ostracism number one; Tokyo, Kokubundō, 1920).
4. Nichi-Bei Shūkō Tsūshō Hyakunen Kinen Gyōji Un'eikai, ed., *Man'en gannen ken-Bei shisetsu shiryō shūsei* (Historical materials on the 1860 mission to the United States, 7 vols.; Tokyo, Kazama Shobō, 1960–61). The journals by Morita and Kimura are found in volume 1, those by Ekitō and Shimmi in volume 2, and that by Nonomiya in volume 3.

10. U.S. ELITE IMAGES OF JAPAN: THE POSTWAR PERIOD, BY PRISCILLA
A. CLAPP AND MORTON H. HALPERIN

1. "The Public's Attitude toward U.S.-Japanese Relations," a study conducted
for the Consulate of Japan by Gallup International, Princeton, March 20–22, 1970.

2. "American Public's View of Japan and the Japanese," *Asahi Evening News,*
March 17, 1971, describing the results of a poll conducted by Louis Harris and
Associates, Inc.

3. *Yomiuri shimbun,* morning edition, November 18, 1971, describing the results
of a poll conducted by Gallup (American Institute of Public Opinion).

4. James Reston, "Tyranny of the Minority in Tokyo and Washington," *New
York Times,* June 17, 1960.

5. Paul A. Samuelson, "Japan Revisited," *Newsweek* (November 15, 1971).

6. The broad common conceptions presented here are based on a more detailed
description of the shared images underlying American foreign policy in Morton
Halperin, *Bureaucratic Politics and Foreign Policy* (Washington, D.C.: Brookings
Institution, 1974).

7. George Kennan, "Japanese Security and American Policy," *Foreign Affairs*
(October 1964), p. 15.

8. U. Alexis Johnson, "The Role of Japan and the Future of American Relations
with the Far East," *Annals of the American Assembly* (July 1970), p. 63.

9. The images described in this section are, in part, based on a series of interviews we have recently held with senior and middle-level officials in the U.S.
government who are concerned with U.S.-Japanese relations. They are also based
on a survey of the literature pertinent to Japan that has been produced by the
U.S. foreign policy community in the postwar period.

10. John K. Emmerson, *Arms, Yen and Power: The Japanese Dilemma* (New
York: Dunellen, 1971), p. 377.

11. *Fiscal Year 1973 Report of the Secretary of Defense* (Washington, D.C.,
1972), pp. 115–116.

12. George Kennan, "Japanese Security and American Policy," *Foreign Affairs*
(October 1964), p. 24.

13. Emmerson, *Arms, Yen and Power,* p. 4.

14. Center for the Study of Democratic Institutions, *Asian Dilemma: United
States, Japan and China* 2.5:130 (October 1969).

15. Ibid, p. 219.

16. Robert Barnett, "United States Policy and Japan," paper prepared for Joint
Conference on Social and External Factors Influencing Japanese Foreign Policies
during the 1970s, Mt. Fuji, Japan, March 1972, p. 6.

17. Edwin O. Reischauer, paper prepared for Conference on U.S.-Japanese Political and Security Relations, New York, February 1972, p. 24.

18. Statement by Edwin O. Reischauer before the House Foreign Affairs Committee, November 1971, as quoted in Barnett, "U.S. Policy and Japan," p. 1.

19. George Ball, "A Shift of Emphasis in U.S.-Japanese Relationship," *Pacific Community* (January 1972), p. 247.

20. *Asian Dilemma,* p. 130.

21. William J. Sebald, *With MacArthur in Japan* (London: Cresset, 1965), pp. 80–82.

22. Hanson Baldwin, "Crisis in the Pacific," *New York Times,* June 18, 1960.

23. William P. Bundy, "Asian Triangle," *Newsweek* (December 6, 1971).

24. Herman Kahn, *The Emerging Japanese Superstate: Challenge and Response* (Englewood Cliffs, N.J.: Prentice-Hall, 1970), p. vii.

25. Address by Edwin Reischauer before Conference on U.S.-Japanese Political and Security Relations, New York, February 1972, pp. 34, 36.

26. Edward Seidensticker, "The Image," quoted in Herbert Passin, ed., *The United States and Japan* (Englewood Cliffs, N.J.: Prentice-Hall, 1966), p. 18.

11. THE VISUAL PANACEA: JAPANESE-AMERICANS IN THE CITY OF SMOG, BY DON TOSHIAKI NAKANISHI

1. Memorandum to the author from Wagatsuma Hiroshi, October 22, 1971.

2. California Senator J. M. Inman, quoted in George Sabage and Dorothy S. Thomas, "Changing Patterns of Fertility and Survival among the Japanese Americans on the Pacific Coast," *American Sociological Review* 10:651 (1945).

3. William Petersen, *Japanese Americans* (New York: Random House, 1971), pp. 4–5.

4. Dennis Ogawa, *From Japs to Japanese: The Evolution of Japanese-American Stereotypes* (Berkeley: McCutchan Publishing Corporation, 1971).

5. In a few cases these questions were asked in Japanese.

6. The picture that will emerge from this brief inventory of panel characteristics is one that shows degrees of both uniformity and difference across generations. In several ways the panel was probably not reflective of the generational units from which it was drawn: (1) it is not numerically representative of the different generations or the sex differences within them; (2) it is not reflective of the educational attainment level of each generation, that is, not all Japanese-Americans have been to college; (3) it is not necessarily representative of the occupational distribution of Japanese-Americans; and (4) most Kibei probably remigrated to the United States before rather than after the war like our panelists.

7. Amos S. Hershey's article, "The Japanese School Question and the Treaty-Making Power," has been the only study on Japanese-Americans to appear in the *American Political Science Review* 1:393–409 (1907).

8. Louis Hartz, *The Founding of New Societies* (New York: Harcourt, 1964). The use of the concept of "fragments" in this essay differs from that of Hartz, especially in relation to immigrant groups.

9. This refers to an advertisement in an Arizona newspaper in July 1971 which stated: "Remember Pearl Harbor, when they tried to take your country from you. They are back with Cheap Imports to take your Jobs, Pensions, and Social Security.

DON'T HELP THEM. Buy Arizona Products when possible, and ALWAYS buy American Made Products," in this case, the Chevy Vega.

10. Marcus Lee Hansen, "The Third Generation in America," *Commentary* 14: 492–500 (1952).

11. Karl W. Deutsch, "External Influences on the Internal Behavior of States," in R. B. Farrell, ed., *Approaches to Comparative and International Politics* (Evanston, Ill.: Northwestern University Press, 1966), pp. 5–26.

12. SOME CONCLUDING REMARKS: THE TURNING MIRRORS, BY HAROLD R. ISAACS

1. *Images of Asia: American Views of China and India* (New York: Harper and Row, 1972).

INDEX

of Teachers of History, 185; Conference of Teachers of Mathematics, 186; and Confucianism, 169–170, 182, 232; Core Curriculum Federation, 179–180; Cultural Center (New York), 172; Dutch in, 56; Education Ordinance (1879), 169; and Europe, economic competition, 75; and European fairs, 36; Japan Exhibit Association, 48; exhibits at Centennial Exposition, 28; exhibits at Paris fair of 1900, 48; Finance Ministry, 219; Foreign Ministry, 195; and Germany, 63, 95–96, 126, 131; and Great Britain, 63, 92–95, 108, 134, 155, 177, 235, 281n7; and Hawaii, 76, 82–86; Home Ministry, 172, 180; Imperial Diet, 37–38; and Korea and Koreans, 98, 239, 251–252; and Louisiana Purchase Exposition, 47–51, 275n71; and Manchuria, 87, 94, 98, 126, 129; and Mexico, 80–81; Ministry of Education, 170–171, 173, 175, 180; Ministry of International Trade and Industry, 219; National Creation Day, 185; Naval Academy, 120–122; naval expansion, 281n9; and New Orleans fair, 36–37; and Pan-Asianism, 127, 129–130, 132, 284nn39 and 50; and Paris fair of 1867, 27; and Paris fair of 1889, 38; and Philippines, 83–85, 263; postwar democracy, 156–157, 161–162; postwar economic expansion, 19, 272n10; postwar education, 169–187; postwar rearmament, 205, 211–212; prewar education, 169, 173–174, 176–178; Rescript on Education (1890), 169–170, 172, 175, 181; and Russia, 154 (*see also* Russo-Japanese War; Soviet Union); and Shimonoseki indemnity, 46, 275n70; Japan Society, 40; and Southeast Asia, 135–136, 263; and Soviet Union, 119, 124, 200; Japan Teachers Union (JTU), 171–172, 178, 182–183; and US naval policies, 282n9; and US Occupation, 156–157, 169, 176–177, 181, 211, 214, 221, 234, 243, 247, 254–

255; US security interests in, 209–215, 221, 250; Japan-US economic competition, 74–76, 86–87, 89; Japan-US Gentlemen's Agreement (1908), 155; Japan-US military competition, 78–86, 89; Japan-US trade relations, 75, 138, 206, 218–219, 221; and Vienna fair of 1873, 27; War Ministry, 123–124, 134; and the West compared, 45; and Western learning, 22, 272n–13; and World's Columbian Exposition, 37–40, 43–46, 48; and world fairs, 30–40, 43–51

Japan-American Society, 227

Japanese: American public opinion polls on, 138–144, 166, 203–204, 207; and Americans, 24–25, 144; and Russia, 10; army's conceptions of war with US, 123–127; army's criticism of the navy, 281n5; in Britain, 11; Buddhists, 69–70; at Centennial Exposition, 28–29, 31, 33; in California, 64, 71–72; Chamber of Commerce, 226; and China, 9, 59; and Christianity, 69–71; in Ecuador, 80; education on America, 62–63; educators in China, 89–90; Exhibitors Association, 48; exhibits at American fairs, 24, 43–51; exhibits at Centennial Exposition, 28–35, 38; exhibits at Louisiana Purchase Exposition, 47–50; exhibits at New Orleans fair, 37; exhibits at World's Columbian Exposition, 38–45; exports to US, 34; first embassy to US, 58–59; and French republicanism, 61; future war stories, 102–114; and Germany, 63, 231; and Hawaii, 195–196, 230; immigrants to Hawaii, 76, 82–84; immigrants to US, 76–80, 82–83; knowledge on US, 55–58; at Louisiana Purchase Exposition, 48–49; Mail and Steamship Company, 48, 51; Marxists, 248nn49–50; and Mexican republicanism, 61; navy's conceptions of war with US, 117–123, 127; in Oakland, 64; origin of study of images, 8; in Peru, 80; in Philippines, 82; radicals favoring Ameri-

HARVARD STUDIES IN AMERICAN–EAST ASIAN RELATIONS